*Approaches to the Novel*

# APPROACHES TO THE NOVEL Materials for a Poetics

Collected and Edited by Robert Scholes,
University of Iowa

*Revised Edition*

CHANDLER PUBLISHING COMPANY
124 Spear Street, San Francisco, California 94105

Science Research Associates, Inc., 259 East Erie Street, Chicago, Illinois 60611
A Subsidiary of IBM

Library of Congress Catalog Card No. 66–26878

Printed in the United States of America

# Contents

# Foreword

"Why should the ordinary reader or the undergraduate student be concerned with literary criticism?"

"Students haven't read enough novels, so why should their heads be stuffed full of critical theories? Let 'em read enough novels, and the criticism will take care of itself."

Attitudes like these are typical reactions to the notion of teaching criticism to those who are not going to be specialists in literature, and they are not, I think, to be laughed off or dismissed with a sneer. The usefulness of a collection such as this to the graduate student of literature or the professional writer or teacher is, I hope, obvious, and should need little justification from me. But of what value can it be to the person who is literate but not literary, an amateur not a professional? This is a question that I very much want to face up to, not only for the sake of this collection of critical writings but because it touches on a larger problem: the growing gap, in our culture, between the technician and the layman, the professional and the amateur, the participant and the spectator. Literary criticism can be seen either as a function of every reader or as an arcane pursuit, like repairing television sets, which the layman had better leave to the "factory-trained specialist."

Obviously, I think criticism is every reader's business. My thinking so is based on my notion of what happens when we read. We make critical judgments just as we make practical or moral choices, either deliberately or inadvertently. Much of whatever progress can be seen in the history of Western civilization has been a matter of gradually coming to know a little better what we are doing: what we are doing when we bake bread or eat it, when we make a law or break it, when we write a book or read it. Criticism helps us to know a little more what we are doing when we read. That, quite simply, is the justification for a book such as this one.

Whatever we read, we read in the light of certain assumptions about the nature of the thing we are reading. The celebrated "plain reader" is simply unaware of the nature of the assumptions he makes, or he regards them not as assumptions but as truths—what everybody knows. A critic, I should like to suggest, differs from the plain reader in that he is aware, gratefully or regretfully, of his assumptions, and of the way they govern his responses. We are sometimes told that the instinctive, untrammeled responses of the uncritical reader are superior to the responses of the self-conscious, limited critic. This notion of the reader as a noble savage whose natural state is superior to that of civilized man should not have as much persuasiveness as it sometimes seems to have; for the uncritical reader is like the actual savage, at the mercy of totems and taboos whose validity he can never think of questioning. Only the critical reader enjoys anything like free choice in esthetic matters, and the true critic knows not only his freedom but its limitations as well. He knows what he knows and what he does not know.

The materials collected here are designed to help readers become critics. They have been selected and arranged so as to open the great critical questions, not to close them; to provide approaches, not an approach. The essays are not tied to specific works for the most part, but present the problems and offer some solutions appropriate to any study of the novel in any language. In this revised edition of the collection, more material directly relevant to French fiction has been included, and perhaps a better balance between general essays pointed toward English and French literature has been achieved. The various approaches may be thought of as presenting methods of criticism to be applied to works of fiction, or theoretical possibilities to be tested against the intractible actualities of specific works. The separate essays may also be seen as introductory illustrations of the aims and methods of their authors. Here we can see many of our finest literary minds engaged in their most crucial intellectual efforts, providing examples (as Eliot said of Aristotle's *Poetics*) "of intelligence itself swiftly operating the analysis of sensation to the point of principle and definition."

## FROM THE FOREWORD TO THE 1961 EDITION

This book is intended to assist all readers of novels who feel the need of some critical orientation. Though it has developed into a book of general usefulness it began as a teacher's solution to a teacher's problem. Better than anyone else, a teacher knows that literature can not be taught. We can use literature to teach history or philosophy or sociology, or some combination of these which we call "the history of ideas"; we can even teach literary history. Or we can teach literary criticism. But literature itself is a subject matter, not a subject; a body of material, not an intellectual discipline.

In teaching the novel it is especially easy to emphasize the historical and sociological aspects of the study, and it is especially difficult to deal with the subject critically. The New Criticism, which despite its vociferous detractors works quite well with lyric poetry, is helpless when confronted by the large, irregular masses of prose fiction which we call novels. And though in approaching the Drama we at least have Aristotle's *Poetics* as a point of departure, Aristotle—as E. M. Forster points out—had read no modern novels, and thus neglected to provide us with a Poetics of the Novel. In fact, really searching criticism of fiction is the product of our own time, and is one of the areas of criticism in which the most progress has been made in this century of notable critical progress.

But, up to now, no one work has been written which we can point to as a Poetics of the Novel. The approaches of the major critics of fiction have been so different, their assumptions and conclusions so various, that the wished-for Poetics seems at times farther away than ever. Yet it may be that the syncretic effort which will reconcile the jarring sects lies not too far in the future. The works of Auerbach and Frye, for example, suggest that we are beginning to know enough about narrative fiction to make some significant and useful generalizations. But even these two men approach the novel from very different directions.

*Approaches to the Novel*

# PART ONE

## Theoretical Matters

# I. Narrative Modes and Forms

Austin Warren, "The Nature and Modes of Narrative Fiction," Chapter 16 of René Wellek and Austin Warren, *Theory of Literature*, reprinted here by permission of Harcourt, Brace and Company, Inc.

Northrop Frye, "Fictional Modes" (from the First Essay) and "Specific Continuous Forms" (from the Fourth Essay) from *Anatomy of Criticism*, reprinted here by permission of the Princeton University Press.

*These two selections represent quite different ways of approaching the great problem of reducing narrative literature to an intelligible order. Warren surveys the field, synthesizing the most useful and reasonable answers that have been proposed for the traditional questions about narrative modes and forms. In doing so, he presents much of the standard terminology employed in discussions of fiction. Frye, on the other hand, is concerned with patterns. He wishes to provide a complete and coherent system of understanding narrative. In the two passages on narrative modes, he offers a total perspective of the historical evolution of narrative. In the essay on narrative forms, he presents a system of four reference points or idealized norms to which all prose fiction can be referred. Both the forms and the modes can be used by readers to put individual works in perspective, and hence to understand them better. Warren accepts a certain formlessness in his essay in order to range widely and freely. Frye risks doing violence to literary actualities in order to offer a perfected system.*

## Austin Warren

### *The Nature and Modes of Narrative Fiction*

Literary theory and criticism concerned with the novel are much inferior in both quantity and quality to theory and criticism of poetry. The cause customarily assigned for this would be the antiquity of poetry, the comparative recency of the novel. But the explanation scarcely seems adequate. The novel as an art form is, as one can say in German, a form of *Dichtung;* is, indeed, in its high form, the modern descendant of the epic—with drama, one of the two great forms. The reasons are rather, one thinks, the widespread association of the novel with entertainment, amusement, and escape rather than serious art—the confounding of the great novels, that is, with manufactures made with a narrow aim at the market. The lingering American popular view, disseminated by pedagogues, that the reading of nonfiction was instructive and meritorious, that of fiction, harmful or at best self-indulgent, was not without implicit backing in the attitude toward the novel of representative critics like Lowell and Arnold.

There is an opposite danger, however, of taking the novel seriously in the wrong way, that is, as a document or case history, as—what for its own purposes of illusion it sometimes professes to be—a confession, a true story, a history of a life and its times. Literature must always be interesting; it must always have a structure and an aesthetic purpose, a total coherence and effect. It must, of course, stand in recognizable relation to life, but the relations are very various: the life can be heightened or burlesqued or antithesized; it is in any case a selection, of a specifically purposive sort, from life. We have to have a knowledge independent of literature in order to know what the relation of a specific work to "life" may be.

Aristotle described poetry (that is, epic and drama) as nearer to philosophy than to history. The dictum seems to have permanent suggestiveness. There is factual truth, truth in specific detail of time and place—truth of history in the narrow sense. Then there is philosophic truth: conceptual, propositional, general. From the points of view of "history," so defined, and philosophy, imaginative literature is "fiction," a lie. The word "fiction" still preserves this old Platonic charge against literature, to which Philip Sidney and Dr. Johnson reply that literature never pretended to be real in that sense;[1] and still preserving this vestigial remnant of the old charge of deception, it can still irritate the earnest writer of novels, who knows well that fiction is less strange and more representative than truth.

Wilson Follett remarks admirably of Defoe's narrative of Mrs. Veal and Mrs. Bargrave that "Everything in the story is true except the whole of it. And mark how difficult Defoe makes it to question even that whole. The tale is told by a third woman of exactly the same stamp as the other two, a life-long friend of Mrs. Bargrave. . . ."[2]

Marianne Moore speaks of poetry as presenting

*for inspection, imaginary gardens with real toads in them.*

The reality of a work of fiction—i.e., its illusion of reality, its effect on the reader as a convincing reading of life—is not necessarily or primarily a reality of circumstance or detail or commonplace routine. By all of these standards, writers like Howells or Gottfried Keller put to shame the writers of *Oedipus Rex, Hamlet,* and *Moby Dick.* Verisimilitude in detail, is a means to illusion, but often used, as in *Gulliver's Travels,* as a decoy to entice the reader into some improbable or incredible situation

[1] Sidney: "Now for the poet, he nothing affirmeth, and therefore never lieth."
[2] Wilson Follett, *The Modern Novel,* New York, 1918, p. 29.

which has "truth to reality" in some deeper than a circumstantial sense.

Realism and naturalism, whether in the drama or the novel, are literary or literary-philosophical movements, conventions, styles, like romanticism or surrealism. The distinction is not between reality and illusion, but between differing conceptions of reality, between differing modes of illusion.[3]

What is the relation of narrative fiction to life? The classical or Neo-Classical answer would be that it presents the typical, the universal—the typical miser (Molière, Balzac), the typical faithless daughters (*Lear, Goriot*). But are not such class concepts for sociology? Or it would have been said that art ennobles or heightens or idealizes life. There is such a style of art, of course, but it is a style, not the essence of art; though all art, to be sure, by giving aesthetic distance, by shaping and articulating, makes that pleasant to contemplate which would be painful to experience or even, in life, to witness. Perhaps it might be said that a work of fiction offers a "case history"—an illustration or exemplification of some general pattern or syndrome. There are instances—in short stories like Cather's "Paul's Case" or "The Sculptor's Funeral"—which approach it. But the novelist offers less a case—a character or event—than a world. The great novelists all have such a world—recognizable as overlapping the empirical world but distinct in its self-coherent intelligibility. Sometimes it is a world which can be mapped out in some area of the globe—like Trollope's counties and cathedral towns, Hardy's Wessex; but sometimes—as with Poe—it is not: Poe's horrendous castles are not in Germany or Virginia but in the soul. Dickens' world can be identified with London; Kafka's with old Prague: but both worlds are so "projected," so creative and created and hereafter recognized in the empirical world as Dickens characters and Kafka situations that the identifications seem rather irrelevant.

Meredith, Conrad, Henry James, and Hardy have all, says Desmond McCarthy, "blown great comprehensive iridescent bubbles, in which the human beings they describe, though they have

[3] The reader's exhortation that the novelist "deal with life" is often "an exhortation to preserve certain conventions of nineteenth-century prose fiction": Kenneth Burke, *Counterstatement,* New York, 1931, p. 238; *cf.* also p. 182 and p. 219.

of course a recognizable resemblance to real people, only attain in that world their full reality." Imagine, McCarthy says, "a character moved from one imaginary world to another. If Pecksniff were transplanted into *The Golden Bowl* he would become extinct. . . . The unforgivable artistic fault in a novelist is failure to maintain consistency of tone."[4]

This world or *Kosmos* of a novelist—this pattern or structure or organism, which includes plot, characters, setting, world-view, "tone"—is what we must scrutinize when we attempt to compare a novel with life or to judge, ethically or socially, a novelist s work. The truth to life, or "reality," is no more to be judged by the factual accuracy of this or that detail than the moral judgment is to be passed, as Boston censors pass it, on whether specific sexual or blasphemous words occur within a novel. The soundly critical appeal is to the whole fictional world in comparison with our own experienced and imagined world, commonly less integrated than that of the novelist. We are content to call a novelist great when his world, though not patterned or scaled like our own, is comprehensive of all the elements which we find necessary to catholic scope or, though narrow in scope, selects for inclusion the deep and central, and when the scale or hierarchy of elements seems to us such as a mature man can entertain.

In using the term "world," one is using a space term. But "narrative fiction"—or better, a term like "story," calls our attention to time, and a sequence in time. "Story" comes from "history": the "Chronicles of Barsetshire." Literature is generally to be classed as a time-art (in distinction from painting and sculpture, space-arts); but in a very active way modern poetry (non-narrative poetry) seeks to escape its destiny—to become a contemplative stasis, a "self-reflexive" pattern; and as Joseph Frank has well shown, the modern art-novel (*Ulysses, Nightwood, Mrs. Dalloway*) has sought to organize itself poetically, i.e., "self-reflexively."[5] This calls our attention to an important cultural phenomenon: the old narrative, or story (epic or novel) happened in time—the traditional time-span for the epic was a year. In

[4] D. McCarthy, *Portraits*, London, 1931, pp. 75, 156.

[5] J. Frank, "Spatial Form in Modern Literature," *Sewanee Review*, LIII (1945), pp. 221-40, 433-56. Reprinted in *Criticism* (Schorer, Miles, McKenzie), New York, 1948, pp. 379-92.

many great novels, men are born, grow up, and die; characters develop, change; even a whole society may be seen to change (*The Forsyte Saga, War and Peace*) or a family's cyclic progress and decline exhibited (*Buddenbrooks*). The novel, traditionally, has to take the time dimension seriously.

In the picaresque novel, the chronological sequence is all there is: this happened and then that. The adventures, each an incident, which might be an independent tale, are connected by the figure of the hero. A more philosophic novel adds to chronology the structure of causation. The novel shows a character deteriorating or improving in consequence of causes operating steadily over a period of time. Or in a closely contrived plot, something has happened in time: the situation at the end is very different from that at the opening.

To tell a story, one has to be concerned about the happening, not merely the outcome. There is or was a kind of reader who must look ahead to see how a story "comes out"; but one who reads only the "concluding chapter" of a nineteenth-century novel would be somebody incapable of interest in story, which is process—even though process toward an end. There are certainly philosophers and moralists like Emerson who cannot take novels seriously primarily, one thinks, because action—or external action—or action in time—seems to them unreal. They cannot see history as real: history is just an unrolling in time of more of the same; and the novel is fictitious history.

A word should be said about the word "narrative," which, as applied to fiction, should imply the contrast of enacted fiction, i.e., drama. A story, or fable, can be represented by mimes, or it can be narrated by a single teller, who will be the epic teller, or one of his successors. The epic poet uses the first person and can, like Milton, make that a lyric or auctorial first person. The nineteenth-century novelist, even though he did not write in the first person, used the epic privilege of comment and generalization—what we might call the "essayistic" (as distinct from lyric) first person. But the chief pattern of narrative is its inclusiveness: it intersperses scenes in dialogue (which might be acted) with summary accounts of what is happening.[6]

[6] The first two chapters of *Pride and Prejudice* are almost exclusively dialogue, while the third chapter opens with narrative summary, then returns to the "scenic" method.

The two chief modes of narrative fiction have, in English, been called the "romance" and the "novel." In 1785, Clara Reeve distinguished them: "The Novel is a picture of real life and manners, and of the time in which it is written. The Romance, in lofty and elevated language, describes what never happened nor is likely to happen."[7] The novel is realistic; the romance is poetic or epic: we should now call it "mythic." Mrs. Radcliffe, Sir Walter Scott, Hawthorne are writers of "romance." Fanny Burney, Jane Austen, Anthony Trollope, George Gissing are novelists. The two types, which are polar, indicate the double descent of prose narrative: the novel develops from the lineage of non-fictitious narrative forms—the letter, the journal, the memoir or biography, the chronicle or history; it develops, so to speak, out of documents; stylistically, it stresses representative detail, "mimesis" in its narrow sense. The romance, on the other hand, the continuator of the epic and the medieval romance, may neglect verisimilitude of detail (the reproduction of individuated speech in dialogue, for example), addressing itself to a higher reality, a deeper psychology. "When a writer calls his work a Romance," writes Hawthorne, "it need hardly be observed that he wishes to claim a certain latitude both as to its fashion and its material. . . ." If such a romance be laid in past time, it is not in order to picture with minute accuracy that past time, but to secure, in Hawthorne's words elsewhere, "a sort of poetic . . . precinct, where actualities would not be . . . insisted upon. . . ."[8]

Analytical criticism of the novel has customarily distinguished three constituents, plot, characterization, and setting: the last, so readily symbolic, becomes, in some modern theories, "atmosphere" or "tone." It is needless to observe that each of these elements is determinant of the others. As Henry James asks in his essay, "The Art of Fiction," "What is character but the determination of incident? What is incident but the illustration of character?"

The narrative structure of play, tale, or novel has traditionally been called the "plot"; and probably the term should be retained. But then it must be taken in a sense wide enough to

[7] Clara Reeve, *Progress of Romance*, London, 1785.
[8] Hawthorne, prefaces to *The House of the Seven Gables* and *The Marble Faun*.

include Chekhov and Flaubert and Henry James as well as Hardy, Wilkie Collins, and Poe: it must not be restricted to mean a pattern of close intrigue like Godwin's *Caleb Williams.*[9] We shall speak rather of types of plots, of looser and of more intricate, of "romantic" plots and "realistic." In a time of literary transition, a novelist may feel compelled to provide two kinds, one of them out of an obsolescent mode. Hawthorne's novels after *The Scarlet Letter* offer, clumsily, an old-fashioned mystery plot, while their real plot is of a looser, more "realistic," variety. In his later novels, Dickens devotes much ingenuity to his mystery plots, which may or may not coincide with the novel's real center of interest. The last third of *Huck Finn,* obviously inferior to the rest, seems prompted by a mistaken sense of responsibility to provide some "plot." The real plot, however, has already been in successful progress: it is a mythic plot, the meeting on a raft and journey down a great river of four who have escaped, for various reasons, from conventional society. One of the oldest and most universal plots is that of the Journey, by land or water: *Huck Finn, Moby Dick, Pilgrim's Progress, Don Quixote, Pickwick Papers, The Grapes of Wrath.* It is customary to speak of all plots as involving conflict (man against nature, or man against other men, or man fighting with himself); but then, like plot, the term must be given much latitude. Conflict is "dramatic," suggests some matching of approximately equal forces, suggests action and counteraction. Yet there are plots which it seems more rational to speak of in terms of a single line or direction, as plots of the chase or the pursuit: *Caleb Williams, The Scarlet Letter, Crime and Punishment,* Kafka's *Trial.*

The plot (or narrative structure) is itself composed of smaller narrative structures (episodes, incidents). The larger and more inclusive literary structures (the tragedy, the epic, the novel) have developed, historically, from earlier, rudimentary forms like the joke, the saying, the anecdote, the letter; and the plot of a play or novel is a structure of structures. The Russian formalists, and German form-analysts like Dibelius, give the term "motive"

[9] Poe's "Philosophy of Composition" opens with a quotation from Dickens: "Are you aware that Godwin wrote his *Caleb Williams* backwards?" Earlier, in a review of *Barnaby Rudge,* Poe had cited Godwin's novel as a masterpiece of close plotting.

(Fr., *motif*, Germ., *motiv*) to the ultimate plot-elements.[10] "Motive," as thus used by literary historians, is borrowed from the Finnish folklorists, who have analyzed fairy and folk tales into their parts.[11] Obvious examples from written literature will be mistaken identities (*The Comedy of Errors*); the marriage of youth and old age ("January and May") filial ingratitude to a father (*Lear, Père Goriot*); the search of a son for his father (*Ulysses*, and *The Odyssey*).[12]

What we call the "composition" of the novel is, by the Germans and Russians, called its "motivation." The term might well be adopted into English as valuable precisely for its double reference to structural or narrative composition and to the inner structure of psychological, social, or philosophical theory of why men behave as they do—some theory of causation, ultimately. Sir Walter Scott asserts early, that "the most marked distinction between a real and fictitious narrative [is] that the former, in reference to the remote causes of the events it relates, is obscure . . . whereas in the latter case it is a part of the author's duty to . . . account for everything."[13]

Composition or motivation (in the largest sense) will include narrative method: "scale," "pace"; devices: the proportioning of scenes or drama to picture or straight narrative and of both to narrative summary or digest.

Motifs and devices have their period character. The Gothic romance has its own; the realistic novel, its. Dibelius repeatedly speaks of Dickens' "realism" as of the *Märchen*, not of the naturalistic novel, the devices being utilized to lead into old-fashioned melodramatic motifs: the man supposed dead who comes

[10] *Motif* is commonly used in English criticism; but A. H. Krappe, *Science of Folklore*, London, 1930, sensibly urges that we use the English *motive* instead of the French form, which in turn acquired *its* sense under the influence of the German *Motiv*.

[11] *Cf.* Aarne-Thompson, *Types of the Folk-Tale*, Helsinki, 1928.

[12] *Cf.* G. Polti, *Thirty-six Dramatic Situations*, New York, 1916; P. Van Tieghem, *La littérature comparée*, Paris, 1931, p. 87 ff.

[13] Sir Walter Scott, quoted by S. L. Whitcomb, *Study of a Novel*, Boston, 1905, p. 6. Whitcomb calls *motivation* "a technical term to denote the causation of the plot-movement, especially in reference to its conscious artistic arrangement."

The opening sentence of *Pride and Prejudice* is a good example of "motivation" explicitly (even parodically) stated: "It is a truth universally acknowledged, that a single man in possession of a good fortune must be in want of a wife."

to life, or the child whose real paternity is finally established, or the mysterious benefactor who turns out to be a convict.[14]

In a work of literary art, the "motivation" must increase the "illusion of reality": that is, its aesthetic function. "Realistic" motivation is an artistic device. In art, seeming is even more important than being.

The Russian formalists distinguish the "fable," the temporal-causal sequence which, however it may be told, is the "story" or story-stuff, from the "sujet," which we might translate as "narrative structure." The "fable" is the sum of all the motifs, while the "sujet" is the artistically ordered presentation of the motifs (often quite different). Obvious instances involve temporal displacement: beginning *in medias res,* like the *Odyssey* or *Barnaby Rudge;* backward and forward movements, as in Faulkner's *Absalom, Absalom.* The "sujet" of Faulkner's *As I Lay Dying* involves the story being narrated in turn by the members of a family as they carry the mother's body to a distant graveyard. "Sujet" is plot as mediated through "point of view," "focus of narration." "Fable" is, so to speak, an abstraction from the "raw materials" of fiction (the author's experience, reading, etc.); the "sujet" is an abstraction from the "fable"; or, better, a sharper focusing of narrative vision.[15]

Fable-time is the total period spanned by the story. But "narrative" time corresponds to "sujet": it is reading-time, or "experienced time," which is controlled, of course, by the novelist, who passes over years in a few sentences but gives two long chapters to a dance or tea-party.[16]

The simplest form of characterization is naming. Each "appellation" is a kind of vivifying, animizing, individuating. The allegoric or quasi-allegoric name appears in eighteenth-century comedy: Fielding's Allworthy and Thwackum, Witwould, Mrs. Malaprop, Sir Benjamin Backbite, with their echo of Jonson, Bunyan, Spenser, and *Everyman.* But the subtler practice is a

[14] Dibelius, *Dickens,* 2nd ed., Leipzig, 1926, p. 383.

[15] We refer here especially to Tomashevsky's treatment of "Thermatology" in his *Teoriyu literatury,* Leningrad, 1931.

[16] *Cf.* the discussion of "tempo" in Carl Grabo's *Technique of the Novel,* New York, 1928, pp. 214-36, and "Zeit" in Petsch's *Wesen und Formen der Erzählkunst,* Halle, 1934, p. 92 ff.

kind of onomatopoeic toning, at which novelists as alien as Dickens and Henry James, Balzac and Gogol, are alike adept: Pecksniff, Pumblechook, Rosa Dartle (dart; startle), Mr. and Miss Murdstone (murder + stony heart). Melville's Ahab and Ishmael show what can be done by literary—in this instance, Biblical—allusion as a form of characterizing economy.[17]

Modes of characterization are many. Older novelists like Scott introduce each of their major persons by a paragraph describing in detail the physical appearance and another analyzing the moral and psychological nature. But this form of block characterization may be reduced to an introductory label. Or the label may turn into a device of mimicry or pantomime—some mannerism, gesture, or saying, which, as in Dickens, recurs whenever the character reappears, serving as emblematic accompaniment. Mrs. Gummidge is "always thinking of the old un"; Uriah Heep has a word, "umble," and also a ritual gesture of the hands. Hawthorne sometimes characterizes by a literal emblem: Zenobia's red flower; Westervelt's brilliantly artificial teeth. The later James of *The Golden Bowl* has one character see another in symbolic terms.

There are static characterizations and dynamic or developmental. The latter seems particularly suited to the long novel like *War and Peace,* as it is obviously less suited to drama, with its confined narrative time. Drama (e.g., Ibsen) can gradually disclose how a character has become what it is; the novel can show the change occurring. "Flat" characterization (which commonly overlaps "static") presents a single trait, seen as the dominant or socially most obvious trait. It may be caricature or may be abstractive idealization. Classical drama (e.g., Racine) applies it to major characters. "Round" characterization, like "dynamic," requires space and emphasis; is obviously usable for characters focal

[17] *Cf.* E. Berend, "Die Namengebung bei Jean Paul," *PMLA,* LVII (1942), pp. 820-50; E. H. Gordon, "The Naming of Characters in the Works of Dickens," *University of Nebraska Studies in Language,* etc., 1917; also John Forster's *Life of Dickens,* Bk. IX, Ch. 7, citing lists of names from the novelist's memoranda.

Henry James talks out the naming of his characters in the memoranda printed at the end of his unfinished novels, *The Ivory Tower* and *The Sense of the Past* (both 1917). *Cf.* also James' *Notebooks* (ed. Matthiessen and Murdock), New York, 1947, pp. 7-8, and *passim.*

On Balzac's character-naming, *cf.* E. Faguet, *Balzac* (Eng. tr., London, 1914), p. 120; and on Gogol's, V. Nabokov's *Gogol,* New York, 1944, p. 85 ff.

for point of view or interest; hence is ordinarily combined with "flat" treatment of background figures—the "chorus."[18]

There is obviously some kind of connection between characterization (literary method) and characterology (theories of character, personality types). There are character-typologies, partly literary tradition, partly folk-anthropology, which are used by novelists. In nineteenth-century English and American fiction, one finds brunettes, male and female (Heathcliffe, Mr. Rochester; Becky Sharp; Maggie Tulliver; Zenobia, Miriam; Ligeia) and blondes (female instances—Amelia Sedley; Lucy Dean; Hilda, Priscilla, and Phoebe [Hawthorne]; Lady Rowena [Poe]). The blonde is the home-maker, unexciting but steady and sweet. The brunette—passionate, violent, mysterious, alluring, and untrustworthy—gathers up the characteristics of the Oriental, the Jewish, the Spanish, and the Italian as seen from the point of view of the "Anglo-Saxon."[19]

In the novel, as in the drama, we have something like a repertory company: the hero, the heroine, the villain, the "character actors" (or "humor characters," or comic relief). There are the juveniles and ingénues and the elderly (the father and mother, the maiden aunt, the duenna, or the nurse). The dramatic art of the Latin tradition (Plautus and Terence, the *commedia dell'arte,* Jonson, Molière) uses a strongly marked and traditional typology of *miles gloriosus,* miserly father, wily servant. But a great novelist like Dickens largely adopts and adapts the types of the eighteenth-century stage and novel; he initiates only two types—the helpless old and young, and the dreamers or fantasts (e.g., Tom Pinch, in *Chuzzlewit*).[20]

Whatever the ultimate social or anthropological basis for literary character-types such as the blonde heroine and the brunette, the affective patterns can both be made out from the

[18] Flat and round characterization: *cf.* E. M. Forster, *Aspects of the Novel,* London, 1927, pp. 103-4

[19] On the typology of English heroines, *cf.* R. P. Utter and G. B. Needham, *Pamela's Daughters,* New York, 1936. On the polarity of light and dark heroines, *cf.* F. Carpenter, "Puritans Preferred Blondes," *New England Quarterly,* IX (1936), pp. 253-72; Philip Rahv, "The Dark Lady of Salem," *Partisan Review,* VIII (1941), pp. 362-81.

[20] Dibelius, *Dickens,* Leipzig, 1916.

novels without documentary aid, and they have, commonly, literary-historical ancestries and lines—like the *femme fatale* and the dark Satanic hero studied by Mario Praz in *The Romantic Agony*.[21]

Attention to setting—the literary element of description as distinguished from narration—would at first thought seem to differentiate "fiction" from drama; our second thought, however, would rather make it a matter of period. Detailed attention to setting, whether in drama or the novel, is Romantic or Realistic (i.e., nineteenth-century) rather than universal. In drama, the setting may be given verbally within the play (as in Shakespeare) or indicated by stage directions to scene designers and carpenters. Some "scenes" in Shakespeare are not to be placed, localized, at all.[22] But within the novel, also, description of the setting is to a high degree variable. Jane Austen, like Fielding and Smollett, rarely describes either interiors or exteriors. The earlier novels of James, written under the influence of Balzac, are detailed for both houses and landscapes; the later novels substitute for how scenes look some symbolic rendering of how they totally *feel*.

Romantic description aims at establishing and maintaining a mood: plot and characterization are to be dominated by tone, effect—Mrs. Radcliffe and Poe are instances. Naturalistic description is a seeming documentation, offered in the interest of illusion (Defoe, Swift, Zola).

Setting is environment; and environments, especially domestic interiors, may be viewed as metonymic, or metaphoric, expressions of character. A man's house is an extension of himself. Describe it and you have described him. Balzac's detailed specifications for the house of the miser Grandet or the Pension Vauquer are neither irrelevant nor wasteful.[23] These houses express their owners; they affect, as atmosphere, those others who must live in them. The petty-bourgeois horror of the Pension is the immediate provocation of Rastignac's reaction and in another sense Vautrin's, while it measures the degradation of Goriot and affords constant contrast with the grandeurs alternately described.

[21] Mario Praz, *The Romantic Agony*, London, 1933.

[22] *Cf.* Arthur Sewell, "Place and Time in Shakespeare's Plays," *Studies in Philology*, XLII (1945), pp. 205-24.

[23] *Cf.* P. Lubbock, *Craft of Fiction*, London, 1921, pp. 205-35.

Setting may be the expression of a human will. It may, if it is a natural setting, be a projection of the will. Says the self-analyst Amiel, "A landscape is a state of mind." Between man and nature there are obvious correlatives, most intensely (but not exclusively) felt by the Romantics. A stormy, tempestuous hero rushes out into the storm. A sunny disposition likes sunlight.

Again, setting may be the massive determinant—environment viewed as physical or social causation, something over which the individual has little individual control. This setting may be Hardy's Egdon Heath or Lewis' Zenith. The great city (Paris, London, New York) is the most real of the characters in many a modern novel.

A story can be told through letters or journals. Or it can develop from anecdotes. The frame-story enclosing other stories is, historically, a bridge between ancedote and novel. In the *Decameron,* the stories are thematically grouped. In the *Canterbury Tales,* such grouping of themes (e.g., marriage) is brilliantly supplemented by the conception of characterization of teller through tale and of a set of characters with psychological and social tensions between them. The story-of-stories has a Romantic version as well: in Irving's *Tales of a Traveller* and Hoffmann's *Tales of the Serapion Brethren.* The Gothic novel, *Melmoth the Wanderer,* is a strange but undeniably effective group of separate tales united only loosely save by their common tone of horror.

Another device, currently out of practice, is the short story included within a novel (e.g., the "Man on the Hill's Tale" in *Tom Jones;* the "Confessions of a Beautiful Soul," in *Wilhelm Meister*). This can be seen as, on one level, the attempt to fill out the size of a work; on another, as the search for variety. Both ends seem better served in the Victorian three-decker novels, which keep two or three plot-sequences in alternate movement (on their revolving stage) and eventually show how they interlock—a compounding of plots already practiced by the Elizabethans, often brilliantly. Artistically handled, one plot parallels the other (in *Lear*) or serves as "comic relief" or parody and hence underlining of the other.

Telling a story in the first person (the *Ich-Erzählung*) is a method carefully to be weighed against others. Such a narrator must not, of course, be confounded with the author. The purpose and effect of narration in the first person vary. Sometimes the effect is to make the teller less sharp and "real" than other characters (*David Copperfield*). On the other hand, Moll Flanders and Huck Finn are central to their own stories. In "The House of Usher," Poe's first-person narration enables the reader to identify himself with Usher's neutral friend and to withdraw with him at the catastrophic finale; but the neurotic or psychotic central character tells his own story in "Ligeia," "Berenice," and "The Tell-Tale Heart": the narrator, with whom we cannot identify, is making a confession, characterizing himself by what he reports and how he reports it.

Interesting is the question of how the story purports to exist. Some tales are elaborately introduced (*Castle of Otranto, Turn of the Screw, Scarlet Letter*): the story proper is given several degrees of detachment from its author or the reader by being represented as told to A by B, or as a manuscript entrusted to A by B, who perhaps wrote down the life-tragedy of C. Poe's first-person narratives are sometimes, ostensibly, dramatic monologues ("Amontillado"), sometimes the written confession of a tormented soul, avowedly unburdening himself ("The Tell-Tale Heart"). Often the assumption is not clear: in "Ligeia," are we to think of the narrator as talking to himself, rehearsing his story to refresh his own sense of horror?

The central problem of narrative method concerns the relation of the author to his work. From a play, the author is absent; he has disappeared behind it. But the epic poet tells a story as a professional story-teller, including his own comments within the poem, and giving the narration proper (as distinct from dialogue) in his own style.

The novelist can similarly tell a story without laying claim to having witnessed or participated in what he narrates. He can write in the third person, as the "omniscient author." This is undoubtedly the traditional and "natural" mode of narration. The author is present, at the side of his work, like the lecturer whose exposition accompanies the lantern slides or the documentary film.

There are two ways of deviating from that mixed mode of

epic narration: one, which may be called the romantic-ironic, deliberately magnifies the role of the narrator, delights in violating any possible illusion that this is "life" and not "art," emphasizes the written literary character of the book. The founder of the line is Sterne, especially in *Tristram Shandy;* he is followed by Jean Paul Richter and Tieck in Germany; by Veltman and Gogol in Russia. *Tristram* might be called a novel about novel-writing, as might Gide's *Les Faux-Monnayeurs* and its derivative, *Point Counterpoint.* Thackeray's much-censured management of *Vanity Fair*—his constant reminder that these characters are puppets he has manufactured—is doubtless a species of this literary irony: literature reminding itself that it is but literature.

The opposite goal for the novel is the "objective" or "dramatic" method, argued for and illustrated by Otto Ludwig in Germany, Flaubert and Maupassant in France, Henry James in England.[24] The exponents of this method, critics as well as artists, have sought to represent it as the only artistic method (a dogma which need not be accepted). It has been admirably expounded in Percy Lubbock's *Craft of Fiction,* a Poetics of the novel based on the practice and the theory of Henry James.

"Objective" is the better term to use, since "dramatic" might mean "dialogue" or "action, behavior" (in contrast to the inner world of thought and feeling); but, quite clearly, it was the drama, the theater, which instigated these movements. Otto Ludwig formed his theories on the basis chiefly of Dickens, whose devices of pantomime and characterization by stock phrase were borrowed from the older eighteenth-century comedy and melodrama. Instead of narrating, Dickens' impulse is always to *present,* in dialogue and pantomime; instead of telling us *about,* he *shows* us. Later modes of the novel learn from other and subtler theaters, as James did from that of Ibsen.[25]

[24] Otto Ludwig, "Romanstudien," *Gesammelte Schriften,* VI (1891), p. 59 ff.; Maupassant, Introduction to *Pierre et Jean* (1887); H. James, Prefaces to the New York Edition (collected as *The Art of the Novel,* New York, 1934). *Cf.* also Oskar Walzel's "Objektive Erzählung," in *Das Wortkunstwerk, Leipzig,* 1926, p. 182 ff., and J. W. Beach, *The Twentieth Century Novel,* New York, 1932.

[25] Ludwig, *op. cit.,* pp. 66-7: The structure of Dickens' novels is analogous to that of plays. "Seine Romane sind erzählte Dramen mit Zwischenmusik, *d.i.,* erzählter."

On James and Ibsen, *cf.* Francis Fergusson, "James' Idea of Dramatic Form," *Kenyon Review,* V (1943), pp. 495-507.

The objective method must not be thought of as limited to dialogue and reported behavior (James' *The Awkward Age;* Hemingway's "The Killers"). Such limitation would bring it into direct, and unequal, rivalry with the theater. Its triumphs have been in the presentation of that psychic life which the theater can handle but awkwardly. Its essentials are the voluntary absence from the novel of the "omniscient novelist" and, instead, the presence of a controlled "point of view." James and Lubbock see the novel as giving us, in turn, "picture" and drama," by which they mean some character's consciousness of what is going on (within and without) in distinction from a "scene," which is partly at least in dialogue and which presents, in some detail, an important episode or encounter.[26] The "picture" is as "objective" as the "drama," only it is the objective rendering of a specific subjectivity—that of one of the characters (Madame Bovary, or Strether), while the "drama" is the objective rendering of speech and behavior. This theory admits of a shift of "point of view" (e.g., from the Prince to the Princess in the second half of *The Golden Bowl*), provided it be systematic. It also admits the author's use of a character within the novel, not unlike the author, who is either telling the narrative to some friends (Marlow, in Conrad's *Youth*) or the consciousness through which all is seen (Strether, in *The Ambassadors*): the insistence is upon the self-consistent objectivity of the novel. If the author is to be present other than "in solution," it must be by reducing himself or his representative to the same size and status as the other characters.[27]

Integral to the objective method is presentation in time, the reader's living through the process with the characters. To some extent, "picture" and "drama" must always be supplemented by "summary" (the "five days elapse between Acts I and II" of the theater); but it should be minimal. The Victorian novel used to end with a chapter summarizing the subsequent careers, marriages, and deaths, of the principal characters; James, Howells, and their contemporaries put an end to this practice, which they

[26] On "picture" and "scene," *cf.* James' *Art of the Novel,* pp. 298-300, 322-3.

[27] *Ibid.*, pp. 320-1, 327-9. James attacks narration in the first person as well as the "mere muffled majesty of irresponsible 'authorship' " (the omniscient narrator).

viewed as an artistic blunder. According to objectivist theory, the author must never anticipate what lies ahead; he must enroll his chart, letting us see only a line at a time. Ramon Fernandez sets up a distinction between the *récit,* the narrative of what has already taken place, and is now being told, according to the laws of exposition and description, and the *roman,* or novel, which represents events taking place in time, according to the order of living production.[28]

A characteristic technical device of the objective novel is what the Germans call *"erlebte Rede,"* and the French *"le style indirect libre"* (Thibaudet) and *"le monologue intérieur"* (Dujardin); and in English, the phrase, "stream of consciousness," which goes back to William James, is the loose, inclusive correspondent.[29] Dujardin defines "interior monologue" as a device for the "direct introduction of the reader into the interior life of the character, without any interventions in the way of explanation or commentary on the part of the author . . ." and as "the expression of the most intimate thoughts, those which lie nearest the unconscious. . . ." In *The Ambassadors,* says Lubbock, James does not "tell the story of Strether's mind; he makes it tell itself, he dramatizes it."[30] The history of these devices, and of their adumbrations in all modern literatures, only begins to be studied: the Shakespearean soliloquy is one ancestor; Sterne, applying Locke on the free association of ideas, is another; the "internal analysis," i.e., the summarizing by the author of a character's movement of thought and feeling, is a third.[31]

[28] R. Fernandez, "La méthode de Balzac: Le récit et l'esthétique du roman," *Messages,* Paris, 1926, p. 59 ff. (English tr., London, 1927, pp. 59-88).

[29] Oskar Walzel, "Von 'erlebter Rede,'" *Das Wortkunstwerk,* Leipzig, 1926, p. 207 ff.; Albert Thibaudet, *Flaubert,* Paris, 1935, pp. 229-32; E. Dujardin, *Le monologue intérieur . . .,* Paris, 1931; William James, *Principles of Psychology,* New York, 1890, Vol. I, p. 243: chap. IX, in which the phrase appears, is called "The Stream of Thought."

[30] Lubbock, *op. cit.,* p. 147. "When Strether's mind is dramatized, nothing is shown but the passing images that anybody might detect, looking down upon a mind grown visible" (*ibid.,* p. 162).

[31] *Cf.* L. E. Bowling, "What Is the Stream of Consciousness Technique?" *PMLA,* LXV (1950), pp. 337-45, and Melvin Friedman, *Stream of Consciousness: A Study in Literary Method,* New Haven, 1955.

## Northrop Frye

### *Fictional Modes and Forms*

FICTIONAL MODES

In the second paragraph of the *Poetics* Aristotle speaks of the differences in works of fiction which are caused by the different elevations of the characters in them. In some fictions, he says, the characters are better than we are, in others worse, in still others on the same level. This passage has not received much attention from modern critics, as the importance Aristotle assigns to goodness and badness seems to indicate a somewhat narrowly moralistic view of literature. Aristotle's words for good and bad, however, are *spoudaios* and *phaulos,* which have a figurative sense of weighty and light. In literary fictions the plot consists of somebody doing something. The somebody, if an individual, is the hero, and the something he does or fails to do is what he can do, or could have done, on the level of the postulates made about him by the author and the consequent expectations of the audience. Fictions, therefore, may be classified, not morally, but by the hero's power of action, which may be greater than ours, less, or roughly the same. Thus:

1. If superior in *kind* both to other men and to the environment of other men, the hero is a divine being, and the story about him will be a *myth* in the common sense of a story about a god. Such stories have an important place in literature, but are as a rule found outside the normal literary categories.

2. If superior in *degree* to other men and to his environment, the hero is the typical hero of *romance,* whose actions are marvelous but who is himself identified as a human being. The hero of romance moves in a world in which the ordinary laws of nature are slightly suspended: prodigies of courage and endurance, unnatural to us, are natural to him, and enchanted weapons, talking animals, terrifying ogres and witches, and talismans of miraculous power violate no rule of probability once the postulates of romance have been established. Here we have moved from myth, properly so called, into legend, folk tale, *märchen,* and their literary affiliates and derivatives.

3. If superior in degree to other men but not to his natural environment, the hero is a leader. He has authority, passions, and powers of expression far greater than ours, but what he does is subject both to social criticism and to the order of nature. This is the hero of the *high mimetic* mode, of most epic and tragedy, and is primarily the kind of hero that Aristotle had in mind.

4. If superior neither to other men nor to his environment, the hero is one of us: we respond to a sense of his common humanity, and demand from the poet the same canons of probability that we find in our own experience. This gives us the hero of the *low mimetic* mode, of most comedy and of realistic fiction. "High" and "low" have no connotations of comparative value, but are purely diagrammatic, as they are when they refer to Biblical critics or Anglicans. On this level the difficulty in retaining the word "hero," which has a more limited meaning among the preceding modes, occasionally strikes an author. Thackeray thus feels obliged to call *Vanity Fair* a novel without a hero.

5. If inferior in power or intelligence to ourselves, so that we have the sense of looking down on a scene of bondage, frustration, or absurdity, the hero belongs to the *ironic* mode. This is still true when the reader feels that he is or might be in the same situation, as the situation is being judged by the norms of a greater freedom.

Looking over this table, we can see that European fiction, during the last fifteen centuries, has steadily moved its center of gravity down the list. In the pre-medieval period literature is closely attached to Christian, late Classical, Celtic, or Teutonic myths. If Christianity had not been both an imported myth and a devourer of rival ones, this phase of Western literature would be easier to isolate. In the form in which we possess it, most of it has already moved into the category of romance. Romance divides into two main forms: a secular form dealing with chivalry and knight-errantry, and a religious form devoted to legends of saints. Both lean heavily on miraculous violations of natural law for their interest as stories. Fictions of romance dominate literature until the cult of the prince and the courtier in the Renaissance brings the high mimetic mode into the foreground. The characteristics of this mode are most clearly seen in the genres of drama, particularly tragedy, and national epic. Then a new kind of middle-class culture introduces the low mimetic, which predominates in English literature from Defoe's time to the end of the nineteenth century. In French literature it begins and ends about fifty years earlier. During the last hundred years, most serious fiction has tended increasingly to be ironic in mode.

Something of the same progression may be traced in Classical literature too, in a greatly foreshortened form. Where a religion is mythological and polytheistic, where there are promiscuous incarnations, deified heroes and kings of divine descent, where the same adjective "godlike" can be applied either to Zeus or to Achilles, it is hardly possible to separate the mythical, romantic, and high mimetic strands completely. Where the religion is theological, and insists on a sharp division between divine and human natures, romance becomes more clearly isolated, as it does in the legends of Christian chivalry and sanctity, in the Arabian Nights of Mohammedanism, in the stories of the judges and thaumaturgic prophets of Israel. Similarly, the inability of the Classical world to shake off the divine leader in its later period has much to do with the abortive development of low mimetic and ironic modes that got barely started with Roman satire. At the same time the establishing of the high mimetic mode, the developing of a literary tradition with a consistent sense of an order of nature in it, is one of the great feats of Greek civilization. Oriental fiction does not, so far as I know, get very far away from mythical and romantic formulas.

We shall here deal chiefly with the five epochs of Western

literature, as given above, using Classical parallels only incidentally. In each mode a distinction will be useful between naive and sophisticated literature. The word naive I take from Schiller's essay on naive and sentimental poetry: I mean by it, however, primitive or popular, whereas in Schiller it means something more like Classical. The word sentimental also means something else in English, but we do not have enough genuine critical terms to dispense with it. In quotation marks, therefore, "sentimental" refers to a later recreation of an earlier mode. Thus romanticism is a "sentimental" form of romance, and the fairy tale, for the most part, a "sentimental" form of folk tale. Also there is a general distinction between fictions in which the hero becomes isolated from his society, and fictions in which he is incorporated into it. This distinction is expressed by the words "tragic" and "comic" when they refer to aspects of plot in general and not simply to forms of drama.

* * * * * *

The conception of a sequence of fictional modes should do something, let us hope, to give a more flexible meaning to some of our literary terms. The words "romantic" and "realistic," for instance, as ordinarily used, are relative or comparative terms: they illustrate tendencies in fiction, and cannot be used as simply descriptive adjectives with any sort of exactness. If we take the sequence *De Raptu Proserpinae, The Man of Law's Tale, Much Ado About Nothing, Pride and Prejudice, An American Tragedy,* it is clear that each work is "romantic" compared to its successors and "realistic" compared to its predecessors. On the other hand, the term "naturalism" shows up in its proper perspective as a phase of fiction which, rather like the detective story, though in a very different way, begins as an intensification of low mimetic, an attempt to describe life exactly as it is, and ends, by the very logic of that attempt, in pure irony. Thus Zola's obsession with ironic formulas gave him a reputation as a detached recorder of the human scene.

The difference between the ironic *tone* that we may find in low mimetic or earlier modes and the ironic *structure* of the ironic mode itself is not hard to sense in practice. When Dickens, for instance, uses irony the reader is invited to share in the irony, because certain standards of normality common to author and reader are assumed. Such assumptions are a mark of a relatively popular mode: as the example of Dickens indicates, the gap between serious and popular fiction is narrower in low mimetic than in ironic writing. The literary acceptance of relatively stable social norms is closely connected with the *reticence* of low mimetic as compared to ironic fiction. In low mimetic modes characters are usually presented as they appear to others, fully dressed and with a large section of both their physical lives and their inner monologue carefully excised. Such an approach is entirely consistent with the other conventions involved.

If we were to make this distinction the basis of a comparative value-judgment, which would, of course, be a moral value-judgment disguised as a critical one, we should be compelled either to attack low mimetic conventions for being prudish and hypocritical and leaving too much of life out, or to attack ironic conventions for not being wholesome, healthy, popular, reassuring, and sound, like the conventions of Dickens. As long as we are concerned simply to distinguish between the conventions, we need only remark that the low mimetic is one step more heroic than the ironic, and that low mimetic reticence has the effect of making its characters, on the average, more heroic, or at least more dignified, than the characters in ironic fiction.

We may also apply our scheme to the principles of selection on which a writer of fiction operates. Let us take, as a random example, the use of ghosts in fiction. In a true myth there can obviously be no consistent distinction between ghosts and living beings. In romance we have real human beings, and consequently ghosts are in a separate category, but in a romance a ghost as a rule is merely one more character: he causes little surprise because his appearance is no more marvellous than many other events. In high mimetic, where we are within the order of nature, a ghost is relatively easy to introduce because the plane of experience is above our own, but when he appears he is an awful and mysterious being from what is perceptibly another world. In low mimetic, ghosts have been, ever since Defoe, almost entirely confined to a separate category of "ghost stories." In ordinary low mimetic fiction they are inadmissible, "in complaisance to the scepticism of a reader," as Fielding puts it, a skepticism which extends only to low mimetic conventions. The few exceptions, such as *Wuthering Heights*, go a long way to prove the rule—that is, we recognize a strong influence of romance in *Wuthering Heights*. In some forms of ironic fiction, such as the later works of Henry James, the ghost begins to come back as a fragment of a disintegrating personality.

Once we have learned to distinguish the modes, however, we must then learn to recombine them. For while one mode constitutes the underlying tonality of a work of fiction, any or all of the other four may be simultaneously present. Much of our sense of the subtlety of great literature comes from this modal counterpoint. Chaucer is a medieval poet specializing mainly in romance, whether sacred or secular. Of his pilgrims, the knight and the parson clearly present the norms of the society in which he functions as a poet, and, as we have them, the *Canterbury Tales* are contained by these two figures, who open and close the series. But to overlook Chaucer's mastery of low mimetic and ironic techniques would be as wrong as to think of him as a modern novelist who got into the Middle Ages by mistake. The tonality of *Antony and Cleopatra* is high mimetic, the story of the fall of a great leader. But it is easy to look at Mark Antony ironically, as a man enslaved by passion; it is easy to recognize his common humanity with ourselves; it is easy to see in him a romantic adventurer of prodigious courage and endurance betrayed by a witch; there are even hints of a superhuman being whose legs bestrid the ocean and whose downfall is a conspiracy of fate, explicable only to a soothsayer. To leave out any of these would oversimplify and belittle the play. Through such an analysis we may come to realize that the two essential facts about a work of art, that it is contemporary with its own time and that it is contemporary with ours, are not opposed but complementary facts.

Our survey of fictional modes has also shown us that the mimetic tendency itself, the tendency to verisimilitude and accuracy of description, is one of two poles of literature. At the other pole is something that seems to be connected both with Aristotle's word *mythos* and with the usual meaning of myth. That is, it is a tendency to tell a story which is in origin a story about characters who can do anything, and only gradually becomes attracted toward a tendency to tell a plausible or credible story. Myths of gods merge into legends of heroes; legends of heroes merge into plots of tragedies and comedies; plots of tragedies and comedies merge into plots of more or less realistic fiction. But these are change of social context rather than of literary form, and the constructive principles of story-telling remain constant through them, though of course they adapt to them. Tom Jones and Oliver Twist are typical enough as low mimetic characters, but the birth-mystery plots in which they are involved are plausible adaptations of fictional formulas that go back to Menander, and from Menander to Euripides' *Ion,* and from Euripides to legends like those of Perseus and Moses. We note in passing that imitation of nature in fiction produces, not truth or reality, but plausibility, and plausibility varies in weight from a mere perfunctory concession in a myth or folk tale to a kind of censor principle in a naturalistic novel. Reading forward in history, therefore, we may think of our romantic, high mimetic and low mimetic modes as a series of *displaced* myths, *mythoi* or plot-formulas progressively moving over towards the opposite pole of verisimilitude, and then, with irony, beginning to move back.

## SPECIFIC CONTINUOUS FORMS

In assigning the term fiction to the genre of the written word, in which prose tends to become the predominating rhythm, we collide with the view that the real meaning of fiction is falsehood or unreality. Thus an autobiography coming into a library would be classified as non-fiction if the librarian believed the author, and as fiction if she thought he was lying. It is difficult to see what use such a distinction can be to a literary critic. Surely the word fiction, which, like poetry, means etymologically something made for its own sake, could be applied in criticism to any work of literary art in a radically continuous form, which almost always means a work of art in prose. Or, if that is too much to ask, at least some protest can be entered against the sloppy habit of identifying fiction with the one genuine form of fiction which we know as the novel.

Let us look at a few of the unclassified books lying on the boundary of "non-fiction" and "literature." Is *Tristram Shandy* a novel? Nearly everyone would say yes, in spite of its easygoing disregard of "story values." Is *Gulliver's Travels* a novel? Here most would demur, including the Dewey decimal system, which puts it under "Satire and Humor." But surely everyone would call it fiction, and if it is fiction, a distinction appears between fiction as a genus and the novel as a species of that genus. Shifting the ground to fiction, then, is *Sartor Resartus* fiction? If not, why not? If it is, is *The Anatomy of Melancholy* fiction? Is it a literary form or only a work of "non-fiction" written with "style"? Is Borrow's *Lavengro* fiction? Everyman's Library says yes; the World's Classics puts it under "Travel and Topography."

The literary historian who identifies fiction with the novel is greatly embarrassed by the length of time that the world managed to get along without the novel, and until he reaches his great deliverance in Defoe, his perspective is intolerably cramped. He is compelled to reduce Tudor fiction to a series of tentative essays in the novel form, which works well enough for Deloney but makes nonsense of Sidney. He postulates a great fictional gap in the seventeenth century which exactly covers the golden age of rhetorical prose. He finally discovers that the word novel, which up to about 1900 was still the name of a more or less recognizable form, has since expanded into a catchall term which can be applied to practically any prose book that is not "on" something. Clearly, this novel-centered view of prose fiction is a Ptolemaic perspective which is now too complicated to be any longer workable, and some more relative and Copernican view must take its place.

When we start to think seriously about the novel, not as fiction, but as a form of fiction, we feel that its characteristics, whatever they are, are such as make, say, Defoe, Fielding, Austen, and James central in its tradition, and Borrow, Peacock, Melville, and Emily Bronte somehow peripheral. This is not an estimate of merit: we may think *Moby Dick* "greater" than *The Egoist* and yet feel that Meredith's book is closer to being a typical novel. Fielding's conception of the novel as a comic epic in prose seems fundamental to the tradition he did so much to establish. In novels that we think of as typical, like those of Jane Austen, plot and dialogue are closely linked to the conventions of the comedy of manners. The conventions of *Wuthering Heights* are linked rather with the tale and the ballad. They seem to have more affinity with tragedy, and the tragic emotions of passion and fury, which would shatter the balance of tone in Jane Austen, can be safely accommodated here. So can the supernatural, or the suggestion of it, which is difficult to get into a novel. The shape of the plot is different: instead of manoeuvering around a central situation, as Jane Austen does, Emily Bronte tells her story with linear accents, and she seems to need the help of a narrator, who would be absurdly out of place in Jane Austen. Conventions so different justify us in regarding *Wuthering Heights* as a different form of prose fiction from the novel, a form which we shall here call the romance. Here again we have to use the same word in several different contexts, but romance seems on the whole better than tale, which appears to fit a somewhat shorter form.

The essential difference between novel and romance lies in the conception of characterization. The romancer does not attempt to create "real people" so much as stylized figures which expand into psychological archetypes. It is in the romance that we find Jung's libido, anima, and shadow reflected in the hero, heroine, and villain respectively. That is why the romance so often radiates a glow of subjective intensity that the novel lacks, and why a suggestion of allegory is constantly creeping in around its fringes. Certain elements of character are released in the romance which make it naturally a more revolutionary form than the novel. The novelist deals with personality, with characters wearing their *personae* or social masks. He needs the framework of a stable society, and many of our best novelists have been conventional to the verge of fussiness. The romancer deals with individuality, with characters *in vacuo* idealized by revery, and, however conservative he may be, something nihilistic and untamable is likely to keep breaking out of his pages.

The prose romance, then, is an independent form of fiction to be distinguished from the novel and extracted from the miscellaneous heap of prose works now covered by that term. Even in the other heap known as short stories one can isolate the tale form used by Poe, which bears the same relation to the full romance that the stories of Chekhov or Katherine Mansfield do to the novel. "Pure" examples of either form are never found;

there is hardly any modern romance that could not be made out to be a novel, and vice versa. The forms of prose fiction are mixed, like racial strains in human beings, not separable like the sexes. In fact the popular demand in fiction is always for a mixed form, a romantic novel just romantic enough for the reader to project his libido on the hero and his anima on the heroine, and just novel enough to keep these projections in a familiar world. It may be asked, therefore, what is the use of making the above distinction, especially when, though undeveloped in criticism, it is by no means unrealized. It is no surprise to hear that Trollope wrote novels and William Morris romances.

The reason is that a great romancer should be examined in terms of the conventions he chose. William Morris should not be left on the side lines of prose fiction merely because the critic has not learned to take the romance form seriously. Nor, in view of what has been said about the revolutionary nature of the romance, should his choice of that form be regarded as an "escape" from his social attitude. If Scott has any claims to be a romancer, it is not good criticism to deal only with his defects as a novelist. The romantic qualities of *The Pilgrim's Progress,* too, its archetypal characterization and its revolutionary approach to religious experience, make it a well-rounded example of a literary form: it is not merely a book swallowed by English literature to get some religious bulk in its diet. Finally, when Hawthorne, in the preface to *The House of the Seven Gables,* insists that his story should be read as romance and not as novel, it is possible that he meant what he said, even though he indicates that the prestige of the rival form has induced the romancer to apologize for not using it.

Romance is older than the novel, a fact which has developed the historical illusion that it is something to be outgrown, a juvenile and undeveloped form. The social affinities of the romance, with its grave idealizing of heroism and purity, are with the aristocracy (for the apparent inconsistency of this with the revolutionary nature of the form just mentioned, see the introductory comment on the *mythos* of romance in the previous essay). It revived in the period we call Romantic as part of the Romantic tendency to archaic feudalism and a cult of the hero, or idealized libido. In England the romances of Scott and, in less degree, the Brontes, are part of a mysterious Northumbrian renaissance, a Romantic reaction against the new industrialism in the Midlands, which also produced the poetry of Wordsworth and Burns and the philosophy of Carlyle. It is not surprising, therefore, that an important theme in the more bourgeois novel should be the parody of the romance and its ideals. The tradition established by *Don Quixote* continues in a type of novel which looks at a romantic situation from its own point of view, so that the conventions of the two forms make up an ironic compound instead of a sentimental mixture. Examples range from *Northanger Abbey* to *Madame Bovary* and *Lord Jim*.

The tendency to allegory in the romance may be conscious, as in *The Pilgrim's Progress,* or unconscious, as in the very obvious sexual mythopoeia in William Morris. The romance, which deals with heroes, is intermediate between the novel, which deals with men, and the myth, which deals with gods. Prose romance first appears as a late development of Classical mythology, and the prose Sagas of Iceland follow close on the mythical Eddas. The novel tends rather to expand into a fictional approach to history. The soundness of Fielding's instinct in calling *Tom Jones* a history is confirmed by the general rule that the larger the scheme of a novel becomes, the more obviously its historical nature appears. As it is creative history, however, the novelist usually prefers his material in a plastic, or roughly contemporary state, and feels cramped by a fixed historical pattern. *Waverley* is dated about sixty years back from the time of writing and *Little Dorrit* about forty years, but the historical pattern is fixed in the romance and plastic in the novel, suggesting the general principle that most "historical novels" are romances. Similarly a novel becomes more romantic in its appeal when the life it reflects has passed away: thus the novels of Trollope were read primarily as romances during the Second World War. It is perhaps the link with history and a sense of temporal context that has confined the novel, in striking contrast to the world-wide romance, to the alliance of time and Western man.

Autobiography is another form which merges with the novel by a series of insensible gradations. Most autobiographies are inspired by a creative, and therefore fictional, impulse to select only those events and experiences in the writer's life that go to build up an integrated pattern. This pattern may be something larger than himself with which he has come to identify himself or simply the coherence of his character and attitudes. We may call this very important form of prose fiction the confession form, following St. Augustine, who appears to have invented it, and Rousseau, who established a modern type of it. The earlier tradition gave *Religio Medici, Grace Abounding,* and Newman's *Apologia* to English literature, besides the related but subtly different type of confession favored by the mystics.

Here again, as with the romance, there is some value in recognizing a distinct prose form in the confession. It gives several of our best prose works a definable place in fiction instead of keeping them in a vague limbo of books which are not quite literature because they are "thought," and not quite religion or philosophy because they are Examples of Prose Style. The confession, too, like the novel and the romance, has its own short form, the familiar essay and Montaigne's *livre de bonne foy* is a confession made up of essays in which only the continuous narrative of the longer form is missing. Montaigne's scheme is to the confession what a work of fiction made up of short stories, such as Joyce's *Dubliners* or Boccaccio's *Decameron,* is to the novel or romance.

After Rousseau—in fact in Rousseau—the confession flows into the novel, and the mixture produces the fictional autobiography, the *Künstler-roman,* and kindred types. There is no literary reason why the subject of a confession should always be the author himself, and dramatic confessions have been used in the novel at least since *Moll Flanders*. The "stream of consciousness" technique permits of a much more concentrated fusion of the two forms, but even here the characteristics peculiar to the confession form show up clearly. Nearly always some theoretical and intellectual interest in religion, politics, or art plays a leading role in the confession. It is his success in integrating his mind on such subjects that makes the author of a confession feel that his life is worth writing about. But this interest in ideas and theoretical statements is alien to the genius of the novel proper, where the technical problem is to dissolve all theory into personal relationships. In Jane Austen, to take a familiar instance, church, state, and culture are never examined except as social data, and Henry James has been described as having a mind so fine that no idea could violate it. The novelist who cannot get along without ideas, or has not the patience to digest them in the way that James did, instinctively resorts to what Mill calls a "mental history" of a single character. And when we find that a technical discussion of a theory of aesthetics forms the climax of Joyce's *Portrait,* we realize that what makes this possible is the presence in that novel of another tradition of prose fiction.

The novel tends to be extroverted and personal; its chief interest is in human character as it manifests itself in society. The romance tends to be introverted and personal: it also deals with characters, but in a more subjective way. (Subjective here refers to treatment, not subject-matter. The characters of romance are heroic and therefore inscrutable; the novelist is freer to enter his characters' minds because he is more objective.) The confession is also introverted, but intellectualized in content. Our next step is evidently to discover a fourth form of fiction which is extroverted and intellectual.

We remarked earlier that most people would call *Gulliver's Travels* fiction but not a novel. It must then be another form of fiction, as it certainly has a form, and we feel that we are turning from the novel to this form, whatever it is, when we turn from Rousseau's *Emile* to Voltaire's *Candide,* or from Butler's *The Way of All Flesh* to the Erewhon books, or from Huxley's *Point Counterpoint* to *Brave New World.* The form thus has its own traditions, and, as the examples of Butler and Huxley show, has preserved some integrity even under the ascendancy of the novel. Its existence is easy enough to demonstrate, and no one will challenge the statement that the literary ancestry of *Gulliver's Travels* and *Candide* runs through Rabelais and Erasmus to Lucian. But while much has been said about the style and thought of Rabelais, Swift, and Voltaire, very little has been made of them as craftsmen working in a specific medium, a point no one dealing with a novelist would ignore. Another great writer in this traditon, Huxley's master Peacock, has fared even worse, for, his form not being understood, a general impression has grown up that his status in the development of prose fiction is that of a slapdash eccentric. Actually, he is as exquisite and precise an artist in his medium as Jane Austen is in hers.

The form used by these authors is the Menippean satire, also more rarely called the Varronian satire, allegedly invented by a Greek cynic named Menippus. His works are lost, but he had two great disciples, the Greek Lucian and the Roman Varro, and the tradition of Varro, who has not survived either except in fragments, was carried on by Petronius and Apuleius. The Menippean satire appears to have developed out of verse satire through the practice of adding prose interludes, but we know it only as a prose form, though one of its recurrent features (seen in Peacock) is the use of incidental verse.

The Menippean satire deals less with people as such than with mental attitudes. Pedants, bigots, cranks, parvenus, vituosi, enthusiasts, rapacious and incompetent professional men of all kinds, are handled in terms of their occupational approach to life as distinct from their social behavior. The Menippean satire thus resembles the confession in its ability to handle abstract ideas and theories and differs from the novel in its characterization, which is stylized rather than naturalistic, and presents people as mouthpieces of the ideas they represent. Here again no sharp boundary lines can or should be drawn, but if we compare a character in Jane Austen with a similar character in Peacock we can immediately feel the difference between the two forms. Squire Western belongs to the novel, but Thwackum and Square have Menippean blood in them. A constant theme in the tradition is the ridicule of the *philosophus gloriosus,* already discussed. The novelist sees evil and folly as social diseases, but the Menippean satirist sees them as diseases of the intellect, as a kind of maddened pedantry which the *philosophus gloriosus* at once symbolizes and defines.

Petronius, Apuleius, Rabelais, Swift, and Voltaire all use a loose-jointed narrative form often confused with the romance. It differs from the romance, however (though there is a strong admixture of romance in Rabelais), as it is not primarily concerned with the exploits of heroes, but relies on the free play of intellectual fancy and the kind of humorous observation that produces caricature. It differs also from the picaresque form, which has the novel's interest in the actual structure of society. At its most concentrated the Menippean satire presents us with a vision of the world in terms of a single intellectual pattern. The intellectual structure built up from the story makes for violent dislocations in the customary logic of narrative, though the appearance of carelessness that results reflects only the carelessness of the reader or his tendency to judge by a novel-centered conception of fiction.

The word "satire," in Roman and Renaissance times, meant either of two specific literary forms of that name, one (this one) prose and the other verse. Now it means a structural principle or attitude, what we have called a *mythos*. In the Menippean satires we have been discussing, the name of the form also applies to the attitude. As the name of an attitude, satire is, we have seen, a combination of fantasy and morality. But as the name of a form, the term satire, though confined to literature (for as a *mythos* it may appear in any art, a cartoon, for example), is more flexible, and can be either entirely fantastic or entirely moral. The Menippean adventure story may thus be pure fantasy, as it is in the literary fairy tale. The Alice books are perfect Menippean satires, and so is *The Water-Babies,* which has been influenced by Rabelais. The purely moral type is a serious vision of society as a single intellectual pattern, in other words a Utopia.

The short form of the Menippean satire is usually a dialogue or colloquy, in which the dramatic interest is in a conflict of ideas rather than of character. This is the favorite form of Erasmus, and is common in Voltaire. Here again the form is not invariably satiric in attitude, but shades off into more purely fanciful or moral discussions, like the *Imaginary Conversations* of Landor or the "dialogue of the dead." Sometimes this form expands to full length, and more than two speakers are used: the setting then is usually a *cena* or symposium, like the one that looms so large in Petronius. Plato, though much earlier in the field than Menippus, is a strong influence on this type, which stretches in an unbroken tradition down through those urbane and leisurely conversations which define the ideal courtier in Castiglione or the doctrine and discipline of angling in Walton. A modern development produces the country-house weekends in Peacock, Huxley, and their imitators in which the opinions and ideas and cultural interests expressed are as important as the love-making.

The novelist shows his exuberance either by an exhaustive analysis of human relationships, as in Henry James, or of social phenomena, as in Tolstoy. The Menippean satirist, dealing with intellectual themes and attitudes, shows his exuberance in intellectual ways, by piling up an enormous mass of erudition about his theme or in overwhelming his pedantic targets with an avalanche of their own jargon. A species, or rather sub-species, of the form is the kind of encyclopaedic farrago represented by Athenaeus' *Deipnosophists* and Macrobius' *Saturnalia,* where people sit at a banquet and pour out a vast mass of erudition on every subject that might conceivably come up in a conversation. The display of erudition had probably been associated with the Menippean tradition by Varro, who was enough of a polymath to make Quintilian, if not stare and gasp, at any rate call him *vir Romanorum eruditissimus*. The tendency to expand into an encyclopaedic farrago is clearly marked in Rabelais notably in the great catalogues of torcheculs and epithets of codpieces and methods of divination. The encyclopaedic compilations produced in the line of duty by Erasmus and Voltaire suggest that a magpie instinct to collect facts is not unrelated to the type of ability that has made them famous as artists. Flaubert's encyclopaedic approach to the construction of *Bouvard et Pecuchet* is quite comprehensible if we explain it as marking an affinity with the Menippean tradition.

This creative treatment of exhaustive erudition is the organizing principle of the greatest Menippean satire in English before Swift, Burton's *Anatomy of Melancholy*. Here human society is studied in terms of the intellectual pattern provided by the conception of melancholy, a symposium of books replaces dialogue, and the result is the most comprehensive survey of human life in one book that English literature had seen since Chaucer, one of Burton's favorite authors. We may note in passing the Utopia in his introduction and his "digressions," which when examined turn out to be scholarly distillations of Menippean forms: the digression of air, of the marvellous journey; the digression of spirits, of the ironic use of erudition; the digression of the miseries of scholars, of the satire on the *philosophus gloriosus*. The word "anatomy" in Burton's title means a dissection or analysis, and expresses very accurately the intellectualized approach of his form. We may as well adopt it as a convenient name to replace the cumbersome and in modern times rather misleading "Menippean satire."

The anatomy, of course, eventually begins to merge with the novel, producing various hybrids including the *roman à these* and novels in which the characters are symbols of social or other ideas, like the proletarian novels of the thirties in this century. It was Sterne, however, the disciple of Burton and Rabelais, who combined them with greatest success. *Tristram Shandy* may be, as was said at the beginning, a novel, but the digressing narrative, the catalogues, the stylizing of character along "humor" lines, the marvellous journey of the great nose, the symposium discussions, and the constant ridicule of philosophers and pedantic critics are all features that belong to the anatomy.

A clearer understanding of the form and traditions of the anatomy would make a good many elements in the history of literature come into focus. Boethius' *Consolation of Philosophy,* with its dialogue form, its verse interludes and its pervading tone of contemplative irony, is a pure anatomy, a fact of considerable importance for the understanding of its vast influence. *The Compleat Angler* is an anatomy because of its mixture of prose and verse, its rural *cena* setting, its dialogue form, its deipnosophistical interest in food, and its gentle Menippean raillery of a society which considers everything more important than fishing and yet has discovered very few better things to do. In nearly every period of literature there are many romances, confessions, and anatomies that are neglected only because the categories to which they belong are unrecognized. In the period between Sterne and Peacock, for example, we have, among romances, *Melmoth the Wanderer;* among confessions, Hogg's *Confessions of a Justified Sinner;* among anatomies, Southey's *Doctor,* Amory's *John Buncle,* and the *Noctes Ambrosianae.*

To sum up then: when we examine fiction from the point of view of form, we can see four chief strands binding it together, novel, confession, anatomy, and romance. The six possible combinations of these forms all exist, and we have shown how the novel has combined with each of the other three. Exclusive concentration on one form is rare: the early novels of George Eliot, for instance, are influenced by the romance, and the later ones by the anatomy. The romance-confession hybrid is found, naturally, in the autobiography of a romantic temperament, and is represented in English by the extroverted George Borrow and the introverted De Quincey. The romance-anatomy one we have noticed in Rabelais; a later example is *Moby Dick,* where the romantic theme of the wild hunt expands into an encyclopaedic anatomy of the whale. Confession and anatomy are united in *Sartor Resartus* and in some of Kierkegaard's strikingly original experiments in prose fiction form, including *Either/Or*. More comprehensive fictional schemes usually employ at least three forms: we can see strains of novel, romance, and confession in *Pamela,* of novel, romance, and anatomy in *Don Quixote,* of novel, confession, and anatomy in Proust, and of romance, confession, and anatomy in Apuleius.

I deliberately make this sound schematic in order to suggest the advantage of having a simple and logical explanation for the form of, say, *Moby Dick* or *Tristram Shandy.* The usual critical approach to the form of such works resembles that of the doctors in Brobdingnag, who after great wrangling finally pronounced Gulliver a *lusus naturae*. It is the anatomy in particular that has baffled critics, and there is hardly any fiction writer deeply influenced by it who has not been accused of disorderly conduct. The reader may be reminded here of Joyce, for describing Joyce's books as monstrous has become a nervous tic. I find "demogorgon," "behemoth," and "white elephant" in good critics; the bad ones could probably do much better. The care that Joyce took to organize *Ulysses* and *Finnegans Wake* amounted nearly to obsession, but as they are not organized on familiar principles of prose fiction, the impression of shapelessness remains. Let us try our formulas on him.

If a reader were asked to set down a list of things that had most impressed him about *Ulysses,* it might reasonably be somewhat as follows. First, the clarity with which the sights and sounds and smells of Dublin come to life, the rotundity of the character-drawing, and the naturalness of the dialogue. Second, the elaborate way that the story and characters are parodied by being set against archetypal heroic patterns, notably the one provided by the *Odyssey.* Third, the revelation of character and incident through the searching use of the stream-of-consciousness technique. Fourth, the constant tendency to be encyclopaedic and exhaustive both in technique and in subject matter, and to see both in highly intellectualized terms. It should not be too hard for us by now to see that these four points describe elements in the book which relate to the novel, romance, confession, and anatomy respectively. *Ulysses,* then, is a complete prose epic with all four forms employed in it, all of practically equal importance, and all essential to one another, so that the book is a unity and not an aggregate.

This unity is built up from an intricate scheme of parallel contrasts. The romantic archetypes of Hamlet and Ulysses are like remote stars in a literary heaven looking down quizzically on the shabby creatures of Dublin obediently intertwining themselves in the patterns set by their influences. In the "Cyclops" and "Circe" episodes particularly there is a continuous parody of realistic patterns by romantic ones which reminds us, though the irony leans in the opposite direction, of *Madame Bovary.* The relation of novel and confession techniques is similar; the author jumps into his characters' minds to follow their stream of consciousness, and out again to describe them externally. In the novel-anatomy combination, too, found in the "Ithaca" chapter, the sense of lurking antagonism between the personal and intellectual aspects of the scene accounts for much of its pathos. The same principle of parallel contrast holds good for the other three combinations: of romance and confession in "Nausicaa" and "Penelope," of confession and anatomy in "Proteus" and "The Lotos-Eaters," of romance and anatomy (a rare and fitful combination) in "Sirens" and parts of "Circe."

In *Finnegans Wake* the unity of design goes far beyond this. The dingy story of the sodden HCE and his pinched wife is not contrasted with the archetypes of Tristram and the divine king: HCE is himself Tristram and the divine king. As the setting is a dream, no contrast is possible between confession and novel, between a stream of consciousness inside the mind and the appearances of other people outside it. Nor is the experiential world of the novel to be separated from the intelligible world of the anatomy. The forms we have been isolating in fiction, and which depend for their existence on the commonsense dichotomies of the daylight consciousness, vanish in *Finnegans Wake* into a fifth and quintessential form. This form is the one traditionally associated with scriptures and sacred books, and treats life in terms of the fall and awakening of the human soul and the creation and apocalypse of nature. The Bible is the definitive example of it; the Egyptian Book of the Dead and the Icelandic Prose Edda, both of which have left deep imprints on *Finnegans Wake*, also belong to it.

# II. The Representation of Reality

Erich Auerbach, "Fortunata," from *Mimesis,* translated from the German by Willard Trask, reprinted here by permission of the Princeton University Press.

Harry Levin, "The Context of Realism" and "The Dynasty of Realism" (sections 6 and 7 of Chapter 2), from *The Gates of Horn,* reprinted here by permission of the Oxford University Press.

Ian Watt, "Realism and the Novel Form," from *The Rise of the Novel,* reprinted here by permission of the University of California Press.

Lionel Trilling, "Manners, Morals, and the Novel," from *The Liberal Imagination* (copyright 1948, 1950 by Lionel Trilling), reprinted here by permission of the Viking Press.

*To understand the novel as a literary form, we must not only see its relationships with other literary forms. We must also see it in terms of social history and the history of ideas; for the novel itself is a historical phenomenon, coming into being at a particular time and showing signs of decay and dissolution at present. To do some justice to this temporal aspect of the novel, it has seemed best to present four essays, which deal with different segments of the history of narrative and which offer certain differences of emphasis in their ways of defining the relationship of art to life. Erich Auerbach is concerned with the concept of mimesis, which he develops in this essay by way of discussing the obstacles which prevented certain ancient writers from achieving a full representation of reality. Ian Watt, focusing on the rise of the English novel, relates this phenomenon to extraliterary developments in thought and life. Harry Levin, considering the great age of the French novel, the nineteenth century, is also concerned with a broadly historical and extraliterary perspective on this literary mode. And Lionel Trilling, with modern American fiction much in mind, looks back over the history of the novel to find its justification in the way it has been able to raise ethical questions by its prolonged scrutiny of appearance and reality. Auerbach's "mimesis," Watt's "formal realism," Levin's "scrupulous critique," and Trilling's "moral realism" are all ways of talking about the peculiar relationship with life held by the novel as a literary form. All of these essays circle around a great paradox. The essence of the novel as a form lies in its presentation of actuality, its working of life into art. But representing reality is not altogether a formal problem; it is also a matter of perception or vision. Formal realism, as Watt points out, is only the novel's "lowest common denominator." We shall find many of the other critics in this volume engaged with aspects of this same central situation.*

## Erich Auerbach

### *Fortunata*

Non potui amplius quicquam gustare, sed conversus ad eum, ut quam plurima exciperem, longe accersere fabulas coepi sciscitarique, quae esset mulier illa, quae huc atque illuc discurreret. Uxor, inquit, Trimalchionis, Fortunata, appellatur, quae nummos modio metitur. Et modo, modo quid fuit? Ignoscet mihi genius tuus, noluisses de manu illius panem accipere. Nunc, nec quid nec quare, in caelum abiit et Trimalchionis topanta est. Ad summam, mero meridie si dixerit illi tenebras esse, credet. Ipse nescit quid habeat, adeo saplutus est; sed haec lupatria providet omnia et ubi non putes. Est sicca, sobria, bonorum consiliorum, est tamen malae linguae, pica pulvinaris. Quem amat, amat; quem non amat, non amat. Ipse Trimalchio fundos habet qua milvi volant, nummorum nummos. Argentum in ostiarii illius cella plus iacet quam quisquam in fortunis habet. Familia vero babae babae, non mehercules puto decumam partem esse quae dominum suum noverit. Ad summam, quemvis ex istis babaecalis in rutae folium coniciet. Nec est quod putes illum quicquam emere. Omnia domi nascuntur: lana, credrae, piper, lacte gallinaceum si quaesieris, invenies. Ad summam, parum illi bona lana nascebatur; arietes a Tarento emit, et eos culavit in gregem . . . Vides tot culcitras: nulla non aut cochyliatum aut coccineum tomentum habet. Tanta est animi beatitudo. Reliquos autem collibertos eius cave contemnas; valde succossi sunt. Vides illum qui in imo imus recumbit; hodie sua octingenta possidet. De nihilo crevit. Modo solebat collo suo ligna portare. Sed quomodo dicunt—ego nihil scio, sed audivi—quom Incuboni pilleum rapuisset, thesaurum invenit. Ego nemini invideo, si quid deus dedit. Est tamen subalapo et non vult sibi male. Itaque proxime casam hoc titulo proscripsit: C. Pompeius Diogenes ex Calendis Iuliis cenaculum locat; ipse enim domum emit. Quid ille qui libertini loco iacet, quam bene se habuit! Non impropero illi. Sestertium suum vidit decies, sed male vacillavit. Non puto illum capillos liberos habere. . . .

This passage is taken from Petronius' romance, of which only one episode—the banquet at the house of the wealthy freedman Trimalchio—is extant in full. Our sample is chapter 37 and part of chapter 38. During dinner, the narrator, Encolpius, asks his neighbor who the woman is who keeps running back and forth through the hall. The following translation of the answer he receives attempts to do justice to its style:

That's Trimalchio's wife. Fortunata they call her. She measures money by the bushel. Yet not so long ago, not so long ago, what was she? I hope you won't mind my putting it that way, but you wouldn't have accepted a piece of bread from her hands. Now she sits on top of the world and is Trimalchio's one and only. If she tells him at high noon it's dark, he'll agree. He can't keep track of what he owns; he's so filthy rich. But that bitch looks out for everything, even where you'd least expect it. She doesn't drink; she's level-headed; her advice is good. But she has a nasty tongue and gossips like a magpie once she gets settled on her cushion. When she likes a person, she really likes him. When she hates one, she certainly hates him. Trimalchio's estates reach as far as a falcon flies. And some money he has! There's more silver in his porter's lodge than any one man's whole estate. And the number of slaves he's got! O my God, I don't think one out of ten knows his master even by sight. Believe me, he could stick any of these louts here in his pocket. And don't you think he ever has to buy anything. Everything is produced on the premises: wool, wax, pepper, everything; if you asked for chicken milk, I'm sure they'd have it. Once, you know, he didn't produce enough high-grade wool. So he bought rams from Tarentum and had them mount his sheep . . . Look at these cushions. Every single one has purple or scarlet stuffing. Not bad to put a man's mind at ease. But his fellow freedmen are not to be despised either. They aren't badly off. Look at the one sitting all the way back there. Today he is worth eight hundred thousand, and when he started out he had nothing. Not so long ago he carried wood around on his back. But they say—of course I don't know, except that I have heard people talk about it—they say he stole a goblin's magic cap and then found a treasure. Well I won't begrudge a fellow what God has given him. Still, he has just been freed and is planning to do a lot for himself. The other day he put a notice on his place: "C. Pompeius Diogenes offers this dwelling for rent as of July 1st because he is buying a house." That one there sitting with the freedmen—he used to have a nicely feathered nest too. I don't want to say anything against him. He had a cool million. But somehow he slipped badly, and now I don't think even the hair on his head doesn't have a lien on it. . . .[1]

The answer, which goes on in the same style for some time longer, turns out, then, to be fairly circumstantial. Not only the woman about whom Encolpius inquires, but the host and some of the guests are also described. In addition, the speaker portrays himself: his language, and the standards of value which he applies, give a clear idea of his personality. His language is the ordinary, rather mushy jargon of an uneducated city businessman, full of clichés (*nummos modio metitur, ignoscet mihi genius tuus, noluisses de manu illius panem accipere, in caelum abiit, topanta est, ad summam*—nearly all of his expressions would have to be transcribed); and it comes out in that lusty tone of voice which expresses lively but trivial feelings: astonishment, wonder, protestation, indifference, pomposity. In short, in their linguistic form the *tam dulces fabulae* (sweet bits of small talk), as they are presently called, reveal themselves unmistakably as what they are, namely, vulgar chatter, although a considerable portion of their content may be true. At the same time too, they reveal what the man who utters them is—namely, one who fits perfectly into

[1] The translator has profited by an English version of this passage contributed by Professors Oates and Raubitchek of Princeton University.

the milieu he is describing. His standards of value provide further evidence of the fact. For obviously, under all that he says, lie three convictions: that wealth is the greatest good, and the more of it the better (*tanta est animi beatitudo*); that the good things of life are simply a superfluity of articles of the best quality and the opportunity to enjoy them in the most vulgar manner possible; and that, in this sense, everyone quite naturally acts for his own material advantage. Yet withal he himself is doubtless only a small or middling man, who looks upon the truly rich with honest awe. Thus the good fellow describes not only Fortunata, Trimalchio, and their guests, but without being aware of it, himself. Although, as we see, he has a rather one-sided viewpoint and speaks more from emotion and association than from logic, he yet speaks circumstantially and, as it were, plastically; he is completely frank and goes into everything that bears on his subject. He leaves nothing obscure; he talks himself out. As in Homer, a clear and equal light floods the persons and things with which he deals; like Homer, he has leisure enough to make his presentation explicit; what he says can have but one meaning, nothing is left mysteriously in the background, everything is expressed.

Of course, there are important differences from Homer's manner. In the first place, the presentation, explicit though it be, is entirely subjective, for what is set before us is not Trimalchio's circle as objective reality, but as a subjective image, as it exists in the mind of the speaker, who himself, however, belongs to the circle. Petronius does not say: This is so. Instead, he lets an "I," who is identical neither with himself nor yet with the feigned narrator Encolpius, turn the spotlight of his perception on the company at table—a highly artful procedure in perspective, a sort of twofold mirroring, which I dare not say is unique in antique literature as it has come down to us, but which is most unusual there. In outward form this procedure is certainly nothing new, for of course throughout antique literature characters speak of their experiences and impressions. But nowhere, except in this passage from Petronius, do we have, on the one hand, the most intense subjectivity, which is even heightened by individuality of language, and, on the other hand, an objective intent—for the aim is an objective description of the company at table, including the speaker, through a subjective procedure. This procedure leads to a more meaningful and more concrete illusion of life. Inasmuch as the guest describes a company to which he himself belongs both by inner convictions and outward circumstances, the viewpoint is transferred to a point within the picture, the picture thus gains in depth, and the light which illuminates it seems to come from within it. Modern writers, Proust for example, work in exactly the same way, only more consistently within the realm of the tragic and problematic—a matter which we shall soon take up. Petronius' procedure is thus in the highest degree artistic, and marks him, if he had no forerunners, as a creative genius: the company at table is measured by its own standards; merely expressing these standards passes judgment upon them, and in addition the vulgarity of these parvenus is brilliantly illuminated by the mere fact that such things can be said of them at their own table. There are germs of such a technique elsewhere in the satirical literature of antiquity. But I know of no other example so well considered and so well carried out.

Another important difference from Homeric procedure is the following: In his description, the guest considers it particularly important to stress what all these people formerly were, in contrast to what they now are. *Et modo, modo quid fuit,* he says with reference to Fortunata; *de nihilo crevit,* and *quam bene se habuit,* referring to two fellow guests. Homer too, as we remarked earlier, likes to bring in the lineage, station, and previous history of his characters. But the facts he gives are of a very different nature. They do not lead us to a situation of change, to something in process; on the contrary, they lead us to a fixed point from which we can take our bearings. His Greek audiences are schooled in mythology and genealogy; Homer undertakes to give them the family-tree of the character in question as a means of placing him. Just so, in modern times, a newcomer into an exclusive aristocratic or bourgeois society can be placed by information concerning his paternal and maternal relatives. Thus, rather than an impression of historical change, Homer evokes the illusion of an unchanging, a basically stable social order, in comparison with which the succession of individuals and changes in personal fortunes appear unimportant. But our guest (and in this, as in everything that he says, his feelings are those of the type he represents) has in mind actual historical change, the ups and downs of fortune. For him, the world is in ceaseless motion, nothing is certain, and wealth and social position are highly unstable. His sense of historical reality is one-sided, since it is centered entirely upon the possession of wealth, but it is genuine. (The other guests too perpetually refer to the instability of life.) The acquisition and loss of worldly goods is what interests him in life, and is what has taught him and his fellows to distrust all stability. Yesterday you were still a slave, a porter, a catamite—yesterday you could still be whipped, sold, deported—today you are suddenly a rich landowner, a speculator, enjoying prodigious luxury—and tomorrow it may be all over. Naturally, he asks: *et modo, modo quid fuit?* It is not, or not only, his envy and jealousy speaking—basically he is doubtless a kindly man; it is his most real and most profound interest.

Now, it is well known that the instability of fortune occupies an important place in antique literature and that antique philosophical ethics often takes the same concept as a starting point. But strangely enough, elsewhere it but rarely conveys the impression of a living historical reality. It appears either in tragedy, as a fate without precedent, far outside the common course of things; or in comedy, as the result of a wholly extraordinary concatenation of events. Whether the subject be King Oedipus, whom the long-prophesied curse finds and casts into the utmost wretchedness; or the poor girl or the slave who, turning out to be children of rich parents, given up for lost after a shipwreck or a kidnapping, can marry as their hearts desire—in both cases, something extraordinary happens, something especially arranged, something which is outside the usual course of events, and which affects only one person or a few people, while the rest of the world appears to remain apart from it and indeed to witness the extraordinary event from a spectator's viewpoint. In the mimetic literary art of antiquity, the instability of fortune almost always appears as a fate which strikes from without and affects only a limited area, not as a fate which results from the inner processes of the real, historical world. And though, to be sure, proverbial literature and the gnomic maxims of popular philosophy conceive of change of fortune as coming to all men in all conditions, they express the idea only theoretically. Sententious reflections upon the instability of earthly happiness are heard often enough at Trimalchio's banquet; and, on the other hand, in the guest's reference to a goblin (*incubo*), there lingers something of the tendency to ascribe changes of fortune to specific interventions from without. But in Petronius' book the highly practical and mundane, or what we may call the intrahistorical, concept of the instability of fortune, predominates; the account which Trimalchio gives of his rise to wealth is entirely practical and mundane, and there are similar passages elsewhere. In the passage before us, however, it is the very similarity of the cases cited, the fact that they are so similar as to constitute a series, which more especially conveys the impression of an intrahistorical process. This is no matter of one person, or a few people, being stricken by a fate without precedent, far outside the common course of things, while the rest of the world remains calm. On the contrary, merely in the guest's narrative, four persons are mentioned who are all in the same boat, all engaged in the same turbulent pursuit of unstable Fortune. Though each of them individually has his private destiny, their destinies are all similar; their lot, for all its turbulence, is the common lot, common and vulgar. And behind the four persons who are described, we see the entire company, every member of which, we surmise, has a similar destiny which can be described in similar terms. Behind them again, we see in imagination a whole world of similar lives, and finally find ourselves contemplating an extremely animated historico-economic picture of the perpetual ups and downs of a mob of fortune-hunters scrambling after wealth and stupid pleasures. It is easy to understand that a society of businessmen of the humblest origins is particularly suitable material for a representation of this nature, for conveying this view of things. Such a society most clearly reflects the ups and downs of existence, because there is nothing to hold the balance for it; its members have neither inward tradition nor outer stability; they are nothing without money. In all of antique literature there is hardly a passage which, in this sense, so strongly exhibits intrahistorical movement as the passage before us.

And now we come to the third and possibly most important difference from the Homeric style, the most significant peculiarity of Petronius' Banquet: it is closer to our modern conception of a realistic presentation than anything else that has come down to us from antiquity; and this not so much because of the common vulgarity of its subject matter but above all because of its precise and completely unschematized fixation of the social milieu. The guests gathered at Trimalchio's party are southern Italian freedmen-parvenus of the first century; they hold the views of such people and speak their language almost without literary stylization. The like can hardly be found anywhere else. Comedy indicates the social milieu much more abstractly and schematically, much less specifically as to time and place; it hardly exhibits the rudiments of individualized speech in its characters. Satire, to be sure, contains much that tends in our direction, but the presentation is never so broad, it is moralistic and concerned with branding some specific vice or ridiculous trait. The romance, finally, *fabula milesiaca,* the genre which doubtless includes Petronius' work, is—in the other specimens and fragments that have come down to us—so crammed with magic, adventure, and mythology, so overburdened with erotic detail, that it cannot possibly be considered an imitation of everyday life as it existed at the time—quite apart from the unrealistic and rhetorical stylization of its language. A broad and truly workaday style of presentation is most nearly approximated by certain products of Alexandrian literature, for instance the two women at the festival of Adonis, by Theocritus, or the brothelkeeper bringing suit, by Herondas. But both these pieces, which are in verse, are more playful in their realistic portrayal of sociological background data, and also more linguistically stylized, than Petronius. Petronius' literary ambition, like that of the realists of modern times, is to imitate a random, everyday, contemporary milieu with its sociological background, and to have his characters speak their jargon without recourse to any form of stylization. Thus he reached the ultimate limit of the advance of realism in antiquity. Whether he was the first and only writer to embark upon such a venture, whether and how far the Roman mime had blazed the trail for him, are questions which need not be taken up in this context.

Now if Petronius marks the ultimate limit to which realism attained in antiquity, his work will accordingly serve to show what that realism could not or would not do. The Banquet is a purely comic work. The individual characters, as well as the connecting narrative, are consciously and consistently kept on the lowest level of style both in diction and treatment. And this necessarily implies that everything problematic, everything psychologically or sociologically suggestive of serious, let alone tragic, complications must be excluded, for its excessive weight would break the style. Let us pause here for a moment and think of the nineteenth-century realists, of Balzac or Flaubert, of Tolstoi or Dostoevski. Old Grandet (in *Eugénie Grandet*) or Fedor Pavlovich Karamazov are not mere caricatures, as Trimalchio is, but terrible realities which must be taken wholly seriously; they are involved in tragic complications, and notwithstanding their grotesqueness, are themselves tragic. In modern literature the technique of imitation can evolve a serious, problematic, and tragic conception of any character regardless of type and social standing, of any occurrence regardless of whether it be legendary, broadly political, or narrowly domestic; and in most cases it actually does so. Precisely that is completely impossible in antiquity. There are, it is true, some transitional forms in bucolic and amatory poetry, but on the whole the rule of the separation of styles, touched upon in the first chapter of this study, remains inviolate. Everything commonly realistic, everything pertaining to everyday life, must not be treated on any level except the comic, which admits no problematic probing. As a result the boundaries of realism are narrow. And if we take the word realism a little more strictly, we are forced to conclude that there could be no serious literary treatment of everyday occupations and social classes—merchants, artisans, peasants, slaves—of everyday scenes and places—home, shop, field, store—of everyday customs and institutions—marriage, children, work, earning a living—in short, of the people and its life. Linked with this is the fact that the realists of antiquity do not make clear the social forces underlying the facts and conditions which they present. This could only be done in the realm of the serio-problematic. But since the characters do not leave the realm of the comic, their relation to the social whole is either a matter of clever adaptation or of grotesquely blameworthy isolation. In the latter case, the realistically portrayed individual is always in the wrong in his conflict with the social whole, which is represented as a given fact, an institution unalterably established in the background of the action and requiring no explanation in regard either to its origin or to its effects. This too has altered in modern times. In the realistic literature of antiquity, the existence of society poses no historical problem; it may at best pose a problem in ethics, but even then the ethical question is more concerned with the individual members of society than with the social whole. No matter how many persons may be branded as given to vice or as ridiculous, criticism of vices and excesses poses the problem as one for the individual; consequently, social criticism never leads to a definition of the motive forces within society.

Hence, behind the bustle which Petronius sets before us, we sense nothing which might help us understand the action in terms of its economic and political context; and the historical movement, of which we spoke above, is here only a surface movement. Of course this observation is not intended to suggest that Petronius ought to have worked an essay in national economy into his Banquet. He need not even have gone as far as Balzac who, in the novel mentioned above, *Eugénie Grandet,* described the growth of Grandet's fortune in a manner which reflects all of French history from the Revolution to the Restoration. An entirely unsystematic but continuous and conscious connection with the events and conditions of the time would have been enough. A modern Petronius would link a portrait of a profiteer to the inflation after the First World War, let us say, or to some other well-known crisis. Thackeray, although his method of elaboration remains ethical rather than historical, already links his great novel to the background of the Napoleonic and post-Napoleonic era. Nothing of the sort is found in Petronius. When the subject is the price of food stuffs (chapter 44), or other aspects of urban life (chapters 44, 45 and *passim*), or the history of the guests' lives and fortunes (the passage quoted and especially chapters 57 and 75f.), he will not even allude to a specific place, a definite time, a particular political and economic situation. True enough, we can easily determine that the place is a town in Southern Italy, the time that of the early emperors; the modern historian can use these indications as sociological raw material, and Petronius' contemporaries of course knew all this, possibly in greater detail than we do—but the author himself attributes no importance whatever to the contemporary-historical aspect of his work. Had he done so, that is, had he established a link between his individual events or relationships and specific political and economic situations of the early imperial period, a distinct historical background would have been provided for the reader, which he could supplement with his own knowledge; and the result would have been a historical third dimension in comparison with which Petronius' perspective, of which we spoke above, must appear but a two-dimensional surface; and we could use the term "historical movement" strictly and not merely in a comparative sense. But that would have violated the style within which Petronius undertook to remain; it would not have been possible without an idea which he could not conceive, that is, the idea of historical "forces." As things are, the kinesis—however animated—is limited to the picture itself; back of it, nothing moves, the world is static. We are clearly dealing with a period sketch, a portrait of a time; but the time is presented as though it had always existed unchanged as it does at present in this place, with masters bequeathing large slices of their wealth to slaves who do their sexual bidding, with enormously profitable deals within the reach of merchants, and so forth. The historicity of all these things, the fact that they are determined by an era, is not in itself of interest to Petronius or his contemporary readers. But we moderns note the fact and our historians of economics base their conclusions upon it.

Here we encounter a difficult question of principle which cannot be circumvented. If the literature of antiquity was unable to represent everyday life seriously, that is, in full appreciation of its problems and with an eye for its historical background; if it could represent it only in the low style, comically or at best idyllically, statically and ahistorically, the implication is that these things mark the limits not only of the realism of antiquity but of its historical consciousness as well. For it is precisely in the intellectual and economic conditions of everyday life that those forces are revealed which underlie historical movements; these, whether military, diplomatic, or related to the inner constitution of the state, are only the product, the final result, of variations in the depths of everyday life.

In this connection we may examine a specimen of antique

historiography. I have selected a text which is not too far removed in time from the Banquet, and indeed one which represents a revolutionary movement from the depths, the beginning of the revolt of the Germanic legions after the death of Augustus, in Tacitus' *Annals,* Book 1, chapters 16f. It reads as follows:

Hic rerum urbanarum status erat, cum Pannonicas legiones seditio incessit, nullis novis causis, nisi quod mutatus princeps licentiam turbarum et ex civili bello spem praemiorum ostendebat. Castris aestivis tres simul legiones habebantur, praesidente Iunio Blaeso, qui fine Augusti et initiis Tiberii auditis ob iustitium aut gaudium intermiserat solita munia. Eo principio lascivire miles, discordare, pessimi cuiusque sermonibus praebere aures, denique luxum et otium cupere, disciplinam et laborem aspernari. Erat in castris Percennius quidam, dux olim theatralium operarum, dein gregarius miles, procax lingua et miscere coetus histrionali studio doctus. Is imperitos animos et, quaenam post Augustum militiae condicio, ambigentes impellere paulatim nocturnis conloquiis aut flexo in vesperam die et dilapsis melioribus deterrimum quemque congregare. Postremo promptis iam et aliis seditionis ministris, velut contionabundus interrogabat, cur paucis centurionibus, paucioribus tribunis in modum servorum oboedirent. Quando ausuros exposcere remedia, nisi novum et adhuc nutantem principem precibus vel armis adirent? Satis per tot annos ignavia peccatum, quod tricena aut quadragena stipendia senes et plerique truncato ex vulneribus corpore tolerent. Ne dimissis quidem finem esse militae, sed aput vexillum tendentes alio vocabulo eosdem labores perferre. Ac si quis tot casus vita superaverit, trahi adhuc diversas in terras, ubi per nomen agrorum uligines paludum vel inculta montium accipiant. Enimvero militiam ipsam gravem, infructuosam: denis in diem assibus animam et corpus aestimari: hinc vestem arma tentoria, hinc saevitiam centurionum et vacationes munerum redimi. At Hercule verbera et vulnera, duram hiemem, exercitas aestates, bellum atrox aut sterilem pacem sempiterna. Nec aliud levamentum, quam si certis sub legibus militia iniretur: ut singulos denarios mererent, sextus decumus stipendii annus finem adferret; ne ultra sub vexillis tenerentur, sed isdem in castris praemium pecunia solveretur. An praetorias cohortes, quae binos denarios acceperint, quae post sedecim annos penatibus suis reddantur, plus periculorum suscipere? Non obtrectari a se urbanas excubias; sibi tamen aput horridas gentes e contuberniis hostem aspice.—Adstrepebat vulgus, diversis incitamentis, hi verberum notas, illi canitiem, plurimi detrita tegmina et nudum corpus exprobrantes. . . .

(Thus stood affairs at Rome, when a sedition made its appearance in the legions in Pannonia, without any fresh grounds, save that the accession of a new prince promised impunity to tumult, and held out the hope of advantages to be derived from a civil war. Three legions occupied a summer camp together, commanded by Junius Blaesus, who, upon notice of the death of Augustus and accession of Tiberius, had granted the soldiers a recess from their wonted duties for some days, as a time either of public mourning or festivity. From this beginning they waxed wanton and quarrelsome, lent their ears to the discourses of every profligate, and at last they longed for a life of dissipation and idleness, and spurned all military discipline and labor. In the camp was one Percennius, formerly a busy leader of theatrical factions, after that a common soldier, of a petulant tongue, and from his experience in theatrical party zeal, well qualified to stir up the bad passions of a crowd. Upon minds uninformed, and agitated with doubts as to what might be the condition of military service now that Augustus was dead, he wrought gradually by confabulations by night, or when day verged towards its close; and when all the better-disposed had retired to their respective quarters, he would congregate all the most depraved about him.

(Lastly, when now also other ministers of sedition were at hand to second his designs, in imitation of a general solemnly haranguing his men, he asked them—"Why did they obey, like slaves, a few centurions and fewer tribunes? When would they be bold enough to demand redress, unless they approached the prince, yet a novice, and tottering on his throne, either with entreaties or arms? Enough had they erred in remaining passive through so many years, since decrepit with age and maimed with wounds, after a course of service of thirty or forty years, they were still doomed to carry arms; nor even to those who were discharged was there any end of service, but they were still kept to the colors, and under another name endured the same hardships. And if any of them survived so many dangers, still were they dragged into countries far remote, where, under the name of lands, they are presented with swampy fens, or mountain wastes. But surely, burdensome and ungainful of itself was the occupation of war;—ten asses a day the poor price of their persons and lives; out of this they must buy clothes, and tents, and arms,—out of this the cruelty of centurions must be redeemed, and occasional exemptions from duty; but, by Hercules, stripes, wounds, hard winters and laborious summers, bloody wars and barren peace, were miseries eternally to be endured; nor remained there other remedy than to enter the service upon certain conditions, as that their pay should be a denarius a day, sixteen years to be the utmost term of serving; beyond that period to be no longer obliged to follow the colors, but have their reward in money, paid them in the camp where they earned it. Did the praetorian guards, who had double pay,—they who after sixteen years' service were sent home, undergo more dangers? This was not said in disparagement of the city guards; their own lot, however, was, serving among uncivilized nations, to have the enemy in view from their tents."

(The general body received this harangue with shouts of applause, but stimulated by various motives,—some showing, in all the bitterness of reproach, the marks of stripes, others their hoary heads, many their tattered vestments and naked bodies.) *The Works of Tacitus*. The Oxford Translation. London: Bell. 1888.

At first sight it may seem that this passage does give really serious expression to a movement of the submerged, that it does painstakingly present the practical everyday motives, the underlying economic factors, and the actual events marking the inception of the movement. The grievances of the soldiers discussed in Percennius' speech—excessive length of service, hardships, insufficient pay, inadequate old-age provision, corruption, envy of the easier life of metropolitan troops—are presented vividly and graphically in a manner not frequently encountered even in modern historians. Tacitus is a great artist. Under his hands things come strikingly alive. The modern historian, we must imagine, would proceed more theoretically (one might say, more bookishly); on this occasion he would not have had Percennius speak;

he would have presented a factually objective, well-documented study of pay-scales and welfare provisions, or he might have referred to such a study elsewhere in his own or in some colleague's publications. He would have gone on to discuss the justification of the soldier's demands; he would have given a brief review of the government's past and future policies in the matter, and so forth. All this Tacitus does not do; and the modern historian of antiquity, in order to apply his characteristic methodology, has to reorganize the material which the antique chroniclers have to offer, and to supplement it by inscriptions, excavators' findings, and various other types of indirect evidence.

Tacitus presents the soldiers' grievances and demands, which cast a light upon the facts of their everyday situation, as utterances of the ringleader Percennius; he sees no reason to discuss them, to inquire whether and how far they were justified, to explain how the Roman soldier's lot had changed since the days of the Republic, and the like. All this, he considers, is not worth treating, and it is evident that he could rely on his readers' not missing anything of the kind either. But this is not all. The factual information he gives on the causes of the revolt—information presented in the form of a ringleader's speech and not discussed further—he invalidates in advance by stating at the outset his own view of the real causes of the revolt in purely ethical terms: *nullis novis causis, nisi quod mutatus princeps licentiam turbarum et ex civili bello spem praemiorum ostendebat*. It would be difficult to put it more contemptuously. In his view, the whole thing is merely a matter of mob effrontery and lack of discipline. The blame is placed on the interruption of the usual schedule of duties (they are idle and therefore they shout, says Pharaoh of the Jews). We must be careful not to read into the word *novis* the admission that older grievances are justified. Nothing could be further from Tacitus' view. Time and again he dwells upon the point that only the worst elements are ready to rebel; and as for the leader Percennius, the former chief claqueur, boasting his *histrionale studium* and playing the general, Tacitus feels only the most profound contempt for him.

So it becomes manifest that Tacitus' vivid recital of the soldiers' grievances and demands is by no means based upon an understanding of those demands. This fact might naturally be explained as the result of Tacitus' characteristic attitude of aristocratic conservatism; to his mind, a rebellious legion is nothing but a lawless mob; a common soldier in the role of a mutinous ringleader defies classification in terms of constitutional law, especially since even during the revolutionary epoch of Roman history the most radical rebels could not attain their goal except by submitting to the established order of a civil service career. It may moreover be assumed that Tacitus viewed with alarm the growing power of the military; during the civil wars it had increased to threatening proportions, as later it came to undermine the very structure of the state. But this explanation is not enough. For Tacitus not only lacks understanding, he actually has no interest whatever in the facts underlying the soldiers' demands. He does not argue against their demands in objective terms; he will not take the trouble to prove that they are not justified; a few purely ethical considerations (*licentia, spes praemiorum, pessimus quisque, inexperti animi*) are quite enough to reject them in advance. Had other views existed in his time, views contrary to his own and based on a more clearly sociological and historical interpretation of human actions, Tacitus would have had to take a stand in regard to the problems thus raised—precisely as during the more recent decades of our own period even the most conservative politician still felt obliged to consider the problems raised by his socialist opponents' conception of politics, or at any rate to discuss them polemically, which often implied an elaborate preoccupation with them. Tacitus felt no such obligation, for no such opponents could exist. Historiography in depth—that is, methodical research into the historical growth of social as well as intellectual movements—is a thing unknown to antiquity. This fact has often been alluded to by modern students. So Norden writes in his *Antike Kunstprosa* (2, 647): "We must bear in mind that the historians of antiquity did not attain, and indeed did not seek to attain, a presentation of general, world-moving ideas." And Rostovtzeff in his *Social and Economic History of the Roman Empire* (p. 88): "The historians were not interested in the economic life of the Empire." These two statements, chosen at random, may at first sight appear to have little to do with each other, but what they express goes back to the same peculiarity of the ancients' way of viewing things; it does not see forces, it sees vices and virtues, successes and mistakes. Its formulation of problems is not concerned with historical developments either intellectual or material, but with ethical judgments. But this is most intimately connected with the prevailing view which is manifested in the stylistic differentiation between the tragic-problematic and realism. Both are based upon an aristocratic reluctance to become involved with growth processes in the depths, for these processes are felt to be both vulgar and orgiastically lawless.

An ethically oriented historiography, which also on the whole proceeds in strict chronological order, is bound to use an unchangeable system of categories and hence cannot produce synthetic-dynamic concepts of the kind we are accustomed to employ today. Concepts like "industrial capitalism" or "absenteeism," which are syntheses of characteristic data, applicable especially to specific epochs, and, on the other hand, concepts like Renaissance, Enlightenment, Romanticism, which first of all designate epochs but are also syntheses of characteristic data, sometimes applicable to epochs other than those originally designated by them, are designed to cover phenomena in motion; such phenomena are traced from their first sporadic appearance, then as they occur with progressive density, and finally as they abate and change and vanish; and an essential aspect of all these concepts is the fact that their growth and transformation—that is, an idea of evolution—is contained in them, is conceived as part of their content. On the contrary, the ethical and even the political concepts of antiquity (aristocracy, democracy, etc.) are fixed, aprioristic model concepts. All the modern authorities in the field, from Vico down to Rostovtzeff, have endeavored to dissolve these, to trace the formulation which lies concealed behind them, and which our thought can grasp, a formulation which we can only achieve by collecting and rearranging the characteristic data. As I open Rostovtzeff's work to check the quotation above, my eyes fall on this sentence: "The question, however, arises, How are we to account for the existence of comparatively large numbers of proletarians in Italy?" Such a sentence, such a question, is unthinkable in an author of classical antiquity. It reaches back behind any foreground movements and seeks the changes of significance to them in processes of historical growth which no antique author observed, still less reduced to system and coherence.

When we read Thucydides we get, aside from a continuous account of foreground events, nothing but considerations which are statically aprioristic and ethical in content, on such matters as human nature or fate, and which, though it is true that they are sometimes applied to specific situations, are of an absolute validity in themselves.

Let us return to our passage from Tacitus. If he was not at all interested in the soldiers' demands and never intended to discuss them objectively, why does he express them so graphically in Percennius' speech? The reasons are purely aesthetic. The grand style of historiography requires grandiloquent speeches, which as a rule are fictitious. Their function is graphic dramatization (*illustratio*) of a given occurrence, or at times the presentation of great political or moral ideas; in either case they are intended as the rhetorical bravura pieces of the presentation. The writer is permitted a certain sympathetic entering into the thoughts of the supposed speaker, and even a certain realism. Essentially, however, such speeches are products of a specific stylistic tradition cultivated in the schools for rhetors. The composition of speeches which one person or another might have delivered on one or another great historical occasion was a favorite exercise. Tacitus is a master of his craft, and his speeches are not sheer display; they are really imbued with the character and the situation of the persons supposed to have delivered them; but they too are primarily rhetoric. Percennius does not speak his own language; he speaks Tacitean, that is, he speaks with extreme terseness, as a master of disposition, and highly rhetorically. Undoubtedly his words—though given as indirect discourse—vibrate with the actual excitement of mutinous soldiers and their leader. Yet even if we assume that Percennius was a gifted demagogue, such brevity, incisiveness, and order are not possible in a rebellious propaganda speech, and of soldiers' slang there is not the slightest trace. The same is true of the soldier Vibulenus' words in chapter 22. In the very next chapter they are discounted as lies. They are certainly profoundly moving, but they nevertheless represent the highest degree of rhetorical stylization. Though anaphora, here repeatedly employed (*quis fratri meo vitam, quis fratrem mihi reddit*), may have been frequent in popular usage, it still remains a rhetorical manifestation of the elevated style and has nothing to do with soldiers' language. And this is the second distinctive characteristic of antique historiography: it is rhetorical. The combination of ethical and rhetorical preoccupations gives it a high degree of order, clarity, and dramatic impact. In the case of the Romans there is further a broad and comprehensive view of the extensive stage on which the political and military events occur. Beyond these characteristics, the greatest writers possess a realistic knowledge of the human heart which, though it is soberly based on experience, is never mean. At times we even find traces of an ontogenetic derivation of individual characters, as for example in Sallust's portrait of Catiline and especially in Tacitus' portrait of Tiberius. But this is the limit which cannot be passed. The ethical and rhetorical approach are incompatible with a conception in which reality is a development of forces. Antique historiography gives us neither social history nor economic history nor cultural history. These can only be inferred indirectly from the data presented. However vast the difference between the two passages here considered—the talk of the dinner guest in Petronius and the Pannonian mutiny in Tacitus—both reveal the limits of antique realism and thus of antique historical consciousness.

It will be assumed that, to find a counter example in which these limits are extended, I should have to take a modern text. Yet here again I have at my disposal documents of Jewish-Christian literature which are approximately contemporaneous with Petronius and Tacitus. I choose the story of Peter's denial and I follow Mark's version of it—the differences in the Synoptists are, in any case, quite insignificant.

After the arrest of Jesus—he alone has been arrested, while his entourage has been allowed to escape—Peter, keeping at a safe distance, follows the armed men who take Jesus away. He has been bold enough to enter the court of the High Priest's palace and there, feigning the curiosity of an uninvolved spectator, he stands by the fire among the servants. In doing so he has displayed greater courage than the others. For, since he was a member of the prisoner's inner circle, the risk of his being recognized was very great. And in fact, as he stands there by the fire, a servant girl tells him to his face that he is one of Jesus' group. He denies this and tries unobtrusively to withdraw from the vicinity of the fire. It seems, however, that the girl has kept an eye on him; she follows him to the outer court and repeats her accusation, so that several bystanders hear it. He repeats his denial, but now his Galilean accent has been noticed and the situation begins to look dangerous for him. We are not told how he managed to get away. It is not likely that his third asseveration was given greater credence than the first two. Perhaps something happened to draw the crowd's attention away from him; or perhaps an order had been issued not to molest the prisoner's followers so long as they offered no resistance, and so it may have seemed enough to tell the suspect to move on.

It is apparent at first glance that the rule of differentiated styles cannot possibly apply in this case. The incident, entirely realistic both in regard to locale and *dramatis personae*—note particularly their low social station—is replete with problem and tragedy. Peter is no mere accessory figure serving as *illustratio,* like the soldiers Vibulenus and Percennius, who are represented as mere scoundrels and swindlers. He is the image of man in the highest and deepest and most tragic sense. Of course this mingling of styles is not dictated by an artistic purpose. On the contrary, it was rooted from the beginning in the character of Jewish-Christian literature; it was graphically and harshly dramatized through God's incarnation in a human being of the humblest social station, through his existence on earth amid humble everyday people and conditions, and through his Passion which, judged by earthly standards, was ignominious; and it naturally came to have—in view of the wide diffusion and strong effect of that literature in later ages—a most decisive bearing upon man's conception of the tragic and the sublime. Peter, whose personal account may be assumed to have been the basis of the story, was a fisherman from Galilee, of humblest background and humblest education. The other participants in the night scene in the court of the High Priest's palace are servant girls and soldiers. From the humdrum existence of his daily life, Peter is called to the most tremendous role. Here, like everything else to do with Jesus' arrest, his appearance on the stage—viewed in the world-historical continuity of the Roman Empire—is nothing but a provincial incident, an insignificant local occurrence, noted by none but those directly involved. Yet how tremendous it is, viewed in relation to the life a fisherman from the Sea of Galilee normally lives, and what enormous "pendulation" (Harnack in discussing the denial scene once used the term *Pendelausschlag*) is going on in him! He has left his home and his work; he has followed his master to Jerusalem; he has been the first to recognize him as the Messiah; when the catastrophe came, he was more courageous than the others; not only was he among those who tried to resist but even when the miracle which he had doubtless expected failed to occur, he once again attempted to follow Jesus as he had followed him before. It is but an attempt, halfhearted and timid, motivated perhaps by a confused hope that the miracle by which the Messiah would crush his enemies might still take place. But since his attempt to follow Jesus is a halfhearted, doubt-ridden venture, furtive and full of fear, he falls deeper than all the others, who at least had no occasion to deny Jesus explicitly. Because his faith was deep, but not deep enough, the worst happened to him that can happen to one whom faith had inspired but a short time before: he trembles for his miserable life. And it is entirely credible that this terrifying inner experience should have brought about another swing of the pendulum—this time in the opposite direction and far stronger. Despair and remorse following his desperate failure prepared him for the visions which contributed decisively to the constitution of Christianity. It is only through this experience that the significance of Christ's coming and Passion is revealed to him.

A tragic figure from such a background, a hero of such weakness, who yet derives the highest force from his very weakness, such a to and fro of the pendulum, is incompatible with the sublime style of classical antique literature. But the nature and the scene of the conflict also fall entirely outside the domain of classical antiquity. Viewed superficially, the thing is a police action and its consequences; it takes place entirely among everyday men and women of the common people; anything of the sort could be thought of in antique terms only as farce or comedy. Yet why is it neither of these? Why does it arouse in us the most serious and most significant sympathy? Because it portrays something which neither the poets nor the historians of antiquity ever set out to portray: the birth of a spiritual movement in the depths of the common people, from within the everyday occurrences of contemporary life, which thus assumes an importance it could never have assumed in antique literature. What we witness is the awakening of "a new heart and a new spirit." All this applies not only to Peter's denial but also to every other occurrence which is related in the New Testament. Every one of them is concerned with the same question, the same conflict with which every human being is basically confronted and which therefore remains infinite and eternally pending. It sets man's whole world astir—whereas the entanglements of fate and passion which Greco-Roman antiquity knows, always directly concern simply the individual, the one person involved in them. It is only by virtue of the most general relations, that is, by virtue of the fact that we too are human beings and thus are subject to fate and passion, that we experience "fear and pity." But Peter and the other characters in the New Testament are caught in a universal movement of the depths which at first remains almost entirely below the surface and only very gradually—the Acts of the Apostles show the beginnings of this development—emerges into the foreground of history, but which even now, from the beginning, lays claim to being limitless and the direct concern of everybody, and which absorbs all merely personal conflicts into itself. What we see here is a world which on the one hand is entirely real, average, identifiable as to place, time, and circumstances, but which on the other hand is shaken in its very foundations, is transforming and renewing itself before our eyes. For the New Testament authors who are their contemporaries, these occurrences on the plane of everyday life assume the importance of world-revolutionary events, as later on they will for everyone. They reveal their identity as a movement, a historically active dynamism, through the fact that time and again the impact of Jesus' teachings, personality, and fate upon this and that individual is described. While the aims upon which the movement is centered can as yet be neither clearly grasped nor expressed (it is after all one of its essential characteristics that it does not lend itself to simple definitions and explanations), its effects are already described in numerous examples of its driving dynamism, its surging hither and thither among the people—something which, as pure fact, no Greek or Roman writer would ever have thought of treating in comparably elaborate detail. A Greek or Roman writer describes a popular movement only as reaction to a specific practical complex of events—as Thucydides for instance describes the Athenians' attitude toward the project of an expedition to Sicily; the movement is characterized as a whole—as approving, disapproving, undecided, or perhaps tumultuous—just as the observer sees it, looking, as it were, from above; but it could not possibly occur that reactions so various among so many individuals of the common people should be made a major subject of literary treatment. What considerable portions of the Gospels and the Acts of the Apostles describe, what Paul's Epistles also often reflect, is unmistakably the beginning of a deep subsurface movement, the unfolding of historical forces. For this, it is essential that great numbers of random persons should make their appearance; for it is not possible to bring to life such historical forces in their surging action except by reference to numerous random persons—the term random being here employed to designate people from all classes, occupations, walks of life, people, that is, who owe their place in the account exclusively to the fact that the historical movement engulfs them as it were accidentally, so that they are obliged to react to it in one way or another.

It goes without saying that the stylistic convention of antiquity fails here, for the reaction of the casually involved person can only be presented with the highest seriousness. The random fisherman or publican or rich youth, the random Samaritan or adulteress, come from their random everyday circumstances to be immediately confronted with the personality of Jesus; and the reaction of an individual in such a moment is necessarily a matter of profound seriousness, and very often tragic. The antique stylistic rule according to which realistic imitation, the description of random everyday life, could only be comic (or at best idyllic), is therefore incompatible with the representation of historical forces as soon as such a representation undertakes to render things concretely; for this procedure entails entering into the random everyday depths of popular life, as well as readiness to take seriously whatever is encountered there; and inversely the rule of style can operate only in cases where the writer abandons any attempt to make historical forces concrete or feels no need to do so. It goes without saying that, in the New Testament writings, any raising of historical forces to the level of consciousness is totally "unscientific": it clings to the concrete and fails to progress to a systematization of experience in new concepts. Yet there is to be observed a spontaneous generation of categories which apply to epochs as well as to states of the inner life and which are much more pliable and dynamic than the categories of Greco-Roman historians. For example, there is the distinction of eras, the era of law or of sin and the era of grace, faith, and justice; there are the concepts of "love," "power," "spirit," and the like; and even such abstract and static concepts as that of justice have assumed a dialectic mobility (Romans 3: 21ff.) which renews them completely. Connected with this is everything concerned with inner rebirth and change—the words sin, death, justice, and so on, coming to express not merely action, event, and quality, but phases of an intrahistorical transformation. To be sure, in all this we must not forget that the transformation is here one whose course progresses to somewhere outside of history, to the end of time or to the coincidence of all times, in other words upward, and does not, like the scientific concepts of evolutionary history, remain on the horizontal plane of historical events. That is a decisive difference; and yet, whatever kind of movement it may be which the New Testament writings introduced into phenomenal observation, the essential point is this: the deep subsurface layers, which were static for the observers of classical antiquity, began to move.

In this view of things there is no room for ethical and rhetorical standards in the sense of the ancients. An occurrence like Peter's denial cannot be fitted into a system of judgments which operates with static categories, if for no other reason than the tremendous "pendulation" in the heart of one specific individual; and with the advent of an attitude which seeks justification not in works but in faith, the ethicism of the ancients has lost its supreme rank. And in regard to rhetoric the situation is the same. Surely, the New Testament writings are extremely effective; the tradition of the prophets and the Psalms is alive in them, and in some of them—those written by authors of more or less pronounced Hellenistic culture—we can trace the use of Greek figures of speech. But the spirit of rhetoric—a spirit which classified subjects in *general,* and invested every subject with a specific form of style as the one garment becoming it in virtue of its nature—could not extend its dominion to them for the simple reason that their subject would not fit into any of the known genres. A scene like Peter's denial fits into no antique genre. It is too serious for comedy, too contemporary and everyday for tragedy, politically too insignificant for history—and the form which was given it is one of such immediacy that its like does not exist in the literature of antiquity. This can be judged by a symptom which at first glance may seem insignificant: the use of direct discourse. The maid says: And thou also wast with Jesus of Nazareth! He answers: I know not, neither understand I what thou sayest. Then the maid says to the bystanders: This is one of them. And, Peter repeating his denial, the bystanders speak up: Surely thou art one of them, for thou art a Galilean by thy speech!—I do not believe that there is a single passage in an antique historian where direct discourse is employed in this fashion in a brief, direct dialogue. Dialogues with few participants are rare in their writings; at best they appear in anecdotal biography, and there the function they serve is almost always to lead up to famous pregnant retorts, whose importance lies not in their realistically concrete content but in their rhetorical and ethical impact—the sort of thing which later on, in the theory of the thirteenth-century Italian novella, was called a *bel parlare.* The celebrated anecdotes of Croesus and Solon may serve as examples. Generally speaking, direct discourse is restricted in the antique historians to great continuous speeches delivered in the Senate or before a popular assembly or a gathering of soldiers, in which connection the reader may remember what we said above in regard to Percennius' speech. But here—in the scene of Peter's denial—the dramatic tension of the moment when the actors stand face to face has been given a salience and immediacy compared with which the dialogue (stichomythy) of antique tragedy appears highly stylized. Comedy, satire, and the like may not properly be adduced for purposes of comparison; but in them too one would have to look hard to find anything of similar immediacy. In the Gospels, however, one encounters numerous face-to-face dialogues. I hope that this symptom, the use of direct discourse in living dialogue, suffices to characterize, for our purposes, the relation of the writings of the New Testament to classical rhetoric, so that I need not go further into the general problem, which has often been discussed. (I refer to Norden's book on the art of prose in antiquity, mentioned above.)

In the last analysis the differences in style between the writings of antiquity and early Christianity are conditioned by the fact that they were composed from a different point of view and for different people. Different as Petronius and Tacitus may be in a great many respects, they have the same viewpoint—they look down from above. Tacitus writes from a vantage point which surveys the fullness of events and transactions; he classifies and judges them as a man of the highest rank and the highest culture. That he does not fall into the dry and unvisualized, is due not only to his genius but to the incomparably successful cultivation of the visual, of the sensory, throughout antiquity. But the audience of his equals for whom he wrote demanded that the visual and sensory element respect the limits of what a long tradition had settled as good taste—in which connection we may note that there are to be found in him symptoms of a change in taste, a change in the direction of greater stress on the somber and gruesome, but this is a point we shall have to take up again in a different context. Petronius too looks from above at the world he depicts. His book is a product of the highest culture, and he expects his readers to have such a high level of social and literary culture that they will perceive, without doubt or hesitation, every shade of social blundering and of vulgarity in language and taste. However coarse and grotesque the subject matter may be, its treatment reveals no trace of the crude humor of a popular farce. Scenes like that of the dinner guest's reply or the quarrel between Trimalchio and Fortunata exhibit, it is true, the basest and commonest ideas, but they do so with such refined cross-purposes, with such an array of sociological and psychological presuppositions, as no popular audience could tolerate. And the vulgarity of language is not designed to arouse laughter in a large crowd but is rather a piquant condiment for the palate of a social and literary elite accustomed to viewing things from above with epicurean composure. It may perhaps be compared with the small talk of the hotel manager Aimé and similar characters in Proust's novel of Things Past; but such comparisons with works of modern realism are never quite to the point, because the latter contain far more in the way of serious problems. So Petronius too writes from above, for the class of the highly cultured—a class which at the time of the early emperors may have been quite large but which melted away later. On the other hand, the story of Peter's denial, and generally almost the entire body of New Testament writings, is written from within the emergent growths and directly for everyman. Here we have neither survey and rational disposition, nor artistic purpose. The visual and sensory as it appears here is no conscious imitation and hence is rarely completely realized. It appears because it is attached to the events which are to be related, because it is revealed in the demeanor and speech of profoundly stirred individuals and no effort need be devoted to the task of elaborating it. Even Tacitus, with his conscious endeavor to condense and summarize, describes human individuals in their outer appearance and inner existence, gives detailed portrayals of given situations. The author of the Gospel according to Saint Mark has no viewpoint which would permit him to present a factual, objective portrait of, let us say, the character of Peter. He is at the core of what goes on; he observes and relates only what matters in relation to Christ's presence and mission; and in the present case it does not even occur to him to tell us how the incident ended, that is, how Peter got away. Tacitus and Petronius endeavor to give us a sensory impression, the former of historical occurrences, the latter of a specific stratum of society, and in doing so they respect the limits of a specific aesthetic tradition. The author of the Gospel according to Saint Mark has no such purpose and knows no such tradition. Without any effort on his part, as it were, and purely through the inner movement of what he relates, the story becomes visually concrete. And the story speaks to everybody; everybody is urged and indeed required to take sides for or against it. Even ignoring it implies taking sides. To be sure, for a time its effectiveness was hampered by practical obstacles. For a time the language as well as the religious and social premises of the message restricted it to Jewish circles. Yet the negative reaction which it aroused in Jerusalem, both among the Jewish leaders and among the majority of the people, forced the movement to embark upon the tremendous venture of missionary work among the Gentiles, which was characteristically begun by a member of the Jewish diaspora, the Apostle Paul. With that, an adaptation of the message to the preconceptions of a far wider audience, its detachment from the special preconceptions of the Jewish world, became a necessity and was effected by a method rooted in Jewish tradition but now applied with incomparably greater boldness, the method of revisional interpretation. The Old Testament was played down as popular history and as the code of the Jewish people and assumed the appearance of a series of "figures," that is of prophetic announcements and anticipations of the coming of Jesus and the concomitant events. We have briefly discussed these matters in our first chapter. The total content of the sacred writings was placed in an exegetic context which often removed the thing told very far from its sensory base, in that the reader or listener was forced to turn his attention away from the sensory occurrence and toward its meaning. This implied the danger that the visual element of the occurrences might succumb under the dense texture of meanings. Let one example stand for many: It is a visually dramatic occurrence that God made Eve, the first woman, from Adam's rib while Adam lay asleep; so too is it that a soldier pierced Jesus' side, as he hung dead on the cross, so that blood and water flowed out. But when these two occurrences are exegetically interrelated in the doctrine that Adam's sleep is a figure of Christ's death-sleep; that, as from the wound in Adam's side mankind's primordial mother after the flesh, Eve, was born, so from the wound in Christ's side was born the mother of all men after the spirit, the Church (blood and water are sacramental symbols)—then the sensory occurrence pales before the power of the figural meaning. What is perceived by the hearer or reader or even, in the plastic and graphic arts, by the spectator, is weak as a sensory impression, and all one's interest is directed toward the context of meanings. In comparison, the Greco-Roman specimens of realistic presentation are, though less serious and fraught with problems and far more limited in their conception of historical movement, nevertheless perfectly integrated in their sensory substance. They do not know the antagonism between sensory appearance and meaning, an antagonism which permeates the early, and indeed the whole, Christian view of reality.

## Ian Watt

### *Realism and the Novel Form*

There are still no wholly satisfactory answers to many of the general questions which anyone interested in the early eighteenth-century novelists and their works is likely to ask: Is the novel a new literary form? And if we assume, as is commonly done, that it is, and that it was begun by Defoe, Richardson and Fielding, how does it differ from the prose fiction of the past, from that of Greece, for example, or that of the Middle Ages, or of seventeenth-century France? And is there any reason why these differences appeared when and where they did?

Such large questions are never easy to approach, much less to answer, and they are particularly difficult in this case because Defoe, Richardson and Fielding do not in the usual sense constitute a literary school. Indeed their works show so little sign of mutual influence and are so different in nature that at first sight it appears that our curiosity about the rise of the novel is unlikely to find any satisfaction other than the meagre one afforded by the terms 'genius' and 'accident,' the twin faces on the Janus of the dead ends of literary history. We cannot, of course, do without them: on the other hand there is not much we can do with them. The present inquiry therefore takes another direction: assuming that the appearance of our first three novelists within a single generation was probably not sheer accident, and that their geniuses could not have created the new form unless the conditions of the time had also been favourable, it attempts to discover what these favourable conditions in the literary and social situation were, and in what ways Defoe, Richardson and Fielding were its beneficiaries.

For this investigation our first need is a working definition of the characteristics of the novel—a definition sufficiently narrow to exclude previous types of narrative and yet broad enough to apply to whatever is usually put in the novel category. The novelists themselves do not help us very much here. It is true that both Richardson and Fielding saw themselves as founders of a new kind of writing, and that both viewed their work as involving a break with the old-fashioned romances; but neither they nor their contemporaries provide us with the kind of characterisation of the new genre that we need; indeed they did not even canonise the changed nature of their fiction by a change in nomenclature—our usage of the term 'novel' was not fully established until the end of the eighteenth century.

With the help of their larger perspective the historians of the novel have been able to do much more to determine the idiosyncratic features of the new form. Briefly, they have seen 'realism' as the defining characteristic which differentiates the work of the early eighteenth-century novelists from previous fiction. With their picture—that of writers otherwise different but alike in this quality of 'realism'—one's initial reservation must surely be that the term itself needs further explanation, if only because to use it without qualification as a defining characteristic of the novel might otherwise carry the invidious suggestion that all previous writers and literary forms pursued the unreal.

The main critical associations of the term 'realism' are with the French school of Realists. 'Réalisme' was apparently first used as an aesthetic description in 1835 to denote the 'vérité humaine' of Rembrandt as opposed to the 'idéalité poétique' of neo-classical painting; it was later consecrated as a specifically literary term by the foundation in 1856 of *Réalisme,* a journal edited by Duranty.[1]

Unfortunately much of the usefulness of the word was soon

[1] See Bernard Weinberg, *French Realism: the Critical Reaction 1830-1870* (London, 1937), p. 114.

lost in the bitter controversies over the 'low' subjects and allegedly immoral tendencies of Flaubert and his successors. As a result, 'realism' came to be used primarily as the antonym of 'idealism,' and this sense, which is actually a reflection of the position taken by the enemies of the French Realists, has in fact coloured much critical and historical writing about the novel. The prehistory of the form has commonly been envisaged as a matter of tracing the continuity between all earlier fiction which portrayed low life: the story of the Ephesian matron is 'realistic' because it shows that sexual appetite is stronger than wifely sorrow; and the fabliau or the picaresque tale are 'realistic' because economic or carnal motives are given pride of place in their presentation of human behaviour. By the same implicit premise, the English eighteenth-century novelists, together with Furetière, Scarron and Lesage in France, are regarded as the eventual climax of this tradition: the 'realism' of the novels of Defoe, Richardson and Fielding is closely associated with the fact that Moll Flanders is a thief, Pamela a hypocrite, and Tom Jones a fornicator.

This use of 'realism,' however, has the grave defect of obscuring what is probably the most original feature of the novel form. If the novel were realistic merely because it saw life from the seamy side, it would only be an inverted romance; but in fact it surely attempts to portray all the varieties of human experience, and not merely those suited to one particular literary perspective: the novel's realism does not reside in the kind of life it presents, but in the way it presents it.

This, of course, is very close to the position of the French Realists themselves, who asserted that if their novels tended to differ from the more flattering pictures of humanity presented by many established ethical, social, and literary codes, it was merely because they were the product of a more dispassionate and scientific scrutiny of life than had ever been attempted before. It is far from clear that this ideal of scientific objectivity is desirable, and it certainly cannot be realised in practice: nevertheless it is very significant that, in the first sustained effort of the new genre to become critically aware of its aims and methods, the French Realists should have drawn attention to an issue which the novel raises more sharply than any other literary form—the problem of the correspondence between the literary work and the reality which it imitates. This is essentially an epistemological problem, and it therefore seems likely that the nature of the novel's realism, whether in the early eighteenth century or later, can best be clarified by the help of those professionally concerned with the analysis of concepts, the philosophers.

## I

By a paradox that will surprise only the neophyte, the term 'realism' in philosophy is most strictly applied to a view of reality diametrically opposed to that of common usage—to the view held by the scholastic Realists of the Middle Ages that it is universals, classes or abstractions, and not the particular, concrete objects of sense-perception, which are the true 'realities.' This, at first sight, appears unhelpful, since in the novel, more than in any other genre, general truths only exist *post res;* but the very unfamiliarity of the point of view of scholastic Realism at least serves to draw attention to a characteristic of the novel which is analogous to the changed philosophical meaning of 'realism' today: the novel arose in the modern period, a period whose general intellectual orientation was most decisively separated from its classical and mediaeval heritage by its rejection—or at least its attempted rejection—of universals.[2]

Modern realism, of course, begins from the position that truth can be discovered by the individual through his senses: it has its origins in Descartes and Locke, and received its first full formulation by Thomas Reid in the middle of the eighteenth century.[3] But the view that the external world is real, and that our senses give us a true report of it, obviously does not in itself throw much light on literary realism; since almost everyone, in all ages, has in one way or another been forced to some such conclusion about the external world by his own experience, literature has always been to some extent exposed to the same epistemological naïveté. Further, the distinctive tenets of realist epistemology, and the controversies associated with them, are for the most part much too specialised in nature to have much bearing on literature.

[2] See R. I. Aaron, *The Theory of Universals* (Oxford, 1952), pp. 18-41.
[3] See S. Z. Hasan, *Realism* (Cambridge, 1928), chs. 1 and 2.

What is important to the novel in philosophical realism is much less specific; it is rather the general temper of realist thought, the methods of investigation it has used, and the kinds of problems it has raised.

The general temper of philosophical realism has been critical, anti-traditional and innovating; its method has been the study of the particulars of experience by the individual investigator, who, ideally at least, is free from the body of past assumptions and traditional beliefs; and it has given a peculiar importance to semantics, to the problem of the nature of the correspondence between words and reality. All of these features of philosophical realism have analogies to distinctive features of the novel form, analogies which draw attention to the characteristic kind of correspondence between life and literature which has obtained in prose fiction since the novels of Defoe and Richardson.

(a)

The greatness of Descartes was primarily one of method, of the thoroughness of his determination to accept nothing on trust; and his *Discourse on Method* (*1637*) and his *Meditations* did much to bring about the modern assumption whereby the pursuit of truth is conceived of as a wholly individual matter, logically independent of the tradition of past thought, and indeed as more likely to be arrived at by a departure from it.

The novel is the form of literature which most fully reflects this individualist and innovating reorientation. Previous literary forms had reflected the general tendency of their cultures to make conformity to traditional practice the major test of truth: the plots of classical and renaissance epic, for example, were based on past history or fable, and the merits of the author's treatment were judged largely according to a view of literary decorum derived from the accepted models in the genre. This literary traditionalism was first and most fully challenged by the novel, whose primary criterion was truth to individual experience—individual experience which is always unique and therefore new. The novel is thus the logical literary vehicle of a culture which, in the last few centuries, has set an unprecedented value on originality, on the novel; and it is therefore well named.

This emphasis on the new accounts for some of the critical

difficulties which the novel is widely agreed to present. When we judge a work in another genre, a recognition of its literary models is often important and sometimes essential; our evaluation depends to a large extent on our analysis of the author's skill in handling the appropriate formal conventions. On the other hand, it is surely very damaging for a novel to be in any sense an imitation of another literary work: and the reason for this seems to be that since the novelist's primary task is to convey the impression of fidelity to human experience, attention to any pre-established formal conventions can only endanger his success. What is often felt as the formlessness of the novel, as compared, say, with tragedy, or the ode, probably follows from this: the poverty of the novel's formal conventions would seem to be the price it must pay for its realism.

But the absence of formal conventions in the novel is unimportant compared to its rejection of traditional plots. Plot, of course, is not a simple matter, and the degree of its originality or otherwise is never easy to determine; nevertheless a broad and necessarily summary comparison between the novel and previous literary forms reveals an important difference: Defoe and Richardson are the first great writers in our literature who did not take their plots from mythology, history, legend or previous literature. In this they differ from Chaucer, Spenser, Shakespeare and Milton, for instance, who, like the writers of Greece and Rome, habitually used traditional plots; and who did so, in the last analysis, because they accepted the general premise of their times that, since Nature is essentially complete and unchanging, its records, whether scriptural, legendary or historical, constitute a definitive repertoire of human experience.

This point of view continued to be expressed until the nineteenth century; the opponents of Balzac, for example, used it to deride his preoccupation with contemporary and, in their view, ephemeral reality. But at the same time, from the Renaissance onwards, there was a growing tendency for individual experience to replace collective tradition as the ultimate arbiter of reality; and this transition would seem to constitute an important part of the general cultural background of the rise of the novel.

It is significant that the trend in favour of originality found its first powerful expression in England, and in the eighteenth century; the very word 'original' took on its modern meaning at this time, by a semantic reversal which is a parallel to the change in the meaning of 'realism.' We have seen that, from the mediaeval belief in the reality of universals, 'realism' had come to denote a belief in the individual apprehension of reality through the senses: similarly the term 'original' which in the Middle Ages had meant 'having existed from the first' came to mean 'underived, independent, first-hand'; and by the time that Edward Young in his epoch-making *Conjectures on Original Composition* (1759) hailed Richardson as 'a genius as well moral as original,'[4] the word could be used as a term of praise meaning 'novel or fresh in character or style.'

The novel's use of non-traditional plots is an early and probably independent manifestation of this emphasis. When Defoe, for example, began to write fiction he took little notice of the dominant critical theory of the day, which still inclined towards the use of traditional plots; instead, he merely allowed his narrative order to flow spontaneously from his own sense of what his protagonists might plausibly do next. In so doing Defoe initiated an important new tendency in fiction: his total subordination of the plot to the pattern of the autobiographical memoir is as defiant an assertion of the primacy of individual experience in the novel as Descartes's *cogito ergo sum* was in philosophy.

After Defoe, Richardson and Fielding in their very different ways continued what was to become the novel's usual practice, the use of non-traditional plots, either wholly invented or based in part on a contemporary incident. It cannot be claimed that either of them completely achieved that interpenetration of plot, character and emergent moral theme which is found in the highest examples of the art of the novel. But it must be remembered that the task was not an easy one, particularly at a time when the established literary outlet for the creative imagination lay in eliciting an individual pattern and a contemporary significance from a plot that was not itself novel.

[4] *Works* (1773), V, 125; see also Max Scheler, *Versuche zu einer Soziologie des Wissens* (München and Leipzig, 1924), pp. 104 ff.; Elizabeth L. Mann, 'The Problem of Originality in English Literary Criticism, 1750-1800,' *PQ*, XVIII (1939), 97-118.

(b)

Much else besides the plot had to be changed in the tradition of fiction before the novel could embody the individual apprehension of reality as freely as the method of Descartes and Locke allowed their thought to spring from the immediate facts of consciousness. To begin with, the actors in the plot and the scene of their actions had to be placed in a new literary perspective: the plot had to be acted out by particular people in particular circumstances, rather than, as had been common in the past, by general human types against a background primarily determined by the appropriate literary convention.

This literary change was analogous to the rejection of universals and the emphasis on particulars which characterises philosophic realism. Aristotle might have agreed with Locke's primary assumption, that it was the senses which 'at first let in particular ideas, and furnish the empty cabinet' of the mind.[5] But he would have gone on to insist that the scrutiny of particular cases was of little value in itself; the proper intellectual task of man was to rally against the meaningless flux of sensation, and achieve a knowledge of the universals which alone constituted the ultimate and immutable reality.[6] It is this generalising emphasis which gives most Western thought until the seventeenth century a strong enough family resemblance to outweigh all its other multifarious differences: similarly when in 1713 Berkeley's Philonous affirmed that 'it is an universally received maxim, that *everything which exists is particular*,'[7] he was stating the opposite modern tendency which in turn gives modern thought since Descartes a certain unity of outlook and method.

Here, again, both the new trends in philosophy and the related formal characteristics of the novel were contrary to the dominant literary outlook. For the critical tradition in the early eighteenth century was still governed by the strong classical preference for the general and universal: the proper object of literature remained *quod semper quod ubique ab omnibus creditum est*. This preference was particularly pronounced in the neo-Platonist

[5] *Essay Concerning Human Understanding* (1690), Bk. I, ch. 2, sect. xv.

[6] See *Posterior Analytics*, Bk. I, ch. 24; Bk. II, ch. 19.

[7] First *Dialogue between Hylas and Philonous*, 1713 (Berkeley, *Works*, ed. Luce and Jessop (London, 1949), II, 192).

tendency, which had always been strong in the romance, and which was becoming of increasing importance in literary criticism and aesthetics generally. Shaftesbury, for instance, in his *Essay on the Freedom of Wit and Humour* (1709), expressed the distaste of this school of thought for particularity in literature and art very emphatically: 'The variety of Nature is such, as to distinguish every thing she forms, by a *peculiar* original character; which, if strictly observed, will make the subject appear unlike to anything extant in the world besides. But this effect the good poet and painter seek industriously to prevent. They hate *minuteness,* and are afraid of *singularity.*'[8] He continued: 'The mere Face-Painter, indeed, has little in common with the Poet; but, like the mere Historian, copies what he sees, and minutely traces every feature, and odd mark'; and concluded confidently that ' 'Tis otherwise with men of invention and design.'

Despite Shaftesbury's engaging finality, however, a contrary aesthetic tendency in favour of particularity soon began to assert itself, largely as a result of the application to literary problems of the psychological approach of Hobbes and Locke. Lord Kames was perhaps the most forthright early spokesman of this tendency. In his *Elements of Criticism* (1762) he declared that 'abstract or general terms have no good effect in any composition for amusement; because it is only of particular objects that images can be formed';[9] and Kames went on to claim that, contrary to general opinion, Shakespeare's appeal lay in the fact that 'every article in his descriptions is particular, as in nature.'

In this matter, as in that of originality, Defoe and Richardson established the characteristic literary direction of the novel form long before it could count on any support from critical theory. Not all will agree with Kames that 'every article' in Shakespeare's description is particular; but particularity of description has always been considered typical of the narrative manner of *Robinson Crusoe* and *Pamela.* Richardson's first biographer, indeed, Mrs. Barbauld, described his genius in terms of an analogy which has continually figured in the controversy between neo-classical generality and realistic particularity. Sir

[8] Pt. IV, sect. 3.
[9] 1763 ed., III, 198-199.

Joshua Reynolds, for example, expressed his neo-classical orthodoxy by preferring the 'great and general ideas' of Italian painting to the 'literal truth and . . . minute exactness in the detail of nature modified by accident' of the Dutch school,[10] whereas the French Realists, it will be remembered, had followed the 'vérité humaine' of Rembrandt, rather than the 'idéalité poétique' of the classical school. Mrs. Barbauld accurately indicated Richardson's position in this conflict when she wrote that he had 'the accuracy of finish of a Dutch painter . . . content to produce effects by the patient labour of minuteness.'[11] Both he and Defoe, in fact were heedless of Shaftesbury's scorn, and like Rembrandt were content to be 'mere face-painters and historians.'

The concept of realistic particularity in literature is itself somewhat too general to be capable of concrete demonstration: for such demonstration to be possible the relationship of realistic particularity to some specific aspects of narrative technique must first be established. Two such aspects suggest themselves as of especial importance in the novel—characterisation, and presentation of background: the novel is surely distinguished from other genres and from previous forms of fiction by the amount of attention it habitually accords both to the individualisation of its characters and to the detailed presentation of their environment.

(c)

Philosophically the particularising approach to character resolves itself into the problem of defining the individual person. Once Descartes had given the thought processes within the individual's consciousness supreme importance, the philosophical problems connected with personal identity naturally attracted a great deal of attention. In England, for example, Locke, Bishop Butler, Berkeley, Hume and Reid all debated the issue, and the controversy even reached the pages of the *Spectator*.[12]

[10] *Idler*, No. 79 (1759). See also Scott Elledge, 'The Background and Development in English Criticism of the Theories of Generality and Particularity,' *PMLA*, LX (1945), 161-174.

[11] *Correspondence of Samuel Richardson*, 1804, I, cxxxvii. For similar comments by contemporary French readers, see Joseph Texte, *Jean-Jacques Rousseau and the Cosmopolitan Spirit in Literature* (London, 1899), pp. 174-175.

[12] No. 578 (1714).

The parallel here between the tradition of realist thought and the formal innovations of the early novelists is obvious: both philosophers and novelists paid greater attention to the particular individual than had been common before. But the great attention paid in the novel to the particularisation of character is itself such a large question that we will consider only one of its more manageable aspects: the way that the novelist typically indicates his intention of presenting a character as a particular individual by naming him in exactly the same way as particular individuals are named in ordinary life.

Logically the problem of individual identity is closely related to the epistemological status of proper names; for, in the words of Hobbes, 'Proper names bring to mind one thing only; universals recall any one of many.'[13] Proper names have exactly the same function in social life: they are the verbal expression of the particular identity of each individual person. In literature, however, this function of proper names was first fully established in the novel.

Characters in previous forms of literature, of course, were usually given proper names; but the kind of names actually used showed that the author was not trying to establish his characters as completely individualised entities. The precepts of classical and renaissance criticism agreed with the practice of their literature in preferring either historical names or type names. In either case, the names set the characters in the context of a large body of expectations primarily formed from past literature, rather than from the context of contemporary life. Even in comedy, where characters were not usually historical but invented, the names were supposed to be 'characteristic,' as Aristotle tells us,[14] and they tended to remain so until long after the rise of the novel.

Earlier types of prose fiction had also tended to use proper names that were characteristic, or non-particular and unrealistic in some other way; names that either, like those of Rabelais, Sidney or Bunyan, denoted particular qualities, or like those of Lyly, Aphra Behn or Mrs. Manley, carried foreign, archaic or literary connotations which excluded any suggestion of real and

[13] *Leviathan* (1651), Pt. I, ch. 4.
[14] *Poetics,* ch. 9.

contemporary life. The primarily literary and conventional orientation of these proper names was further attested by the fact that there was usually only one of them—Mr. Badman or Euphues; unlike people in ordinary life, the characters of fiction did not have both given name and surname.

The early novelists, however, made an extremely significant break with tradition, and named their characters in such a way as to suggest that they were to be regarded as particular individuals in the contemporary social environment. Defoe's use of proper names is casual and sometimes contradictory; but he very rarely gives names that are conventional or fanciful—one possible exception, Roxana, is a pseudonym which is fully explained; and most of the main characters such as Robinson Crusoe or Moll Flanders have complete and realistic names or aliases. Richardson continued this practice, but was much more careful and gave all of his major characters, and even most of his minor ones, both a given name and a surname. He also faced a minor but not unimportant problem in novel writing, that of giving names that are subtly appropriate and suggestive, yet sound like ordinary realistic ones. Thus the romance-connotations of Pamela are controlled by the commonplace family name of Andrews; both Clarissa Harlowe and Robert Lovelace are in many ways appropriately named; and indeed nearly all Richardson's proper names, from Mrs. *Sin*clair to Sir Charles *Grand*ison, sound authentic and are yet suited to the personalities of the bearers.

Fielding, as an anonymous contemporary critic pointed out, christened his characters 'not with fantastic high-sounding Names, but such as, tho' they sometimes had some reference to the Character, had a more modern termination.'[15] Such names as Heartfree, Allworthy and Square are certainly modernised versions of the type name, although they are just credible; even Western or Tom Jones suggest very strongly that Fielding had his eye as much on the general type as on the particular individual. This, however, does not controvert the present argument, for it will surely be generally agreed that Fielding's practice in the naming, and in-

[15] *Essay on the New Species of Writing Founded by Mr. Fielding,* 1751, p. 18. This whole question is treated more fully in my 'The Naming of Characters in Defoe, Richardson and Fielding,' *RES,* XXV (1949), 322-338.

deed in the whole portrayal of his characters, is a departure from the usual treatment of these matters in the novel. Not, as we have seen in Richardson's case, that there is no place in the novel for proper names that are in some way appropriate to the character concerned: but that this appropriateness must not be such as to impair the primary function of the name, which is to symbolise the fact that the character is to be regarded as though he were a particular person and not a type.

Fielding, indeed, seems to have realised this by the time he came to write his last novel, *Amelia*: there his neo-classical preference for type-names finds expression only in such minor characters as Justice Thrasher and Bondum the bailiff; and all the main characters—the Booths, Miss Matthews, Dr. Harrison, Colonel James, Sergeant Atkinson, Captain Trent and Mrs. Bennet, for example—have ordinary and contemporary names. There is, indeed, some evidence that Fielding, like some modern novelists, took these names somewhat at random from a printed list of contemporary persons—all the surnames given above are in the list of subscribers to the 1724 folio edition of Gilbert Burnet's *History of His Own Time,* an edition which Fielding is known to have owned.[16]

Whether this is so or not, it is certain that Fielding made considerable and increasing concessions to the custom initiated by Defoe and Richardson of using ordinary contemporary proper names for their characters. Although this custom was not always followed by some of the later eighteenth-century novelists, such as Smollett and Sterne, it was later established as part of the tradition of the form; and, as Henry James pointed out with respect to Trollope's fecund cleric Mr. Quiverful,[17] the novelist can only break with the tradition at the cost of destroying the reader's belief in the literal reality of the character concerned.

(d)

Locke had defined personal identity as an identity of consciousness through duration in time; the individual was in touch with his own continuing identity through memory of his past

[16] See Wilbur L. Cross, *History of Henry Fielding* (New Haven, 1918), I, 342-343.
[17] *Partial Portraits* (London, 1888), p. 118.

thoughts and actions.[18] This location of the source of personal identity in the repertoire of its memories was continued by Hume: 'Had we no memory, we never should have any notion of causation, nor consequently of that chain of causes and effects, which constitute our self or person.'[19] Such a point of view is characteristic of the novel; many novelists, from Sterne to Proust, have made their subject the exploration of the personality as it is defined in the interpenetration of its past and present self-awareness.

Time is an essential category in another related but more external approach to the problem of defining the individuality of any object. The 'principle of individuation' accepted by Locke was that of existence at a particular locus in space and time: since, as he wrote, 'ideas become general by separating from them the circumstances of time and place,'[20] so they become particular only when both these circumstances are specified. In the same way the characters of the novel can only be individualised if they are set in a background of particularised time and place.

Both the philosophy and the literature of Greece and Rome were deeply influenced by Plato's view that the Forms or Ideas were the ultimate realities behind the concrete objects of the temporal world. These forms were conceived as timeless and unchanging,[21] and thus reflected the basic premise of their civilisation in general that nothing happened or could happen whose fundamental meaning was not independent of the flux of time. This premise is diametrically opposed to the outlook which has established itself since the Renaissance, and which views time, not only as a crucial dimension of the physical world, but as the shaping force of man's individual and collective history.

The novel is in nothing so characteristic of our culture as in the way that it reflects this characteristic orientation of modern thought. E. M. Forster sees the portrayal of 'life by time' as the distinctive role which the novel has added to literature's more ancient preoccupation with portraying 'life by values,'[22] Spengler's

[18] *Human Understanding*, Bk. II, ch. 27, sects. ix, x.

[19] *Treatise of Human Nature*, Bk. I, pt. 4, sect. vi.

[20] *Human Understanding*, Bk. III, ch. 3, sect. vi.

[21] Plato does not specifically state that the Ideas are timeless, but the notion, which dates from Aristotle (*Metaphysics*, Bk. XII ch. 6), underlies the whole system of thought with which they are associated.

[22] *Aspects of the Novel* (London, 1949), pp. 29-31.

perspective for the rise of the novel is the need of 'ultrahistorical' modern man for a literary form capable of dealing with 'the whole of life';[23] while more recently Northrop Frye has seen the 'alliance of time and Western man' as the defining characteristic of the novel compared with other genres.[24]

We have already considered one aspect of the importance which the novel allots the time dimension: its break with the earlier literary tradition of using timeless stories to mirror the unchanging moral verities. The novel's plot is also distinguished from most previous fiction by its use of past experience as the cause of present action: a causal connection operating through time replaces the reliance of earlier narratives on disguises and coincidences, and this tends to give the novel a much more cohesive structure. Even more important, perhaps, is the effect upon characterisation of the novel's insistence on the time process. The most obvious and extreme example of this is the stream of consciousness novel which purports to present a direct quotation of what occurs in the individual mind under the impact of the temporal flux; but the novel in general has interested itself much more than any other literary form in the development of its characters in the course of time. Finally, the novel's detailed depiction of the concerns of everyday life also depends upon its power over the time dimension: T. H. Green pointed out that much of man's life had tended to be almost unavailable to literary representation merely as a result of its slowness;[25] the novel's closeness to the texture of daily experience directly depends upon its employment of a much more minutely discriminated time-scale than had previously been employed in narrative.

The role of time in ancient, mediaeval and renaissance literature is certainly very different from that in the novel. The restriction of the action of tragedy to twenty-four hours, for example, the celebrated unity of time, is really a denial of the importance of the temporal dimension in human life; for, in accord with the classical world's view of reality as subsisting in timeless universals, it implies that the truth about existence can

[23] *Decline of the West,* trans. Atkinson (London, 1928), I, 130-131.

[24] 'The Four Forms of Fiction', *Hudson Review,* II (1950), 596.

[25] 'Estimate of the Value and Influence of Works of Fiction in Modern Times' (1862), *Works,* ed. Nettleship (London, 1888), III, 36.

be as fully unfolded in the space of a day as in the space of a lifetime. The equally celebrated personifications of time as the winged chariot or the grim reaper reveal an essentially similar outlook. They focus attention, not on the temporal flux, but on the supremely timeless fact of death; their role is to overwhelm our awareness of daily life so that we shall be prepared to face eternity. Both these personifications, in fact, resemble the doctrine of the unity of time in that they are fundamentally a-historical, and are therefore equally typical of the very minor importance accorded to the temporal dimension in most literature previous to the novel.

Shakespeare's sense of the historical past, for example, is very different from the modern one. Troy and Rome, the Plantagenets and the Tudors, none of them are far enough back to be very different from the present or from each other. In this Shakespeare reflects the view of his age: he had been dead for thirty years before the word 'anachronism' first appeared in English,[26] and he was still very close to the mediaeval conception of history by which, whatever the period, the wheel of time churns out the same eternally applicable *exempla*.

This a-historical outlook is associated with a striking lack of interest in the minute-by-minute and day-to-day temporal setting, a lack of interest which has caused the time scheme of so many plays both by Shakespeare and by most of his predecessors from Aeschylus onwards, to baffle later editors and critics. The attitude to time in early fiction is very similar; the sequence of events is set in a very abstract continuum of time and space, and allows very little importance to time as a factor in human relationships. Coleridge noted the 'marvellous independence and true imaginative absence of all particular space or time in the "Faerie Queene" ';[27] and the temporal dimension of Bunyan's allegories or the heroic romances is equally vague and unparticularised.

Soon, however, the modern sense of time began to permeate many areas of thought. The late seventeenth century witnessed the rise of a more objective study of history and therefore of a

[26] See Herman J. Ebeling, 'The Word Anachronism,' *MLN*, LII (1937), 120-121.
[27] *Selected Works*, ed. Potter (London, 1933), p. 333.

deeper sense of the difference between the past and the present.[28] At the same time Newton and Locke presented a new analysis of the temporal process;[29] it became a slower and more mechanical sense of duration which was minutely enough discriminated to measure the falling of objects or the succession of thoughts in the mind.

These new emphases are reflected in the novels of Defoe. His fiction is the first which presents us with a picture both of the individual life in its larger perspective as a historical process, and in its closer view which shows the process being acted out against the background of the most ephemeral thoughts and actions. It is true that the time scales of his novels are sometimes both contradictory in themselves, and inconsistent with their pretended historical setting, but the mere fact that such objections arise is surely a tribute to the way the characters are felt by the reader to be rooted in the temporal dimension. We obviously could not think of making such objections seriously to Sidney's *Arcadia* or *The Pilgrim's Progress*; there is not enough evidence of the reality of time for any sense of discrepancies to be possible. Defoe does give us such evidence. At his best, he convinces us completely that his narrative is occurring at a particular place and at a particular time, and our memory of his novels consists largely of these vividly realised moments in the lives of his characters, moments which are loosely strung together to form a convincing biographical perspective. We have a sense of personal identity subsisting through duration and yet being changed by the flow of experience.

This impression is much more strongly and completely realised in Richardson. He was very careful to locate all his events of his narrative in an unprecedentedly detailed time-scheme: the superscription of each letter gives us the day of the week, and often the time of the day; and this in turn acts as an objective framework for the even greater temporal detail of the letters themselves—we are told, for example, that Clarissa died at

[28] See G. N. Clark, *The Later Stuarts, 1660-1714* (Oxford, 1934), pp. 362-366; René Wellek, *The Rise of English Literary History* (Chapel Hill, 1941), ch. 2.

[29] See especially Ernst Cassirer, 'Raum und Zeit,' *Das Erkenntnisproblem* . . . (Berlin, 1922-23), II, 339-374.

6:40 P.M. on Thursday, 7th September. Richardson's use of the letter form also induced in the reader a continual sense of actual participation in the action which was until then unparalleled in its completeness and intensity. He knew, as he wrote in the 'Preface' to *Clarissa,* that it was 'Critical situations . . . with what may be called *instantaneous* descriptions and reflections' that engaged the attention best; and in many scenes the pace of the narrative was slowed down by minute description to something very near that of actual experience. In these scenes Richardson achieved for the novel what D. W. Griffith's technique of the 'close-up' did for the film: added a new dimension to the representation of reality.

Fielding approached the problem of time in his novels from a more external and traditional point of view. In *Shamela* he poured scorn on Richardson's use of the present tense: 'Mrs. Jervis and I are just in bed, and the door unlocked; if my master should come—Ods-bobs! I heard him just coming in at the door. You see I write in the present tense, as Parson William says. Well, he is in bed between us . . .'[30] In *Tom Jones* he indicated his intention of being much more selective than Richardson in his handling of the time dimension: 'We intend . . . rather to pursue the method of those writers who profess to disclose the revolutions of countries, than to imitate the painful and voluminous historian, who, to preserve the regularity of his series, thinks himself obliged to fill up as much paper with the detail of months and years in which nothing remarkable happened, as he employs upon those notable eras when the greatest scenes have been transacted on the human stage.'[31] At the same time, however, *Tom Jones* introduced one interesting innovation in the fictional treatment of time. Fielding seems to have used an almanac, that symbol of the diffusion of an objective sense of time by the printing press: with slight exceptions, nearly all the events of his novel are chronologically consistent, not only in relation to each other, and to the time that each stage of the journey of the various characters from the West Country to London would actually have taken, but also in relation to such external considerations as the

[30] Letter 6.
[31] Bk. II, ch. I.

proper phases of the moon and the time-table of the Jacobite rebellion in 1745, the supposed year of the action.[32]

(e)

In the present context, as in many others, space is the necessary correlative of time. Logically the individual, particular case is defined by reference to two co-ordinates, space and time. Psychologically, as Coleridge pointed out, our idea of time is 'always blended with the idea of space.'[33] The two dimensions, indeed, are for many practical purposes inseparable, as is suggested by the fact that the words 'present' and 'minute' can refer to either dimension; while introspection shows that we cannot easily visualize any particular moment of existence without setting it in its spatial context also.

Place was traditionally almost as general and vague as time in tragedy, comedy and romance. Shakespeare, as Johnson tells us, 'had no regard to distinction of time or place';[34] and Sidney's *Arcadia* was as unlocalized as the Bohemian limbos of the Elizabethan stage. In the picaresque novel, it is true, and in Bunyan, there are many passages of vivid and particularised physical description; but they are incidental and fragmentary. Defoe would seem to be the first of our writers who visualised the whole of his narrative as though it occurred in an actual physical environment. His attention to the description of milieu is still intermittent; but occasional vivid details supplement the continual implication of his narrative and make us attach Robinson Crusoe and Moll Flanders much more completely to their environments than is the case with previous fictional characters. Characteristically, this solidity of setting is particularly noticeable in Defoe's treatment of movable objects in the physical world: in *Moll Flanders* there is much linen and gold to be counted, while Robinson Crusoe's island is full of memorable pieces of clothing and hardware.

Richardson, once again occupying the central place in the development of the technique of narrative realism, carried the

[32] As was shown by F. S. Dickson (Cross, *Henry Fielding,* II, 189-193).

[33] *Biographia Literaria,* ed. Shawcross (London, 1907), I, 87.

[34] 'Preface' (1765), *Johnson on Shakespeare,* ed. Raleigh (London, 1908), pp. 21-22.

process much further. There is little description of natural scenery, but considerable attention is paid to interiors throughout his novels. Pamela's residences in Lincolnshire and Bedfordshire are real enough prisons; we are given a highly detailed description of Grandison Hall; and some of the descriptions in *Clarissa* anticipate Balzac's skill in making the setting of the novel a pervasive operating force—the Harlowe mansion becomes a terrifyingly real physical and moral environment.

Here, too, Fielding is some way from Richardson's particularity. He gives us no full interiors, and his frequent landscape descriptions are very conventionalised. Nevertheless *Tom Jones* features the first Gothic mansion in the history of the novel:[35] and Fielding is as careful about the topography of his action as he is about its chronology; many of the places on Tom Jones's route to London are given by name, and the exact location of the others is implied by various other kinds of evidence.

In general, then, although there is nothing in the eighteenth-century novel which equals the opening chapters of *Le Rouge et le noir* or *Le Père Goriot,* chapters which at once indicate the importance which Stendhal and Balzac attach to the environment in their total picture of life, there is no doubt that the pursuit of verisimilitude led Defoe, Richardson and Fielding to initiate that power of 'putting man wholly into his physical setting' which constitutes for Allen Tate the distinctive capacity of the novel form;[36] and the considerable extent to which they succeeded is not the least of the factors which differentiate them from previous writers of fiction and which explain their importance in the tradition of the new form.

(f)

The various technical characteristics of the novel described above all seem to contribute to the furthering of an aim which the novelist shares with the philosopher—the production of what purports to be an authentic account of the actual experiences of individuals. This aim involved many other departures from the

[35] See Warren Hunting Smith, *Architecture in English Fiction* (New Haven, 1934), p. 65.

[36] 'Techniques of Fiction,' in *Critiques and Essays on Modern Fiction, 1920-1951,* ed. Aldridge (New York, 1952), p. 41.

traditions of fiction besides those already mentioned. What is perhaps the most important of them, the adaptation of prose style to give an air of complete authenticity, is also closely related to one of the distinctive methodological emphases of philosophical realism.

Just as it was the Nominalist scepticism about language which began to undermine the attitude to universals held by the scholastic Realists, so modern realism soon found itself faced with the semantic problem. Words did not all stand for real objects, or did not stand for them in the same way, and philosophy was therefore faced with the problem of discovering their rationale. Locke's chapters at the end of the third Book of the *Essay Concerning Human Understanding* are probably the most important evidence of this trend in the seventeenth century. Much of what is said there about the proper use of words would exclude the great bulk of literature, since, as Locke sadly discovers, 'eloquence, like the fair sex,' involves a pleasurable deceit.[37] On the other hand, it is interesting to note that although some of the 'abuses of language' which Locke specifies, such as figurative language, had been a regular feature of the romances, they are much rarer in the prose of Defoe and Richardson than in that of any previous writer of fiction.

The previous stylistic tradition for fiction was not primarily concerned with the correspondence of words to things, but rather with the extrinsic beauties which could be bestowed upon description and action by the use of rhetoric. Heliodorus's *Aethiopica* had established the tradition of linguistic ornateness in the Greek romances and the tradition had been continued in the Euphuism of John Lyly and Sidney, and in the elaborate conceits, or 'phébus,' of La Calprenède and Madeleine de Scudéry. So even if the new writers of fiction had rejected the old tradition of mixing poetry with their prose, a tradition which had been followed even in narratives as completely devoted to the portrayal of low life as Petronius's *Satyricon,* there would still have remained a strong literary expectation that they would use language as a source of interest in its own right, rather than as a purely referential medium.

[37] Bk. III, ch. 10, sects. xxxiii-xxxiv.

In any case, of course, the classical critical tradition in general had no use for the unadorned realistic description which such a use of language would imply. When the 9th *Tatler* (1709) introduced Swift's 'Description of the Morning' as a work where the author had 'run into a way perfectly new, and described things as they happen,' it was being ironical. The implicit assumption of educated writers and critics was that an author's skill was shown, not in the closeness with which he made his words correspond to their objects, but in the literary sensitivity with which his style reflected the linguistic decorum appropriate to its subject. It is natural, therefore, that it is to writers outside the circle of wit that we should have to turn for our earliest examples of fictional narrative written in a prose which restricts itself almost entirely to a descriptive and denotative use of language. Natural, too, that both Defoe and Richardson should have been attacked by many of the better educated writers of the day for their clumsy and often inaccurate way of writing.

Their basically realistic intentions, of course, required something very different from the accepted modes of literary prose. It is true that the movement towards clear and easy prose in the late seventeenth century had done much to produce a mode of expression much better adapted to the realistic novel than had been available before; while the Lockean view of language was beginning to be reflected in literary theory—John Dennis, for example, proscribed imagery in certain circumstances on the ground that it was unrealistic: 'No sort of imagery can ever be the language of grief. If a man complains in simile, I either laugh or sleep.'[38] Nevertheless the prose norm of the Augustan period remained much too literary to be the natural voice of Moll Flanders or Pamela Andrews: and although the prose of Addison, for example, or Swift, is simple and direct enough, its ordered economy tends to suggest an acute summary rather than a full report of what it describes.

It is therefore likely that we must regard the break which Defoe and Richardson made with the accepted canons of prose style, not an incidental blemish, but rather as the price they had to pay for achieving the immediacy and closeness of the text to

[38] Preface, *The Passion of Byblis, Critical Works,* ed. Hooker (Baltimore, 1939-43), I, 2.

what is being described. With Defoe this closeness is mainly physical, with Richardson mainly emotional, but in both we feel that the writer's exclusive aim is to make the words bring his object home to us in all its concrete particularity, whatever the cost in repetition or parenthesis or verbosity. Fielding, of course, did not break with the traditions of Augustan prose style or outlook. But it can be argued that this detracts from the authenticity of his narratives. Reading *Tom Jones* we do not imagine that we are eavesdropping on a new exploration of reality; the prose immediately informs us that exploratory operations have long been accomplished, that we are to be spared that labour, and presented instead with a sifted and clarified report of the findings.

There is a curious antinomy here. On the one hand, Defoe and Richardson make an uncompromising application of the realist point of view in language and prose structure, and thereby forfeit other literary values. On the other hand, Fielding's stylistic virtues tend to interfere with his technique as a novelist, because a patent selectiveness of vision destroys our belief in the reality of report, or at least diverts our attention from the content of the report to the skill of the reporter. There would seem to be some inherent contradiction between the ancient and abiding literary values and the distinctive narrative technique of the novel.

That this may be so is suggested by a parallel with French fiction. In France, the classical critical outlook, with its emphasis on elegance and concision, was not fully challenged until the coming of Romanticism. It is perhaps partly for this reason that French fiction from *La Princesse de Clèves* to *Les Liaisons dangereuses* stands outside the main tradition of the novel. For all its psychological penetration and literary skill, we feel it is too stylish to be authentic. In this Madame de La Fayette and Choderlos de Laclos are the polar opposites of Defoe and Richardson, whose very diffuseness tends to act as a guarantee of the authenticity of their report, whose prose aims exclusively at what Locke defined as the proper purpose of language, 'to convey the knowledge of things,'[39] and whose novels as a whole pretend to be no more than a transcription of real life—in Flaubert's words, 'le réel écrit.'

[39] *Human Understanding,* Bk. III, ch. 10, sect. xxiii.

It would appear, then, that the function of language is much more largely referential in the novel than in other literary forms; that the genre itself works by exhaustive presentation rather than by elegant concentration. This fact would no doubt explain both why the novel is the most translatable of the genres; why many undoubtedly great novelists, from Richardson and Balzac to Hardy and Dostoevsky, often write gracelessly, and sometimes with downright vulgarity; and why the novel has less need of historical and literary commentary than other genres—its formal convention forces it to supply its own footnotes.

## II

So much for the main analogies between realism in philosophy and literature. They are not proposed as exact; philosophy is one thing and literature is another. Nor do the analogies depend in any way on the presumption that the realist tradition in philosophy was a cause of the realism of the novel. That there was some influence is very likely, especially through Locke, whose thought everywhere pervades the eighteenth-century climate of opinion. But if a causal relationship of any importance exists it is probably much less direct: both the philosophical and the literary innovations must be seen as parallel manifestations of larger change—that vast transformation of Western civilisation since the Renaissance which has replaced the unified world picture of the Middle Ages with another very different one—one which presents us, essentially, with a developing but unplanned aggregate of particular individuals having particular experiences at particular times and at particular places.

Here, however, we are concerned with a much more limited conception, with the extent to which the analogy with philosophical realism helps to isolate and define the distinctive narrative mode of the novel. This, it has been suggested, is the sum of literary techniques whereby the novel's imitation of human life follows the procedures adopted by philosophical realism in its attempt to ascertain and report the truth. These procedures are by no means confined to philosophy; they tend, in fact, to be followed whenever the relation to reality of any report of an event is being investigated. The novel's mode of imitating reality may therefore be equally well summarised in terms of the procedures of another group of specialists in epistemology, the jury in a court of law. Their expectations, and those of the novel reader coincide in many ways: both want to know 'all the particulars' of a given case—the time and place of the occurrence; both must be satisfied as to the identities of the parties concerned, and will refuse to accept evidence about anyone called Sir Toby Belch or Mr. Badman—still less about a Chloe who has no surname and is 'common as the air'; and they also expect the witnesses to tell the story 'in his own words.' The jury, in fact, takes the 'circumstantial view of life,' which T. H. Green[40] found to be the characteristic outlook of the novel.

The narrative method whereby the novel embodies this circumstantial view of life may be called its formal realism; formal, because the term realism does not here refer to any special literary doctrine or purpose, but only to a set of narrative procedures which are so commonly found together in the novel, and so rarely in other literary genres, that they may be regarded as typical of the form itself. Formal realism, in fact, is the narrative embodiment of a premise that Defoe and Richardson accepted very literally, but which is implicit in the novel form in general: the premise, or primary convention, that the novel is a full and authentic report of human experience, and is therefore under an obligation to satisfy its reader with such details of the story as the individuality of the actors concerned, the particulars of the times and places of their actions, details which are presented through a more largely referential use of language than is common in other literary forms.

Formal realism is, of course, like the rules of evidence, only a convention; and there is no reason why the report on human life which is presented by it should be in fact any truer than those presented through the very different conventions of other literary genres. The novel's air of total authenticity, indeed, does tend to authorise confusion on this point: and the tendency of some Realists and Naturalists to forget that the accurate transcription of actuality does not necessarily produce a work of any real

[40] 'Estimate,' *Works,* III, 37.

truth or enduring literary value is no doubt partly responsible for the rather widespread distaste for Realism and all its works which is current today. This distaste, however, may also promote critical confusion by leading us into the opposite error; we must not allow an awareness of certain shortcomings in the aims of the Realist school to obscure the very considerable extent to which the novel in general, as much in Joyce as in Zola, employs the literary means here called formal realism. Nor must we forget that, although formal realism is only a convention, it has, like all literary conventions, its own peculiar advantages. There are important differences in the degree to which different literary forms imitate reality; and the formal realism of the novel allows a more immediate imitation of individual experience set in its temporal and spatial environment than do other literary forms. Consequently the novel's conventions make much smaller demands on the audience than do most literary conventions; and this surely explains why the majority of readers in the last two hundred years have found in the novel the literary form which most closely satisfies their wishes for a close correspondence between life and art. Nor are the advantages of the close and detailed correspondence to real life offered by formal realism limited to assisting the novel's popularity; they are also related to its most distinctive literary qualities, as we shall see.

In the strictest sense, of course, formal realism was not discovered by Defoe and Richardson; they only applied it much more completely than had been done before. Homer, for example, as Carlyle pointed out,[41] shared with them that outstanding 'clearness of sight' which is manifested in the 'detailed, ample and lovingly exact' descriptions that abound in their works; and there are many passages in later fiction, from *The Golden Ass* to *Aucassin and Nicolette,* from Chaucer to Bunyan, where the characters, their actions and their environment are presented with a particularity as authentic as that in any eighteenth-century novel. But there is an important difference: in Homer and in earlier prose fiction these passages are relatively rare, and tend to stand out from the surrounding narrative; the total literary structure was not consistently oriented in the direction of formal realism,

[41] 'Burns,' *Critical and Miscellaneous Essays* (New York, 1899), I, 276-277.

and the plot especially, which was usually traditional and often highly improbable, was in direct conflict with its premises. Even when previous writers had overtly professed a wholly realistic aim, as did many seventeenth-century writers, they did not pursue it wholeheartedly. La Calprenède, Richard Head, Grimmelshausen, Bunyan, Aphra Behn, Furetière,[42] to mention only a few, had all asserted that their fictions were literally true; but their prefatory asseverations are no more convincing than the very similar ones to be found in most works of mediaeval hagiography. The aim of verisimilitude had not been deeply enough assimilated in either case to bring about the full rejection of all the non-realistic conventions that governed the genre.

For reasons to be considered in the next chapter, Defoe and Richardson were unprecedentedly independent of the literary conventions which might have interfered with their primary intentions, and they accepted the requirements of literal truth much more comprehensively. Of no fiction before Defoe's could Lamb have written, in terms very similar to those which Hazlitt used of Richardson,[43] 'It is like reading evidence in a court of Justice.'[44] Whether that is in itself a good thing is open to question; Defoe and Richardson would hardly deserve their reputation unless they had other and better claims on our attention. Nevertheless there can be little doubt that the development of a narrative method capable of creating such an impression is the most conspicuous manifestation of that mutation of prose fiction which we call the novel; the historical importance of Defoe and Richardson therefore primarily depends on the suddenness and completeness with which they brought into being what may be regarded as the lowest common denominator of the novel genre as a whole, its formal realism.

[42] See A. J. Tieje, 'A Peculiar Phase of the Theory of Realism in Pre-Richardsonian Prose-Fiction,' *PMLA,* XXVII (1913), 213-252.

[43] 'He sets about describing every object and transaction, as if the whole had been given in on evidence by an eye-witness' (*Lectures on the English Comic Writers* (New York, 1845), p. 138).

[44] Letter to Walter Wilson, Dec. 16, 1822, printed in the latter's *Memoirs of the Life and Times of Daniel de Foe* (London, 1830, III, 428).

# Harry Levin

## *Realism in Perspective*

### THE CONTEXT OF REALISM

We are dealing with a general tendency, and not a specific doctrine. Since no hard and fast definition of realism will cover all the manifestations occurring under its name, we must examine them for its pertinent meaning in each case. " 'Realism,' " says Karl Mannheim, "means different things in different contexts." The same word, Benedetto Croce points out, is applied by some critics in praise and by others in blame. Zola's meat was Brunetière's poison. "Men and women as they are," as they are for Howells, barely exist for his successors. *Jane Eyre,* which preserves a schoolgirlish innocence for us, so shocked its reviewers that they could not believe it had been written by a respectable woman. Charlotte Brontë, for her part, found Jane Austen's fiction "more *real* than *true.*" Diderot praised Richardson for achieving "toute la réalité possible." Fielding would not have agreed. The history of taste, by lending its comparative standards, may resolve these conflicts of opinion. It suggests a sense in which Racine, though we do not ordinarily classify him as a realist, could be more realistic than Corneille. But, as between two contemporaries, one refining the analysis and the other broadening the scope of literature, which is the realist? Is it Trollope, with his accurate notations of provincial or parliamentary life, or Dickens, with his exaggerated efforts to delve in dust heaps which Trollope so quietly ignored? Is the penetrating self-portrait of *Adolphe* less realistic than the panoramic irreality of *Les Misérables?* Some novelists, evidently, go as far as they can within a restricted sphere; others, in enlarging those restrictions, overstep the borderline of romance. Every novel is realistic in some respects and unrealistic in others. Criticism can but try to estimate the proportions by comparing what the writer endeavors to show with what the reader is able to see.

When realism appeals neither to ontological argument nor to scientific experiment but to human experience, philosophers consider it "naïve." This is the kind of everyday realism that interests us most, but it would be naïve indeed if we expected reality to be the same for everyone. And we should be disappointed, like the princess in the fairy tale, if we supposed that nature could be perfectly reproduced by any artifice. Even the purely visual reproduction of the painter or the sculptor is admittedly angled, heightened, foreshortened. The brand of realism that has had the widest application in recent years is the politician's, which, instead of committing itself to a set of principles, rather implies the rejection of principle. The political objective of bourgeois society, freedom, seems to be undefinable in positive terms. "Freedom from what?" is the question that liberalism undertakes to answer, and its answers constitute a negative catalogue of our age's problems. Absolute liberty is as meaningless as realism in a vacuum. Both are relative terms, referring us back to a definite series of restraints from which we have managed to secure some degree of release. When we call a book realistic, we mean that it is relatively free from bookish artificialities; it convinces us, where more conventional books do not. It offers us *realiora,* if not *realia,* as Eugene Zamyatin succinctly put it: not quite the real things, but things that seem more real than those offered by others. By rereading those other books too and reconstructing their conventions, we can relate them to our comparatively realistic book and specify its new departures more precisely. We can define realism by its context.

Our excuse for studying literary history is that the mediocre works help us to place the masterpieces. By establishing the rules we learn to recognize the exceptions. It is the exceptional writer who changes the context of literature, and who—from generation to generation—readjusts it to the vicissitudes of life. Among such writers, Rabelais is doubly exceptional, one of the most original of originals, and he should be saluted in passing as a realist by any criterion, historical or otherwise. Though he preached a naturalistic ethic, he adorned it with an extravagant learning which could scarcely have belonged to a child of nature. Such an attitude is never primordial or spontaneous; it is always a stringent revision of more complicated views. When Schiller ascribed *Realism*—his word was not *Realismus*—to the Greeks, he meant that their outlook was not as idealistic as that of himself and his romantic contemporaries; but this was premised upon his nostalgic contrast between the self-consciousness of the moderns and the simplicity of the ancients. It remained for the twentieth century to perceive, with Léon-Paul Fargue: "There is no genuine simplicity; there are only simplifications. The natural in literature presupposes the utmost effort, or else mannerism." Insofar as realism presupposes an idealism to be corrected, a convention to be superseded, or an orthodoxy to be criticized, George Moore is right: "No more literary school than the realists has ever existed." No writers have been more intensely conscious of what was already written. We can measure their contributions by a sliding scale which moves from literature toward life, but which likewise gravitates in the opposite direction under the counter-influence of romance.

Any work of imagination is likely to exhibit both tendencies, romantic and realistic; they are by no means confined to those historical movements which we respectively associate with the première of *Hernani* in 1830 and the prosecution of *Madame Bovary* in 1857. "Realism had existed long before this great controversy," Baudelaire had written in 1846, under the caption "What is Romanticism?" Nor can we assume, without considerable qualification, that romanticism and realism are historically opposed. "Romanticism is the most recent, the most up-to-date expression of the beautiful . . . To say romanticism is to say modern art." In their eagerness to garner local color, to tackle forbidding subjects, and to break down classical genres, the romanticists anticipated the realists; while the realists, we must bear in mind, took over a considerable residue of romance. These intermixtures are strikingly evident in the romantic realism of Dickens, the "fantastic" realism of Dostoevsky, and the "poetic" realism of Otto Ludwig and Adalbert Stifter. In France there was Victor Hugo; but, on the whole, the transition was more homogeneous. Yet, when Georges Pellissier stressed the continuities in a suggestive study, *Le Réalisme du romantisme,* Emile Faguet repeated the usual textbook distinctions by way of review. Mario Praz does not avoid this verbal impasse by applying the term Biedermeier to the bourgeois romanticism of the mid-Victorians or by illustrating from Dutch genre-paintings. More precise definition should clarify both the extent to which the elder generation paved the way for the younger and the extent to which the younger generation reacted against the elder.

Of the successive generations that have been shaken by literary revolution, only one—the middle generation of the nineteenth century—claims the explicit label of realism. Like most critical categories, the term comes after the fact, and comes later to other languages than to French. English seems to have borrowed it, in 1853, through an article on Balzac in the *Westminster Review*. The first independently relevant instance cited by the *New English Dictionary* came in 1857, when Ruskin criticized the "base grotesque" of Bronzino, the attempt to compensate for lack of imagination by "startling realism." The context here, as in so many early instances, refers to painting and expresses hostility. The previous year Emerson had employed the adjective "realistic," as a synonym for "materialistic" and an antonym for "idealistic," in characterizing Swift. Here the word betrays its ultimately philosophical origin, and its long association with the dualistic arguments of the metaphysicians. In France, though Littré still classifies *réalisme* as a neologism in 1872, the word had been utilized by literary criticism as early as 1826. Through the 'thirties it was used occasionally to designate some of the same things that romanticism stood for; it was consistently attacked, in the *Revue des deux mondes* and other conservative periodicals, as an artistic symptom of the growing radicalism of the epoch. It was usually mentioned in a disparaging sense, until some of the younger bohemians, protesting against the outmoded pomp of the academic tradition, began to pride themselves on the designation. Arsène Houssaye's history of Flemish painting, published in 1846, proved that there was also a realistic tradition. Théophile Gautier and other friendly critics defended the new esthetic by invoking the ancient concept of the imitation of nature.

It was "the landscape-painter of humanity," as Gustave Courbet was known to his admirers, who first proclaimed himself a realist—or rather, accepted the epithet thrust upon him. When the Salons objected to his literal treatment of peasants and laborers and the middle classes, he retorted by issuing manifestoes in the name of realism. When the Paris exposition of 1855 refused to hang his pictures, he erected his own *Pavillon du Réalisme,* and began to publicize the movement on an international scale. Later years brought out the socialistic and anticlerical implications of his work, and he was finally exiled for the part he had taken in the Commune. Whenever his critics complained that he had caricatured his models, he would insist, as Balzac did: "Les bourgeois sont ainsi!" Meanwhile realism was being widely popularized by the quasi-photographic genre-painting of the Barbizon school. The technique of photography, which had been invented by Niepce de Saint-Victor in 1824 and subsequently developed by Jacques Daguerre, had been acquired by the state and divulged to the public in 1839. Neither painters nor writers welcomed the new invention, for it drew them into a competition which they were both destined to lose. Nothing short of the *Comédie humaine* could compete with the daguerreotype; Balzac's ingenuity and facility, in reproducing characters and exhibiting scenes, was hardly less inventive; and Daguerre's other novelty, the diorama, echoes across the dinner-table in *Le Père Goriot*. Once perfected, photography served to demonstrate the difference between artistic means and mechanical processes of reproduction. Its ultimate effect was to discourage photographic realism. Painters became impressionists, writers rediscovered the personality of the observer, and even photographers called art to the aid of technology.

Though Balzac won retrospective recognition as the archrealist, chronologically he belonged to the romantic generation. And though *Madame Bovary* was the most notable and the most notorious book of the realistic generation, Flaubert cultivated an aloofness from his contemporaries. The fanfares were sounded by a pair of journalists whose own novels stirred up less excitement than their articles on contemporary art and literature. Jules Fleury-Husson, under the pseudonym of Champfleury, collected some of his criticism into a volume, *Le Réalisme,* which came out in 1857. Edmond Duranty edited seven numbers of a little magazine, *Réalisme,* at monthly intervals between November 1856 and May 1857. Both men were acute enough to sense that the trend, which they followed rather than led, was far too fundamental to be identified with the special program of a single group. "That terrible word 'realism' is the reverse of the word 'school,' " announced Duranty. "To say 'realistic school' is nonsense. Realism signifies the frank and complete expression of individualities; it is actually an attack upon convention, imitation, every sort of school." More affirmatively, he went on to describe the envisaged result as "the exact, complete, sincere reproduction of the social milieu and the epoch in which one lives." But this was merely to make the description vary with the individual consciousness of one's place and time. As the slogan of a school, announced Champfleury, realism was only "a transitional term which will last no longer than thirty years."

While it lasted, Balzac and Courbet were avenging gods, and Champfleury was their publicist and prophet. He was also the historian of French caricature, which was even then reaching its height and leaving its incisive mark upon fiction. In an embittered tale of bohemian life, *Chien-Caillou,* he schematized the formula of Cervantes by printing side by side in parallel columns the idealistic expectations of his readers and the disappointments that reality would hold for them. His own laconic definition of realism, "sincerity in art," was based upon one of the most elusive words in the critical vocabulary; but it meant something against a context of artistic affectation, and against the constant enthymeme that the lower classes were more rewarding than upper-class subjects because they were more sincere. Here critical logic is overtaken by revolutionary zeal. Champfleury reminds us that realism is the insurrection of a minority, one of those "religions in -ism" like socialism that gained headway with the Revolution of 1848. Even then, while Marx and Engels were framing *The Communist Manifesto,* Champfleury and Baudelaire were conducting a republican paper. Champfleury's distrust of form, and his attempt to judge works of art by their content, foreshadowed the Marxist critics. Disliking poetry, he distinguished the friends and enemies of realism as *sincéristes* and *formistes*—a distinction which left little room for the ironic interplay of Baudelaire or of Flaubert. Political expression, submerged with the failure of the socialist Republic, came to the surface in controversies over realism. Both *Madame Bovary* and *Les Fleurs du mal* were prosecuted by the imperial regime.

Literature was taking stranger and more sensational shapes, artists were making private gestures of opposition to the Empire, while the realists were expressing, in Champfleury's terms, "a latent and unconscious aspiration toward democracy." These impulses converge in the rejected picture, *L'Atelier du peintre: allégorie réelle,* where Courbet has depicted himself, his easel and canvas, a number of cast-off romantic properties, a nude woman, a group of working-class models, and several friends, including Champfleury, Baudelaire, the folk-poet Büchon, and the socialist Proudhon. Here the real allegory is that of the self-portraying artist, whose world is the studio and whose studio is the world, whose symbols are actualities and whose ideology is his art. Even more paradoxically, the distance between Flaubert's material and his style illustrates the ambivalence of realism, as a characteristic product of middle-class society and an unsparing commentary upon it. "As an expression of manners and social conditions, the school seems to correspond in art with the bourgeois element that has become predominant in the new society, reproducing its spirit and image as the novel does in literature," wrote a hostile critic, Louis Peisse, in 1851, the year that witnessed the enthronement of Napoleon III. In 1857, M. Prudhomme himself, succumbing to the vogue, subscribed a letter with assurances of his "distinguished consideration and realism."

With the predominance of the bourgeoisie, with the grandeur and decadence of Birotteau, it was certainly time to explore fresh fields. In 1864, the year of Claude Bernard's *Introduction à l' étude de la médecine expérimentale,* the Goncourts prefaced their *Germinie Lacerteux* with the usual declaration outdating all previous fiction: "The public likes false novels; this is a true novel." They were now proposing a further extension of the literary franchise, *le droit au roman*: "Living in the nineteenth century, in a time of universal suffrage, of democracy, of liberalism, we have asked ourselves whether those we call 'the lower classes' have not their right to the novel." French literature, in all its critical awareness and circumstantial candor, was ready to investigate the servant problem. "Today, when the novel undertakes the investigations and obligations of science, it may also claim the privileges and freedoms." Realism had fully crystallized by 1858, when Taine's essay on Balzac appeared. After the appearance of Darwin's *Origin of Species* in the following year, every mode of interpreting human experience had to be gradually revised. A younger generation, children of the realists and grandchildren of the romanticists, demanded still another readjustment. During the 'seventies Zola sought to consolidate Taine's critical position with Bernard's experimental method, within the widening—or was it the narrowing?—orientation of Darwin's naturalism.

Heretofore "naturalism" had occasionally figured in the critical vocabulary; on occasion it was loosely synonymous with impressionism; but it had never been sharply differentiated from the connotations of realism, the more inclusive term. Zola, the literary executor of Duranty, sought to reinvigorate the realistic novel by substituting a naturalistic slogan. Just as the realists had adopted Balzac, so the naturalists adopted Flaubert, though Flaubert had never accepted the label, and Zola admitted in cynical moments that it was mere publicity. In serious moments, his naturalism looked beyond Flaubert's hatred of the bourgeoisie to an interest in the proletariat, and beyond the conventions of art to the investigations of science. A novel, though it might be impeded by political barriers, was free to lose itself in the uncharted contexts of nature. But the naturalistic novel also involved certain deterministic premises that realism ignored, that inhibited freedom of action and relieved the characters from responsibility for the degrading condition in which the novelist found them. The novelist himself was now a passive observer, a rigorous compiler of what Edmond de Goncourt first termed "human documents." Observation, it was presumed, would eliminate imagination and convert the art of fiction into a branch of scientific research. For Zola the realism of the Empire had been "too exclusively bourgeois." He in turn, with greater success than his forerunners, founded a school. He virtually established naturalism as an official doctrine of the Third Republic, a hardening orthodoxy from which the divergent movements of the twentieth century still take their departure.

Neither Stendhal nor Balzac nor Flaubert nor Zola nor Proust belonged to the French Academy—a sequence of omissions which throws light on the relationship of the novel to the establishment. Novelists less distinguished have been admitted, since the immortalization of the bland Octave Feuillet in 1863. Through one of the most carefully managed ironies of literary history, plus a bequest from Edmond de Goncourt, naturalism established its own academy in 1903. The issue is internationally reflected in the terms by which the Nobel Prize has been awarded, from 1901, to an author of idealistic tendency. Nonetheless most of its laureates, like the winners of the Prix Goncourt, have written in what became the naturalistic tradition. Now that the naturalists, the realists, and the romanticists are venerated alike by literary historians, we must not forget how often—during the nineteenth century—they were damned by critics, ignored by professors, turned down by publishers, opposed by the academies and the Salons, and censored and suppressed by the state. Whatever creed of realism they professed, their work was regarded as a form of subversion, and all the forces of convention were arrayed against them. While art propagandized against the middle class, the middle class invoked morality as a weapon against art. Literature had come too close to life for comfort. Brunetière, who led the counter-attack against the naturalists, accused them of overstressing the grosser aspects of reality, and pleaded for a revival of idealism. The naturalists hinted, by way of reply, that the traditionalists preferred the timeless to the timely because they were out of touch with their own time.

We have something to learn from their objections to specific details; traditionalism, however, objected in principle to the use of detail, and predisposed its critics to find realism tedious or trivial, ugly or obscene, decadent or improbable. On the other hand, the realists, in their revolt against tradition, felt impelled to exaggerate "the true in the horrible and the horrible in the true."

Jules Janin's horrendous parody, *L'Âne mort et la femme guillotinée,* is worth remembering, if only because it proves that the popular novelists of *le bas romantisme* had scarcely been less sensational than Zola. Incidentally, it characterizes the bourgeois idealist who prefers romance to realism as "a Don Quixote in a cotton nightcap," surmounting his shop with battlements and surrounding it with a moat. Thus realism, as Georg Lukács puts it, moves in cycles. Proust, who used the word pejoratively, put his finger on the impetus: "From age to age a certain realism is reborn, by way of reaction against the art that has been theretofore admired." Consequently Erich Auerbach could range across many ages, cultures, and languages, from the *Odyssey* to Virginia Woolf, in order to show us "the representation of reality in western literature." His *Mimesis* is a magistral explication of a rich and eclectic series of texts. It illustrates the stylistic interplay between the grandiose and the plain-spoken, demonstrates the way symbolic conceptions yield to more materialistic approaches, and indicates the realistic component in the formal artistry of Dante and Shakespeare. *A fortiori* the weight of authority must be accorded to Auerbach's considered opinion that historic realism, fully conscious of socio-politico-economic circumstance, is a strictly modern phenomenon beginning with Stendhal.

## THE DYNASTY OF REALISM

Not every age, unfortunately, can be a great age of poetry; and a flourishing drama seems to require a rare conjunction of time and place. If any literary form has flourished in the modern epoch of the western world, it has been prose fiction. And surely, if this form has any nucleus of tradition, it has been the parallel and interconnected development of the novel in England and France. The Occidental novel harks back to brilliant beginnings in Italy and Spain; perhaps it registers its highest degree of imaginative intensity in Russia and America; and it has some interesting later offshoots in the Scandinavian countries and elsewhere. But it was England which led the way in the eighteenth century, and France in the nineteenth century seems to have taken the lead. The fact that Germany has had so few novelists of distinction is clarified by a remark of André Gide's: "The fatherlands of the novel are the lands of individualism." Admitting that German fiction lacks European significance, a sociological study has concluded that it identified itself too uncritically with the interests of the middle class. No land has been more self-critical or more individualistic than France, and no literature has spoken for all of Europe with more authority. Recognizing this authority, Tolstoy advised Maxim Gorky to read the French realists; Henry James wrote Howells that they were the only contemporaries whose work he respected; and George Moore never ceased to tell English novelists how much they could learn from Balzac, Flaubert, and Zola. "Yes, when I read a novel I mostly read a French one," says one of James's heroines, "for I seem with it to get hold of more of the real thing—to get more life for my money."

Circulating in foreign translations or between its original yellow covers, the French novel has acquired an international notoriety, which is based not merely on its pioneer frankness in the matter of sex but on its intransigent refusal to take any human relationship for granted. Its abiding preoccupation might be summed up in the single word *moeurs,* which must be translated by two different English words, "manners" and "morals," but which retains the impersonality of the Latin *mores*. In English literature, ever since the debate between Congreve and Collier, there seems to have been a gradual divorce between manners and morals. Novels of manners, like Meredith's, have been rather eccentric and superficial; novels of morals, like George Eliot's, have been more earnest and didactic. There has been an irresistible temptation, indelibly exemplified in the happy endings of Dickens, to sacrifice the real to the ideal. Too often, when the novelist has not arranged for the triumph of virtue, or modified the conduct of his characters to suit the ethical prepossessions of his readers, they have held him responsible for immoralities which he has simply attempted to describe. Mrs. Grundy equated "realistic" with "pornographic." Guizot, who was an Anglophile as well as an official spokesman for middle-class morality, publicly regretted that French novels were not as respectable as *The Heir of Redclyffe.* Brunetière—that exponent of universality—preferred George Eliot, and even Rhoda Broughton, to Flaubert and Zola. For Flaubert and Zola there could be no compromise with domesticated taste. Morals were the criteria of manners, and manners the test of morals; and, where the practice failed to live up to the theory, nothing less than an uncompromising realism could deal with the situation.

"French novelists are very lucky in having the French to write about," Stephen Spender has remarked. Supremely articulate and gesticulative, their consistent reactions to concrete situations invite such aphoristic remarks; but an almost proverbial example may prove more illuminating, particularly when it is borrowed from Molière. The very title of his comedy, *L'Amour médecin,* characteristically inclines toward a clinical view of an emotional theme. Sganarelle's daughter, having secretly fallen in love, displays symptoms of melancholia, and the father consults his neighbors in the opening scene. M. Josse recommends some gift to cheer her spirits, a diamond necklace or some piece of jewelry, and the others make various other recommendations. Sganarelle listens patiently until they all have spoken, and then tells them off one by one, pointing out that M. Josse happens to be a jeweler—who would profit by the occasion to sell his wares—and that the advice of the others is no more disinterested. "Vous êtes orfèvre, M. Josse!" The line is more than a gag; it is a flash of revelation. Another writer, taken in by the show of pathos and benevolence, might have taken M. Josse at his neighborly word; or, having detected the ulterior economic motive, might have cried out in righteous indignation. Molière, in a mood which is seldom too far from detached amusement, sees through the characters, grasps the situation, and lays bare the *moeurs.* Now there is nothing about a lovesick girl or a worried parent or a merchant with his eye on the main chance that could not be encountered anywhere else. What is characteristic is not the pattern of behavior but the exposure of motivation: the dissembled emotions and calculations of the personalities, the conflicting interests and responsibilities of the group.

French literature has been preoccupied, not so much with

the individual in isolation or with society in the mass, as with the problem of keeping the balance between them. Psychology and sociology have contributed in equal measure to whet the analysis. Long before those twin sciences in -ology had been professionally exploited, their potentialities had been explored by the self-knowledge of Montaigne and the introspection of Pascal, by the maxims of La Rochefoucauld and the memoirs of Saint-Simon. The method of Descartes had located the ego against its context. La Bruyère had subtitled his character-sketches *Les Moeurs de ce siècle*. Voltaire had condensed the history of civilization into an *Essai sur les moeurs*. Even Rousseau, in probing the subjective, had retained a quantum of objectivity. We often hear that the French language is better accommodated to prose than to poetry, that the Gallic genius rises to greater heights in comedy than in tragedy, or that the most creative achievements of this particular culture are the most critical. Though these generalizations are far too sweeping to pass unqualified, they are borne out by the achievements of French fiction. The comparatively short distance between fiction and criticism is due, in Harold Laski's phrase, to "the great French tradition of making criticism a commentary on life." In other countries literature and society are two distinct things, said Renan. "In our country . . . they interpenetrate." Hence the novelist is *ex officio* a social critic. Theory without practice or practice without theory might subsist elsewhere, fostered by German metaphysics or British empiricism. French philosophy, under the aspect of Cartesian dualism, has insisted upon a clear-cut distinction and a running parallel between material reality and the realm of ideas. Realism, as we define it, is therefore implicit in the traditional structure of French thought.

An incomparable control of the instruments of culture has made France's experience available to the rest of the world, but it is the experience itself that has made France, and has made it the second fatherland of educated foreigners. Its explicative talents have reinforced its diagrammatic position. Geographically and historically France has played the typical role of *l'homme sensuel moyen*, as Matthew Arnold was so acutely aware, for Arnold faced the thankless task of upholding a critical tradition in a more decentralized culture. The centrality of France among nations strengthened the centripetal position of Paris among cities, making it the geographical and historical capital of bourgeois democracy. "France is at the heart, and is the heart, of Europe; if it beats too hard or too fast, fever and disorder may spread through the whole body," warned Bonald, fearful lest cultural continuities had been destroyed by the Revolution of 1789. The Revolution of 1830 brought to Michelet, at the other extreme of political opinion, a sense of France's mission: to reveal the social Word, as Judea and Greece had revealed the moral Word. "All social and intellectual solutions are fruitless for Europe until France has interpreted, translated, and popularized them." Bonald's organic metaphor differs significantly from Michelet's conception of the French people, piloting the ship of humanity. "But today this ship is navigating in a hurricane; it goes so fast, so fast that dizziness overcomes the sturdiest, and every breast is troubled. What can I do in this beautiful and terrible movement? One thing—understand it. I shall try, at least."

Why should French writers, with such unflinching effort, have dedicated themselves to that comprehensive task? The reason is the salient circumstance of modern history. It was revolution that inspired both the reactionary Bonald and the radical Michelet. Not less than ten times during the hundred and fifty years that divide the *ancien régime* from the Vichy government, Frenchmen were called upon to overthrow their leaders and to establish a new order. Alas, these overturns have since continued, and Michelet's trepidations would be even stronger today. The record, repeating itself with cumulative emphasis, testifies to a high degree of social consciousness, and to an equally high degree of individualism. Revolutionary movements end in Napoleonic careers, and the cult of Napoleon ends in the Commune.

> Napoleon introduces the need for success, unbridled emulation, unscrupulous ambition—crass egoism, in short, primarily his own egoism—as the central motive and the universal spring. This spring breaks, stretched too far, and ruins his machine. After him, under his successors, the same mechanism will operate in the same way, and will break down in the same way after a more or less protracted period. Up to

the present day, the longest of these periods has lasted less than twenty years.

When Taine was writing this passage in 1889, just a century after the first revolution, he was expecting another man on horseback, General Boulanger, to trample down the Third Republic. But the democratic regime, having already lasted nineteen years, and having proved more durable than its predecessors, was to live fifty years longer. The statue of Liberty Enlightening the World, its gift to a sister republic, retains an undimmed image in a poem by Marianne Moore, written upon the dark days of collapse and capitulation under Marshal Pétain:

*. . . we with re-*
*enforced Bartholdi's*
*Liberty holding up her*
*torch beside the port, hear France*
*demand, "Tell me the truth,*
*especially when it is*
*unpleasant." And we*
*cannot but reply,*
*"The word France means*
*enfranchisement . . ."*

Enfranchisement prompted mingled reverberations of despair and hope in 1941. "French writers, the freest in the universe"—so began a pamphlet published that year by Kléber Haedens, *Paradoxe sur le roman,* which terminated with the imprimatur of the Vichy censorship. The calculated irony was a bid for independence in the very teeth of disheartening odds.

Fanny Burney, who as Madame d'Arblay had lived under the Napoleonic Empire, declared upon her return to England that it would henceforth be impossible to delineate "any picture of actual human life without reference to the French Revolution." Yet it never occurred to Jane Austen that the young officers, who figure as dancing partners for the heroines of her novels, were on furlough from Trafalgar and Waterloo. One had then to breathe the air of France to be fully conscious of the difference between the eighteenth and nineteenth centuries. The new issues were quite as urgent in England, but not so desperately clear; the French were tearing down and building up institutions, while the English were preserving and adapting them. The English novel was free to go its own way, if it chose, and to be content with domestic life; the French novel, for lack of answerable government, assumed certain quasi-public obligations. In the absence of regular institutions, literature became one, whose leadership was conceded in Europe, if not in France. Since the breakdown of the old Latin republic of letters, French books had kept up a kind of International among the intellectuals. Elsewhere, when modern ideas penetrated, they were recognized and ticketed as overtly French. It was the French Revolution of July 1830, according to the historian of materialism, Friedrich Lange, that subverted German idealism. "It was toward France—'realistic' France—that men loved to look even from a political point of view. But what so specially endeared the July Monarchy and French constitutionalism to the men who now gave the tone in Germany was their relation to the material interests of the moneyed classes."

Revolution secured, not the realization of its own slogans, but the enthronement of the middle class. Writers thereafter could only express their doubts and disappointments, and hope for another revolution. The hopes of the first revolutionists had been dashed by the Terror; the grand illusion of Napoleon's Empire had been lost at Waterloo. The monumental past, with its legend of conquest and its rhetoric of freedom, could only reduce the present to mock-heroic dimensions. Alfred de Musset, in his *Confession d'un enfant du siècle,* gave a first-hand diagnosis of the disillusioned state of mind that was inciting his contemporaries to realism. "All the sickness of the present century comes from two causes: the people who have gone through '93 and 1814 bear two wounds in their hearts. Everything that was is no more; everything that will be is not yet. Look no farther for the secret of our troubles." Though the nobleman had been deprived of his prerogatives, it was not the common man who profited. M. Prudhomme, rushing into the breach, was the man of the hour. Eulogizing himself, he parodied Musset. "No matter what you do or say, everything today is bourgeois. Aristocracy exists no more, democracy does not yet exist, there is nothing but bourgeoisie. Your ideas, your opinions, your manners [*moeurs*], your literature, your arts, your instincts are transitional; then hail to Joseph Prudhomme, the man of transition—that is to say, of the bourgeoisie!" Perhaps Musset, as he himself had confessed, had been born too late. Stendhal, who was old enough to be a child of the previous century, liked to think that he had been born too early. But Prudhomme, emerging between revolutions, was the personification of self-conscious modernity, immune to the disenchantments and undeceptions of the *maladie du siècle*.

When the Goncourts portrayed the generic man of letters in *Charles Demailly,* they confronted him with the generic theme. His novel, *La Bourgeoisie,* would apparently have been a French equivalent of *The Way of All Flesh* or *Buddenbrooks*. But, since it was French, it would also have been a "social synthesis"; it would have traced, through three generations of a single family, the evolution of society and behavior (*moeurs*); it would have depicted "the plutocracy of the nineteenth century in its full expansion." The grandfather would have been "the incarnation of the sense of property," the son an ardent believer in "the religions of human and national solidarity," and the grandson a degenerate embodiment of "all the practical skepticisms of modern youth." And, since Charles Demailly depended on observation rather than imagination, like a dutiful disciple of the Goncourts, his characterizations would have been historically sound. At any rate, other observers confirm the story. They show how, through political agitation and dynastic change, the bourgeois dynasties continued to enrich themselves; how the French nation as a whole enacted, in the ambivalent phrase of the intellectual historian, Bernhard Groethuysen, "a virtual epos of the bourgeoisie." The development of capitalism has been divided by the economic historian, Werner Sombart, into two phases. During the first phase, from the Renaissance to the latter part of the eighteenth century, manners and morals were restricted by the sanctions of orthodox Christianity. The second phase, the period of individual competition in a dynamic society, has been unrestricted and expansive. If we accept Sombart's criteria, the presence or the absence of restrictions, it requires no prophet to point out that, since the second World War, this phase has been moving toward a cyclical ending.

This period of bourgeois capitalism, roughly from 1789 to

1939, happens by no accident to be the heyday of the realistic novel. With due allowance for lag and experiment, we are concerned with exactly a hundred years—from Stendhal's first novel, *Armance,* published in 1827, to Proust's last volume, *Le Temps retrouvé,* published in 1927. Our five novelists, posted at intervals, chronicle the intervening century and bear witness for their interconnected generations. Thus in 1842, when Stendhal died and Flaubert came of age, the foreword to the *Comédie humaine* marked Balzac's prime, and Zola's birth had just occurred. If we consider the symbolist overtones of Proust as an epilogue and the classical origins of Stendhal as a prologue, there is a consistent and continuous tendency from romanticism through realism proper to naturalism, which we can follow through the work of Balzac, Flaubert, and Zola. All five, realists according to their respective lights, explicitly render an account of their day, and address themselves directly to posterity—a title which seems for the moment to have devolved upon ourselves. Looking back upon the total configuration of their work, we can hardly fail to notice its chronological links with politics, and with comparable revolutions in the advancing sciences and the plastic arts. We notice that their respective accounts are soon corroborated: Mérimée refines upon Stendhal, Charles de Bernard emulates Balzac, Maupassant sits at the feet of Flaubert, Zola's disciples form the school of Médan, and the influence of Proust is still with us. The imitators lead us back to the innovators. They are the dynasts of realism, and their authority has outlasted the Bourbons and the Bonapartes. Their books, not less than Vigny's, may be read as successive cantos in an epic poem of disillusionment.

By a series of approximations, we arrive at our subject. Novels are such bulky, opaque, and many-faceted items, so easy to conjure with and so much harder to analyze. We have not analyzed a novel until we have discovered its place in the mind of the novelist, in the movement of the age, and in the tradition of literature. Every great novelist has his own solutions to the technical and historical problems that I have been too summarily reviewing. In touching upon some ancestors of the French realists, some of their rivals in English and other literatures, and some of the efforts to formulate their genre, I have tried to test the generality of certain definitions before applying them to these specific examples. The question remains . . . whether I have chosen the best examples. It can only be hoped that the choice of this sequence of novelists is not arbitrary, but would agree with the consensus of readers and critics and other novelists over the years. The reasons for literary survival, depending as they do upon a peculiar combination of powers and circumstances, are never single or simple. If popular appeal were our criterion, we should have to discuss Eugène Sue and Georges Ohnet. If every author lived up to his literary pretensions, none would be greater than Edmond de Goncourt or Anatole France. If we wanted skillful story-tellers, and did not want them to tell us very much more, we should find them in Alexandre Dumas and Guy de Maupassant. If we rated authors by their humanitarian sympathies, rather than by their comprehension of human beings, we should rate George Sand and Victor Hugo above the authors on our list.

If all books belonged to their period like furniture and bric-a-brac, Octave Feuillet would be the novelist of the Second Empire. His novels fit as neatly into Louis Bonaparte's world as the boulevards of Haussmann, the opera-house of Garnier, the music of Offenbach, the drama of Meilhac and Halévy, or the painting of Meissonier and Winterhalter. But that world, though self-satisfied, was not self-sustaining. The Salon des Refusés opened more spacious vistas with the art of Manet and Pissarro; the suppressed poems of Baudelaire uncovered gulfs beneath the very pavements of Paris; and the exile of Hugo held out to later writers the alternatives of intransigence and conformity. Convention dried up Mérimée's inspiration and weakened Daudet's talents, but realism stiffened Flaubert's opposition. Where Feuillet belonged, Flaubert detached himself; and *Madame Bovary* is still alive, where *Le Roman d'un jeune homme pauvre* is as dead as the Empress Eugénie. But Flaubert's detachment, which has kept his work from fading into the debris of his period, is not to be confused with indifference, nor is it an empty gesture; rather it indicates broken attachments, and asserts stronger allegiances to higher standards of integrity. No lack of conviction but too many convictions troubled him, he told George Sand. To conclude that

Flaubert and our other realists were misanthropic and negativistic would be to accept the short-sighted view of their contemporaries. Taking advantage of an enlarged perspective, we shall see them—without exception—as men of generous enthusiasms, positive values, and fruitful ideas. They belong, as I would interpret them, to that world which is inhabited by the greatest writers of all time; for all great writers, in so far as they are committed to a searching and scrupulous critique of life as they know it, may be reckoned among the realists.

## Lionel Trilling

### *Manners, Morals, and the Novel*

The invitation that was made to me to address you this evening was couched in somewhat uncertain terms. Time, place, and cordiality were perfectly clear, but when it came to the subject our hosts were not able to specify just what they wanted me to talk about. They wanted me to consider literature in its relation to manners—by which, as they relied on me to understand, they did not really mean *manners*. They did not mean, that is, the rules of personal intercourse in our culture; and yet such rules were by no means irrelevant to what they did mean. Nor did they quite mean manners in the sense of *mores*, customs, although, again, these did bear upon the subject they had in mind.

I understood them perfectly, as I would not have understood them had they been more definite. For they were talking about a nearly indefinable subject.

Somewhere below all the explicit statements that a people makes through its art, religion, architecture, legislation, there is a dim mental region of intention of which it is very difficult to become aware. We now and then get a strong sense of its existence when we deal with the past, not by reason of its presence in the past but by reason of its absence. As we read the great formulated monuments of the past, we notice that we are reading them without the accompaniment of something that always goes along with the formulated monuments of the present. The voice of multifarious intention and activity is stilled, all the buzz of implication which always surrounds us in the present, coming to us from what never gets fully stated, coming in the tone of greetings and the tone of quarrels, in slang and humor and popular songs, in the way children play, in the gesture the waiter makes when he puts down the plate, in the nature of the very food we prefer.

Some of the charm of the past consists of the quiet—the great distracting buzz of implication has stopped and we are left only with what has been fully phrased and precisely stated. And part of the melancholy of the past comes from our knowledge that the huge, unrecorded hum of implication was once there and left no trace—we feel that because it is evanescent it is especially human. We feel, too, that the truth of the great preserved monuments of the past does not fully appear without it. From letters and diaries, from the remote, unconscious corners of the great works themselves, we try to guess what the sound of the multifarious implication was and what it meant.

Or when we read the conclusions that are drawn about our own culture by some gifted foreign critic—or by some stupid native one—who is equipped only with a knowledge of our books, when we try in vain to say what is wrong, when in despair we say that he has read the books "out of context," then we are aware of the matter I have been asked to speak about tonight.

What I understand by manners, then, is a culture's hum and buzz of implication. I mean the whole evanescent context in which its explicit statements are made. It is that part of a culture which is made up of half-uttered or unuttered or unutterable expressions of value. They are hinted at by small actions, sometimes by the arts of dress or decoration, sometimes by tone, gesture, emphasis, or rhythm, sometimes by the words that are used with a special frequency or a special meaning. They are the things that for good or bad draw the people of a culture together and that separate them from the people of another culture. They make the part of a culture which is not art, or religion, or morals, or politics, and yet it relates to all these highly formulated departments of culture. It is modified by them; it modifies them; it is generated by them; it generates them. In this part of culture assumption rules, which is often so much stronger than reason.

The right way to begin to deal with such a subject is to gather together as much of its detail as we possibly can. Only by doing so will we become fully aware of what the gifted foreign critic or the stupid native one is not aware of, that in any complex culture there is not a single system of manners but a conflicting variety of manners, and that one of the jobs of a culture is the adjustment of this conflict.

But the nature of our present occasion does not permit this accumulation of detail and so I shall instead try to drive toward a generalization and an hypothesis which, however wrong they turn out to be, may at least permit us to circumscribe the subject. I shall try to generalize the subject of American manners by talking about the attitude of Americans toward the subject of manners itself. And since in a complex culture there are, as I say, many different systems of manners and since I cannot talk about them all, I shall select the manners and the attitude toward manners of the literate, reading, responsible middle class of people who are ourselves. I specify that they be reading people because I shall draw my conclusions from the novels they read. The hypothesis I propose is that our attitude toward manners is the expression of a particular conception of reality.

All literature tends to be concerned with the question of reality—I mean quite simply the old opposition between reality and appearance, between what really is and what merely seems. "Don't you *see*?" is the question we want to shout at Oedipus as he stands before us and before fate in the pride of his rationalism. And at the end of *Oedipus Rex* he demonstrates in a particularly direct way that he now sees what he did not see before. "Don't you *see*?" we want to shout again at Lear and Gloucester, the two deceived, self-deceiving fathers: blindness again, resistance to the clear claims of reality, the seduction by mere appearance. The same with Othello—reality is right under your stupid nose, how *dare* you be such a gull? So with Molière's Orgon—my good man, my honest citizen, merely *look* at Tartuffe and you will know what's what. So with Milton's Eve—"Woman, watch out! Don't you see—anyone can see—that's a *snake*!"

The problem of reality is central, and in a special way, to the great forefather of the novel, the great book of Cervantes, whose four-hundredth birthday was celebrated in 1947. There are two movements of thought in *Don Quixote,* two different and opposed notions of reality. One is the movement which leads toward saying that the world of ordinary practicality *is* reality in its fullness. It is the reality of the present moment in all its powerful immediacy of hunger, cold, and pain, making the past and the future, and all ideas, of no account. When the conceptual, the ideal, and the fanciful come into conflict with this, bringing their notions of the past and the future, then disaster results. For one thing, the ordinary proper ways of life are upset—the chained prisoners are understood to be good men and are released, the whore is taken for a lady. There is general confusion. As for the ideal, the conceptual, the fanciful, or romantic—whatever you want to call it—it fares even worse: it is shown to be ridiculous.

Thus one movement of the novel. But Cervantes changed horses in midstream and found that he was riding Rosinante. Perhaps at first not quite consciously—although the new view is latent in the old from the very beginning—Cervantes begins to show that the world of tangible reality is not the real reality after all. The real reality is rather the wildly conceiving, the madly fantasying mind of the Don: people change, practical reality changes, when they come into its presence.

In any genre it may happen that the first great example contains the whole potentiality of the genre. It has been said that all philosophy is a footnote to Plato. It can be said that all prose fiction is a variation on the theme of *Don Quixote*. Cervantes sets for the novel the problem of appearance and reality: the shifting and conflict of social classes becomes the field of the problem of knowledge, of how we know and of how reliable our knowledge is, which at that very moment of history is vexing the philosophers and scientists. And the poverty of the Don suggests that the novel is born with the appearance of money as a social element—money, the great solvent of the solid fabric of the old society, the great generator of illusion. Or, which is to say much the same thing, the novel is born in response to snobbery.

Snobbery is not the same thing as pride of class. Pride of class may not please us but we must at least grant that it reflects a social function. A man who exhibited class pride—in the day when it was possible to do so—may have been puffed up about what he *was*, but this ultimately depended on what he *did*. Thus, aristocratic pride was based ultimately on the ability to fight and administer. No pride is without fault, but pride of class may be thought of as today we think of pride of profession, toward which we are likely to be lenient.

Snobbery is pride in status without pride in function. And it is an uneasy pride of status. It always asks, "Do I belong—do I really belong? And does he belong? And if I am observed talking to him, will it make me seem to belong or not to belong?" It is the peculiar vice not of aristocratic societies which have their own appropriate vices, but of bourgeois democratic societies. For us the legendary strongholds of snobbery are the Hollywood studios, where two thousand dollars a week dare not talk to three hundred dollars a week for fear he be taken for nothing more than fifteen hundred dollars a week. The dominant emotions of snobbery are uneasiness, self-consciousness, self-defensiveness, the sense that one is not quite real but can in some way acquire reality.

Money is the medium that, for good or bad, makes for a fluent society. It does not make for an equal society but for one in which there is a constant shifting of classes, a frequent change in the personnel of the dominant class. In a shifting society great emphasis is put on appearance—I am using the word now in the common meaning, as when people say that "a good appearance is very important in getting a job." To appear to be established is one of the ways of becoming established. The old notion of the solid merchant who owns far more than he shows increasingly gives way to the ideal of signalizing status by appearance, by showing more than you have: status in a democratic society is presumed to come not with power but with the tokens of power. Hence the development of what Tocqueville saw as a mark of democratic culture, what he called the "hypocrisy of luxury"—instead of the well-made peasant article and the well-made middle-class article, we have the effort of all articles to appear as the articles of the very wealthy.

And a shifting society is bound to generate an interest in appearance in the philosophical sense. When Shakespeare lightly touched on the matter that so largely preoccupies the novelist—

that is, the movement from one class to another—and created Malvolio, he immediately involved the question of social standing with the problem of appearance and reality. Malvolio's daydreams of bettering his position present themselves to him as reality, and in revenge his enemies conspire to convince him that he is literally mad and that the world is not as he sees it. The predicament of the characters in *A Midsummer Night's Dream* and of Christopher Sly seems to imply that the meeting of social extremes and the establishment of a person of low class in the privileges of a high class always suggested to Shakespeare's mind some radical instability of the senses and the reason.

The characteristic work of the novel is to record the illusion that snobbery generates and to try to penetrate to the truth which, as the novel assumes, lies hidden beneath all the false appearances. Money, snobbery, the ideal of status, these become in themselves the objects of fantasy, the support of the fantasies of love, freedom, charm, power, as in *Madam Bovary,* whose heroine is the sister, at a three-centuries' remove, of Don Quixote. The greatness of *Great Expectations* begins in its title: modern society bases itself on great expectations which, if ever they are realized, are found to exist by reason of a sordid, hidden reality. The real thing is not the gentility of Pip's life but the hulks and the murder and the rats and decay in the cellarage of the novel.

An English writer, recognizing the novel's central concern with snobbery, recently cried out half-ironically against it. "Who cares whether Pamela finally exasperates Mr. B. into marriage, whether Mr. Elton is more or less than moderately genteel, whether it is sinful for Pendennis nearly to kiss the porter's daughter, whether young men from Boston can ever be as truly refined as middle-aged women in Paris, whether the District Officer's financée ought to see so much of Dr. Aziz, whether Lady Chatterley ought to be made love to by the gamekeeper, even if he was an officer during the war? Who cares?"

The novel, of course, tells us much more about life than this. It tells us about the look and feel of things, how things are done and what things are worth and what they cost and what the odds are. If the English novel in its special concern with class does not, as the same writer says, explore the deeper layers of personality, then the French novel in exploring these layers must start and end in class, and the Russian novel, exploring the ultimate possibilities of spirit, does the same—every situation in Dostoevski, no matter how spiritual, starts with a point of social pride and a certain number of rubles. The great novelists knew that manners indicate the largest intentions of men's souls as well as the smallest and they are perpetually concerned to catch the meaning of every dim implicit hint.

The novel, then, is a perpetual quest for reality, the field of its research being always the social world, the material of its analysis being always manners as the indication of the direction of man's soul. When we understand this we can understand the pride of profession that moved D. H. Lawrence to say, "Being a novelist, I consider myself superior to the saint, the scientist, the philosopher and the poet. The novel is the one bright book of life."

Now the novel as I have described it has never really established itself in America. Not that we have not had very great novels but that the novel in America diverges from its classic intention, which, as I have said, is the investigation of the problem of reality beginning in the social field. The fact is that American writers of genius have not turned their minds to society. Poe and Melville were quite apart from it; the reality they sought was only tangential to society. Hawthorne was acute when he insisted that he did not write novels but romances—he thus expressed his awareness of the lack of social texture in his work. Howells never fulfilled himself because, although he saw the social subject clearly, he would never take it with full seriousness. In America in the nineteenth century, Henry James was alone in knowing that to scale the moral and aesthetic heights in the novel one had to use the ladder of social observation.

There is a famous passage in James's life of Hawthorne in which James enumerates the things which are lacking to give the American novel the thick social texture of the English novel—no state; barely a specific national name; no sovereign; no court; no aristocracy; no church; no clergy; no army; no diplomatic service; no country gentlemen; no palaces; no castles; no manors; no old country houses; no parsonages; no thatched cottages; no ivied ruins; no cathedrals; no great universities; no public schools; no political society; no sporting class—no Epsom, no Ascot! That is, no sufficiency of means for the display of a variety of manners, no opportunity for the novelist to do his job of searching out reality, not enough complication of appearance to make the job interesting. Another great American novelist of very different temperament had said much the same thing some decades before: James Fenimore Cooper found that American manners were too simple and dull to nourish the novelist.

This is cogent but it does not explain the condition of the American novel at the present moment. For life in America has increasingly thickened since the nineteenth century. It has not, to be sure, thickened so much as to permit our undergraduates to understand the characters of Balzac, to understand, that is, life in a crowded country where the competitive pressures are great, forcing intense passions to express themselves fiercely and yet within the limitations set by a strong and complicated tradition of manners. Still, life here has become more complex and more pressing. And even so we do not have the novel that touches significantly on society, on manners. Whatever the virtues of Dreiser may be, he could not report the social fact with the kind of accuracy it needs. Sinclair Lewis is shrewd, but no one, however charmed with him as a social satirist, can believe that he does more than a limited job of social understanding. John Dos Passos sees much, sees it often in the great way of Flaubert, but can never use social fact as more than either backdrop or "condition." Of our novelists today perhaps only William Faulkner deals with society as the field of tragic reality and he has the disadvantage of being limited to a provincial scene.

It would seem that Americans have a kind of resistance to looking closely at society. They appear to believe that to touch accurately on the matter of class, to take full note of snobbery, is somehow to demean themselves. It is as if we felt that one cannot touch pitch without being defiled—which, of course, may possibly be the case. Americans will not deny that we have classes and snobbery, but they seem to hold it to be indelicate to take precise cognizance of these phenomena. Consider that Henry James is, among a large part of our reading public, still held to be at fault for noticing society as much as he did. Consider the conversation that has, for some interesting reason, become a part of our literary folklore. Scott Fitzgerald said to Ernest Hemingway, "The very rich are different from us." Hemingway replied, "Yes, they have more money." I have seen the exchange quoted many times and always with the intention of suggesting that Fitzgerald was infatuated by wealth and had received a salutary rebuke from his democratic friend. But the truth is that after a certain point quantity of money does indeed change into quality of personality: in an important sense the very rich *are* different from us. So are the very powerful, the very gifted, the very poor. Fitzgerald was right, and almost for that remark alone he must surely have been received in Balzac's bosom in the heaven of novelists.

It is of course by no means true that the American reading class has no interest in society. Its interest fails only before society as it used to be represented by the novel. And if we look at the commercially successful serious novels of the last decade, we see that almost all of them have been written from an intense social awareness—it might be said that our present definition of a serious book is one which holds before us some image of society to consider and condemn. What is the situation of the dispossessed Oklahoma farmer and whose fault it is, what situation the Jew finds himself in, what it means to be a Negro, how one gets a bell for Adano, what is the advertising business really like, what it means to be insane and how society takes care of you or fails to do so—these are the matters which are believed to be most fertile for the novelist, and certainly they are the subjects most favored by our reading class.

The public is probably not deceived about the quality of most of these books. If the question of quality is brought up, the answer is likely to be: no, they are not great, they are not imaginative, they are not "literature." But there is an unexpressed addendum: and perhaps they are all the better for not being imaginative, for not being literature—they are not literature, they are reality, and *in a time like this* what we need is reality in large doses.

When, generations from now, the historian of our times undertakes to describe the assumptions of our culture, he will surely discover that the word *reality* is of central importance in his understanding of us. He will observe that for some of our philosophers the meaning of the word was a good deal in doubt, but that for our political writers, for many of our literary critics, and for most of our reading public, the word did not open discussion but, rather, closed it. Reality, as conceived by us, is whatever is external and hard, gross, unpleasant. Involved in its meaning is the idea of power conceived in a particular way. Some time ago I had occasion to remark how, in the critical estimates of Theodore Dreiser, it is always being said that Dreiser has many faults but that it cannot be denied that he has great power. No one ever says "a kind of power." Power is assumed to be always "brute" power, crude, ugly, and undiscriminating, the way an elephant appears to be. It is seldom understood to be the way an elephant actually is, precise and discriminating; or the way electricity is, swift and absolute and scarcely embodied.

The word *reality* is a honorific word and the future historian will naturally try to discover our notion of its pejorative opposite, appearance, mere appearance. He will find it in our feeling about the internal; whenever we detect evidences of style and thought we suspect that reality is being a little betrayed, that "mere subjectivity" is creeping in. There follows from this our feeling about complication, modulation, personal idiosyncrasy, and about social forms, both the great and the small.

Having gone so far, our historian is then likely to discover a puzzling contradiction. For we claim that the great advantage of reality is its hard, bedrock, concrete quality, yet everything we say about it tends toward the abstract and it almost seems that what we want to find in reality is abstraction itself. Thus we believe that one of the unpleasant bedrock facts is social class, but we become extremely impatient if ever we are told that social class is indeed so real that it produces actual difference of personality. The very people who talk most about class and its evils think that Fitzgerald was bedazzled and Hemingway right. Or again, it might be observed that in the degree that we speak in praise of the "individual" we have contrived that our literature should have no individuals in it—no people, that is, who are shaped by our liking for the interesting and memorable and special and precious.

Here, then, is our generalization: that in proportion as we have committed ourselves to our particular idea of reality we have lost our interest in manners. For the novel this is a definitive condition because it is inescapably true that in the novel manners make men. It does not matter in what sense the word manners is taken—it is equally true of the sense which so much interested Proust or of the sense which interested Dickens or, indeed, of the sense which interested Homer. The Duchesse de Guermantes unable to delay departure for the dinner party to receive properly from her friend Swann the news that he is dying but able to delay to change the black slippers her husband objects to; Mr. Pickwick and Sam Weller; Priam and Achilles—they exist by reason of their observed manners.

So true is this, indeed, so creative is the novelist's awareness of manners, that we may say that it is a function of his love. It is some sort of love that Fielding has for Squire Western that allows him to note the great, gross details which bring the insensitive sentient man into existence for us. If that is true, we are forced to certain conclusions about our literature and about the particular definition of reality which has shaped it. The reality we admire tells us that the observation of manners is trivial and even malicious, that there are things much more important for the novel to consider. As a consequence our social sympathies have indeed broadened, but in proportion as they have done so we have lost something of our power of love, for our novels can never create characters who truly exist. We make public demands for love, for we know that broad social feeling should be infused with warmth, and we receive a kind of public product which we try to believe is not cold potatoes. The reviewers of Helen Howe's novel of a few years ago, *We Happy Few,* thought that its satiric first part, an excellent comment on the manners of a small but significant segment of society, was ill-natured and unsatisfactory, but they approved the second part, which is the record of the heroine's self-accusing effort to come into communication with the great soul of America. Yet it should have been clear that the satire had its source in a kind of affection, in a real community of feeling, and told the truth, while the second part, said to be so "warm," was mere abstraction, one more example of our public idea of ourselves and our national life. John Steinbeck is generally praised both for his reality and his warmheartedness, but in *The Way-*

*ward Bus* the lower-class characters receive a doctrinaire affection in proportion to the suffering and sexuality which define their existence, while the ill-observed middle-class characters are made to submit not only to moral judgment but to the withdrawal of all fellow-feeling, being mocked for their very misfortunes and almost for their susceptibility to death. Only a little thought or even less feeling is required to perceive that the basis of his creation is the coldest response to abstract ideas.

Two novelists of the older sort had a prevision of our present situation. In Henry James's *The Princess Casamassima* there is a scene in which the heroine is told about the existence of a conspiratorial group of revolutionaries pledged to the destruction of all existing society. She has for some time been drawn by a desire for social responsibility; she has wanted to help "the people," she has longed to discover just such a group as she now hears about, and she exclaims in joy, "Then it's real, it's solid!" We are intended to hear the Princess's glad cry with the knowledge that she is a woman who despises herself, "that in the darkest hour of her life she sold herself for a title and a fortune. She regards her doing so as such a terrible piece of frivolity that she can never for the rest of her days be serious enough to make up for it." She seeks out poverty, suffering, sacrifice, and death because she believes that these things alone are real; she comes to believe that art is contemptible; she withdraws her awareness and love from the one person of her acquaintance who most deserves them, and she increasingly scorns whatever suggests variety and modulation, and is more and more dissatisfied with the humanity of the present in her longing for the more perfect humanity of the future. It is one of the great points that the novel makes that with each passionate step that she takes toward what she calls the real, the solid, she in fact moves further away from the life-giving reality.

In E. M. Forster's *The Longest Journey* there is a young man named Stephen Wonham who, although a gentleman born, has been carelessly brought up and has no real notion of the responsibilities of his class. He has a friend, a country laborer, a shepherd, and on two occasions he outrages the feelings of certain intelligent, liberal, democratic people in the book by his treatment of this friend. Once, when the shepherd reneges on a bargain, Stephen quarrels with him and knocks him down; and in the matter of the loan of a few shillings he insists that the money be paid back to the last farthing. The intelligent, liberal, democratic people know that this is not the way to act to the poor. But Stephen cannot think of the shepherd as the poor nor, although he is a country laborer, as an object of research by J. L. and Barbara Hammond; he is rather a reciprocating subject in a relationship of affection—as we say, a friend—and therefore liable to anger and required to pay his debts. But this view is held to be deficient in intelligence, liberalism, and democracy.

In these two incidents we have the premonition of our present cultural and social situation, the passionate self-reproachful addiction to a "strong" reality which must limit its purview to maintain its strength, the replacement by abstraction of natural, direct human feeling. It is worth noting, by the way, how clear is the line by which the two novels descend from *Don Quixote*—how their young heroes come into life with large preconceived ideas and are knocked about in consequence; how both are concerned with the problem of appearance and reality, *The Longest Journey* quite explicitly, *The Princess Casamassima* by indirection; how both evoke the question of the nature of reality by contriving a meeting and conflict of diverse social classes and take scrupulous note of the differences of manners. Both have as their leading characters people who are specifically and passionately concerned with social injustice and both agree in saying that to act against social injustice is right and noble but that to choose to act so does not settle all moral problems but on the contrary generates new ones of an especially difficult sort.

I have elsewhere given the name of moral realism to the perception of the dangers of the moral life itself. Perhaps at no other time has the enterprise of moral realism ever been so much needed, for at no other time have so many people committed themselves to moral righteousness. We have the books that point out the bad conditions, that praise us for taking progressive attitudes. We have no books that raise questions in our minds not only about conditions but about ourselves, that lead us to refine our motives and ask what might lie behind our good impulses.

There is nothing so very terrible in discovering that something does lie behind. Nor does it need a Freud to make the discovery. Here is a publicity release sent out by one of our oldest and most respectable publishing houses. Under the heading "What Makes Books Sell?" it reads, "Blank & Company reports that the current interest in horror stories has attracted a great number of readers to John Dash's novel . . . because of its depiction of Nazi brutality. Critics and readers alike have commented on the stark realism of Dash's handling of the torture scenes in the book. The publishers originally envisaged a woman's market because of the love story, now find men reading the book because of the other angle." This does not suggest a more than usual depravity in the male reader, for "the other angle" has always had a fascination, no doubt a bad one, even for those who would not themselves commit or actually witness an act of torture. I cite the extreme example only to suggest that something may indeed lie behind our sober intelligent interest in moral politics. In this instance the pleasure in the cruelty is protected and licensed by moral indignation. In other instances moral indignation, which has been said to be the favorite emotion of the middle class, may be in itself an exquisite pleasure. To understand this does not invalidate moral indignation but only sets up the conditions on which it ought to be entertained, only says when it is legitimate and when not.

But, the answer comes, however important it may be for moral realism to raise questions in our minds about our motives, is it not at best a matter of secondary importance? Is it not of the first importance that we be given a direct and immediate report on the reality that is daily being brought to dreadful birth? The novels that have done this have effected much practical good, bringing to consciousness the latent feelings of many people, making it harder for them to be unaware or indifferent, creating an atmosphere in which injustice finds it harder to thrive. To speak of moral realism is all very well. But it is an elaborate, even fancy, phrase and it is to be suspected of having the intention of sophisticating the simple reality that is easily to be conceived. Life presses us so hard, time is so short, the suffering of the world is so huge, simple, unendurable—anything that complicates our moral fervor in dealing with reality as we immediately see it and wish to drive head-long upon it must be regarded with some impatience.

True enough: and therefore any defense of what I have called moral realism must be made not in the name of some high-flown fineness of feeling but in the name of simple social practicality. And there is indeed a simple social fact to which moral realism has a simple practical relevance, but it is a fact very difficult for us nowadays to perceive. It is that the moral passions are even more willful and imperious and impatient than the self-seeking passions. All history is at one in telling us that their tendency is to be not only liberating but also restrictive.

It is probable that at this time we are about to make great changes in our social system. The world is ripe for such changes and if they are not made in the direction of greater social liberality, the direction forward, they will almost of necessity be made in the direction backward, of a terrible social niggardliness. We all know which of those directions we want. But it is not enough to want it, not even enough to work for it—we must want it and work for it with intelligence. Which means that we must be aware of the dangers which lie in our most generous wishes. Some paradox of our natures leads us, when once we have made our fellow men the objects of our enlightened interest, to go on to make them the objects of our pity, then of our wisdom, ultimately of our coercion. It is to prevent this corruption, the most ironic and tragic that man knows, that we stand in need of the moral realism which is the product of the free play of the moral imagination.

For our time the most effective agent of the moral imagination has been the novel of the last two hundred years. It was never, either aesthetically or morally, a perfect form and its faults and failures can be quickly enumerated. But its greatness and its practical usefulness lay in its unremitting work of involving the reader himself in the moral life, inviting him to put his own motives under examination, suggesting that reality is not as his conventional education has led him to see it. It taught us, as no other genre ever did, the extent of human variety and the value of this variety. It was the literary form to which the emotions of understanding and forgiveness were indigenous, as if by the definition of the form itself. At the moment its impulse does not seem strong, for there never was a time when the virtues of its greatness were so likely to be thought of as weaknesses. Yet there never was a time when its particular activity was so much needed, was of so much practical, political, and social use—so much so that if its impulse does not respond to the need, we shall have reason to be sad not only over a waning form of art but also over our waning freedom.

# PART TWO

# Questions of Craft

# III. What Is Technique?

Mark Schorer, "Technique as Discovery," reprinted by permission from the *Hudson Review*, Spring 1948.

Martin Turnell, "The Language of Fiction," from *The Novel in France*, reprinted here by permission of New Directions. The footnotes have been renumbered to run in series throughout the selection.

*Just two of the many possible answers to the broad question posed by the title of this chapter are presented here, and some of the essays from other sections of this book should also be thought of as contributing ideas and attitudes to this discussion. But here, at least, we have two of the major positions likely to be taken on the question of technique in modern considerations of the novel. Schorer sees technique as "any selection, structure or distortion, any form or rhythm imposed upon the world of action," though in his essay he concentrates on point of view and language. Turnell, in a more extreme approach, reduces the whole question of technique to the problem of language or style: "words on a page." These, then, are not opposed approaches, only different emphases. Both writers believe that achievement in fiction can be described and evaluated technically. They share an im-*

*portant assumption about the relationship between life and art: that the greater the craft of the novelist, the greater justice he will do to experience. Like most critics whose emphasis is esthetic, both Schorer and Turnell see technique as in some sense prior to perception, as a methodology which enables perception to occur.*

**Mark Schorer**

# *Technique as Discovery*

I

Modern criticism, through its exacting scrutiny of literary texts, has demonstrated with finality that in art beauty and truth are indivisible and one. The Keatsian overtones of these terms are mitigated and an old dilemma solved if for beauty we substitute form, and for truth, content. We may, without risk of loss, narrow them even more, and speak of technique and subject matter. Modern criticism has shown us that to speak of content as such is not to speak of art at all, but of experience; and that it is only when we speak of the *achieved* content, the form of the work of art as a work of art, that we speak as critics. The difference between content, or experience, and achieved content, or art, is technique.

When we speak of technique, then, we speak of nearly everything. For technique is the means by which the writer's experience, which is his subject matter, compels him to attend to it; technique is the only means he has of discovering, exploring, developing his subject, of conveying its meaning, and, finally, of evaluating it. And surely it follows that certain techniques are sharper tools than others, and will discover more; that the writer capable of the most exacting technical scrutiny of his subject matter will produce works with the most satisfying content, works with thickness and resonance, works which reverberate, works with maximum meaning.

We are no longer able to regard as seriously intended criticism of poetry which does not assume these generalizations; but the case for fiction has not yet been established. The novel is still read as though its content has some value in itself, as though the subject matter of fiction has greater or lesser value in itself, and as though technique were not a primary but a supplementary element, capable perhaps of not unattractive embellishments upon the surface of the subject, but hardly of its essence. Or technique is thought of in blunter terms than those which one associates with poetry, as such relatively obvious matters as the arrangement of events to create plot; or, within plot, of suspense and climax; or as the means of revealing character motivation, relationship, and development; or as the use of point of view, but point of view as some nearly arbitrary device for the heightening of dramatic interest through the narrowing or broadening of perspective upon the material, rather than as a means toward the positive definition of theme. As for the resources of language, these, somehow, we almost never think of as a part of the technique of fiction—language as used to create a certain texture and tone which in themselves state and define themes and meanings; or language, the counters of our ordinary speech, as forced, through conscious manipulation, into all those larger meanings which our ordinary speech almost never intends. Technique in fiction, all this is a way of saying, we somehow continue to regard as merely a means to organizing material which is "given" rather than as the means of exploring and defining the values in an area of experience which, for the first time *then,* are being given.

Is fiction still regarded in this odd, divided way because it is really less tractable before the critical suppositions which now seem inevitable to poetry? Let us look at some examples: two well-known novels of the past, both by writers who may be described as "primitive," although their relative innocence of technique is of a different sort—Defoe's *Moll Flanders* and Emily Brontë's *Wuthering Heights;* and three well-known novels of this century—*Tono-Bungay,* by a writer who claimed to eschew technique; *Sons and Lovers,* by a novelist who, because his ideal of subject matter ("the poetry of the immediate present") led him at last into the fallacy of spontaneous and unchangeable composition, in effect eschewed technique; and *A Portrait of the Artist as a Young Man,* by a novelist whose practice made claims for the supremacy of technique beyond those made by anyone in the past or by anyone else in this century.

Technique in fiction is, of course, all those obvious forms of it which are usually taken to be the whole of it, and many others; but for the present purposes, let it be thought of in two respects particularly: the uses to which language, as language, is put to express the quality of the experience in question; and the uses of point of view not only as a mode of dramatic delimitation, but more particularly, of thematic definition. Technique is really what T. S. Eliot means by "convention"—any selection, structure, or distortion, any form or rhythm imposed upon the world of action; by means of which—it should be added—our apprehension of the world of action is enriched or renewed. In this sense, everything is technique which is not the lump of experience itself, and one cannot properly say that a writer has no technique or that he eschews technique, for, being a writer, he cannot do so. We can speak of good and bad technique, of adequate and inadequate, of technique which serves the novel's purpose, or disserves.

## 2

In the prefatory remarks to *Moll Flanders,* Defoe tells us that he is not writing fiction at all, but editing the journals of a woman of notorious character, and rather to instruct us in the necessities and the joys of virtue than to please us. We do not, of course, take these professions seriously, since nothing in the conduct of the narrative indicates that virtue is either more necessary or more enjoyable than vice. On the contrary, we discover that Moll turns virtuous only after a life of vice has enabled her to do so with security; yet it is precisely for this reason that Defoe's profession of didactic purpose has interest. For the actual morality which the novel enforces is the morality of any commercial culture, the belief that virtue pays—in worldly goods. It is a morality somewhat less than skin deep, having no relation to motives arising from a sense of good and evil, least of all, of evil-*in*-good, but exclusively from the presence or absence of food, drink, linen, damask, silver, and time-pieces. It is the morality of measurement, and without in the least intending it, *Moll Flanders* is our classic revelation of the mercantile mind: the morality of measurement, which Defoe has completely neglected to measure. He fails not only to evaluate this material in his announced way, but to evaluate it at all. His announced purpose is, we admit, a pious humbug, and he meant us to read the book as a series of scandalous events; and thanks to his inexhaustible pleasure in excess and exaggeration, this element in the book continues to amuse us. Long before the book has been finished, however, this element has also become an absurdity; but not half the absurdity as that which Defoe did not intend at all—the notion that Moll could live a rich and full life of crime, and yet, repenting, emerge spotless in the end. The point is, of course, that she has no moral being, nor has the book any moral life. Everything is external. Everything can be weighed, measured, handled, paid for in gold, or expiated by a prison term. To this, the whole texture of the novel testifies: the bolts of goods, the inventories, the itemized accounts, the landlady's bills, the lists, the ledgers: all this, which taken together comprises what we call Defoe's method of circumstantial realism.

He did not come upon that method by any deliberation: it represents precisely his own world of value, the importance of external circumstance to Defoe. The point of view of Moll is indistinguishable from the point of view of her creator. We discover the meaning of the novel (at unnecessary length, without economy, without emphasis, with almost none of the distortions or the advantages of art) in spite of Defoe, not because of him. Thus the book is not the true chronicle of a disreputable female, but the true allegory of an impoverished soul—the author's; not an anatomy of the criminal class, but of the middle class. And we read it as an unintended comic revelation of self and of a social mode. Because he had no adequate resources of technique to separate himself from his material, thereby to discover and to define the meanings of his material, his contribution is not to fiction but to the history of fiction, and to social history.

The situation in *Wuthering Heights* is at once somewhat the same and yet very different. Here, too, the whole novel turns upon itself, but this time to its estimable advantage; here, too, is a revelation of what is perhaps the author's secret world of value, but this time, through what may be an accident of technique, the revelation is meaningfully accomplished. Emily Brontë may merely have stumbled upon the perspectives which define the form and the theme of her book. Whether she knew from the outset, or even at the end, what she was doing, we may doubt; but what she did and did superbly we can see.

We can assume, without at all becoming involved in the author's life but merely from the tone of somnambulistic excess which is generated by the writing itself, that this world of monstrous passion, of dark and gigantic emotional and nervous energy, is for the author, or was in the first place, a world of ideal value; and that the book sets out to persuade us of the moral significance of such unmoral passion. We are, I think, expected, in the first place, to take at their own valuation these demonic beings, Heathcliff and Cathy: as special creatures, set apart from the cloddish world about them by their heightened capacity for feeling, set apart, even, from the ordinary objects of human passion as, in their transcendental, sexless relationship, they identify themselves with an uncompromising landscape and cosmic force. Yet this is absurd, as much of the detail that surrounds it ("Other dogs lurked in other recesses") is absurd. The novelist Emily Brontë had to discover these absurdities to the girl Emily; her technique had to evaluate them for what they were, so that we are persuaded that it is not Emily who is mistaken in her estimate of her characters, but they who are mistaken in their estimate of themselves The theme of the moral magnificence of unmoral passion is an impossible theme to sustain, and what interests us is that it was device—and this time, mere, mechanical device—which taught Emily Brontë that, the needs of her temperament to the contrary, all personal longing and reverie to the contrary, perhaps—that this was indeed not at all what her material must mean as art. Technique objectifies.

To lay before us the full character of this passion, to show us how it first comes into being and then comes to dominate the world about it and the life that follows upon it, Emily Brontë gives her material a broad scope in time, lets it, in fact, cut across three generations. And to manage material which is so extensive, she must find a means of narration, points of view, which can encompass that material, and, in her somewhat crude concept of motive, justify its telling. So she chooses a foppish traveller who stumbles into this world of passionate violence, a traveller representing the thin and conventional emotional life of the far world of fashion, who wishes to hear the tale: and for her teller she chooses, almost inevitably, the old family retainer who knows everything, a character as conventional as the other, but this one representing not the conventions of fashion, but the conventions of the humblest moralism. What has happened is, first, that she has chosen as her narrative perspective those very elements, conventional emotion and conventional morality, which her hero and heroine are meant to transcend with such spectacular magnificence; and second, that she has permitted this perspective to operate throughout a long period of time. And these two elements compel the novelist to see what her unmoral passions come to. Moral magnificence? Not at all; rather, a devastating spectacle of human waste; ashes. For the time of the novel is carried on long enough to show Heathcliff at last an emptied man, burned out by his fever ragings, exhausted and will-less, his passion meaningless at last. And it goes even a little further, to Lockwood, the fop, in the graveyard, sententiously contemplating headstones. Thus in the end the triumph is all on the side of the cloddish world, which survives.

Perhaps not all on that side. For, like Densher at the end of *The Wings of the Dove,* we say, and surely Hareton and the second Cathy say, "We shall never be again as we were!" But there is more point in observing that a certain body of materials, a girl's romantic daydreams, have, through the most conventional devices of fiction, been pushed beyond their inception in fancy to their meanings, their conception as a written book—that they, that is, are not at all as they were.

## 3

Technique alone objectifies the materials of art; hence technique alone evaluates those materials. This is the axiom which demonstrates itself so devastatingly whenever a writer declares, under the urgent sense of the importance of his materials (whether these are autobiography, or social ideas, or personal passions)—whenever such a writer declares that he cannot linger with technical refinements. That art will not tolerate such a writer H. G. Wells handsomely proves. His enormous literary energy included no respect for the techniques of his medium, and his medium takes its revenge upon his bumptiousness. "I have never taken any very great pains about writing. I am outside the hierarchy of conscious and deliberate writers altogether. I am the absolute antithesis of Mr. James Joyce. . . . Long ago, living in close conversational proximity to Henry James, Joseph Conrad, and Mr. Ford Madox Hueffer, I escaped from under their immense artistic preoccupations by calling myself a journalist." Precisely. And he escaped—he disappeared—from literature into the annals of an era.

Yet what confidence! "Literature," Wells said, "is not jewelry, it has quite other aims than perfection, and the more one thinks of 'how it is done' the less one gets it done. These critical indulgences lead along a fatal path, away from every natural interest towards a preposterous emptiness of technical effort, a monstrous egotism of artistry, of which the later work of Henry James is the monumental warning. 'It,' the subject, the thing or the thought, has long since disappeared in these amazing works; nothing remains but the way it has been manipulated.' " Seldom has a literary theorist been so totally wrong; for what we learn as James grows for us and Wells disappears, is that without what he calls "manipulation," there *is* no "it," no "subject" in art. There is again only social history.

The virtue of the modern novelist—from James and Conrad down—is not only that he pays so much attention to his medium, but that, when he pays most, he discovers through it a new subject matter, and a greater one. Under the "immense artistic preoccupations" of James and Conrad and Joyce, the form of the novel changed, and with the technical change, analogous changes took place in substance, in point of view, in the whole conception of fiction. And the final lesson of the modern novel is that technique is not the secondary thing that it seems to Wells, some external machination, a mechanical affair, but a deep and primary operation; not only that technique *contains* intellectual and moral implications, but that it *discovers* them. For a writer like Wells, who wished to give us the intellectual and the moral history of our times, the lesson is a hard one: it tells us that the order of intellect and the order of morality do not exist at all, in art, except as they are organized in the order of art.

Wells's ambitions were very large. "Before we have done, we will have all life within the scope of the novel." But that is where life already is, within the scope of the novel; where it needs to be brought is into novels. In Wells we have all the important topics in life, but no good novels. He was not asking too much of art, or asking that it include more than it happily can; he was not asking anything of it—as art, which is all that it can give, and that is everything.

A novel like *Tono-Bungay,* generally thought to be Wells's best, is therefore instructive. "I want to tell—*myself,*" says George, the hero, "and my impressions of the thing as a whole"—the thing as a whole being the collapse of traditional British institutions in the twentieth century. George "tells himself" in terms of three stages in his life which have rough equivalents in modern British social history, and this is, to be sure, a plan, a framework; but it is the framework of Wells's abstract thinking, not of his craftsmanship, and the primary demand which one makes of such a book as this, that means be discovered whereby the dimensions of the hero contain the experiences he recounts, is never met. The novelist flounders through a series of literary imitations—from an early Dickensian episode, through a kind of Shavian interlude, through a Conradian episode, to a Jules Verne vision at the end. The significant failure is in that end, and in the way that it defeats not only the entire social analysis of the bulk of the novel, but Wells's own ends as a thinker. For at last George finds a purpose in science. "I decided that in power and knowledge lay the salvation of my life, the secret that would fill my need; that to these things I would give myself."

But science, power and knowledge, are summed up at last in a destroyer. As far as one can tell Wells intends no irony, although he may here have come upon the essence of the major irony in modern history. The novel ends in a kind of meditative rhapsody which denies every value that the book had been aiming toward. For of all the kinds of social waste which Wells has been describing, this is the most inclusive, the final waste. Thus he gives us in the end not a novel, but a hypothesis; not an individual destiny, but a theory of the future; and not his theory of the future, but a nihilistic vision quite opposite from everything that he meant to represent. With a minimum of attention to the virtues of technique, Wells might still not have written a good novel; but he would at any rate have established a point of view and a tone which would have told us what he meant.

To say what one means in art is never easy, and the more intimately one is implicated in one's material, the more difficult it is. If, besides, one commits fiction to a therapeutic function which is to be operative not on the audience but on the author, declaring, as D. H. Lawrence did, that "One sheds one's sicknesses in books, repeats and presents again one's emotions to be master of them," the difficulty is vast. It is an acceptable theory only with the qualification that technique, which objectifies, is under no other circumstances so imperative. For merely to repeat one's emotions, merely to look into one's heart and write, is also merely to repeat the round of emotional bondage. If our books are to be exercises in self-analysis, then technique must—and alone can—take the place of the absent analyst.

Lawrence, in the relatively late Introduction to his *Collected Poems,* made that distinction of the amateur between his "real" poems and his "composed" poems, between the poems which expressed his demon directly and created their own form "willy-nilly," and the poems which, through the hocus pocus of technique, he spuriously put together and could, if necessary, revise. His belief in a "poetry of the immediate present," poetry in which nothing is fixed, static, or final, where all is shimmeriness and impermanence and vitalistic essence, arose from this mistaken notion of technique. And from this notion, an unsympathetic critic like D. S. Savage can construct a case which shows Lawrence driven "concurrently to the dissolution of personality and the dissolution of art." The argument suggests that Lawrence's early, crucial novel, *Sons and Lovers,* is another example of meanings confused by an impatience with technical resources.

The novel has two themes: the crippling effects of a mother's love on the emotional development of her son; and the "split" between kinds of love, physical and spiritual, which the son develops, the kinds represented by two young women, Clara and Miriam. The two themes should, of course, work together, the second being, actually, the result of the first: this "split" is the "crippling." So one would expect to see the novel developed, and so Lawrence. in his famous letter to Edward Garnett, where he says that Paul is left at the end with the "drift towards death," apparently thought he had developed it. Yet in the last few sentences of the novel, Paul rejects his desire for extinction and turns towards "the faintly humming, glowing town," to life—as nothing in his previous history persuades us that he could unfalteringly do.

The discrepancy suggests that the book may reveal certain confusions between intention and performance.

The first of these is the contradiction between Lawrence's explicit characterizations of the mother and father and his tonal evaluations of them. It is a problem not only of style (of the contradiction between expressed moral epithets and the more general texture of the prose which applies to them) but of point of view. Morel and Lawrence are never separated, which is a way of saying that Lawrence maintains for himself in this book the confused attitude of his character. The mother is a "proud, *honorable* soul," but the father has a "small, *mean* head." This is the sustained contrast; the epithets are characteristic of the whole; and they represent half of Lawrence's feelings. But what is the other half? Which of these characters is given his real sympathy—the hard, self-righteous, aggressive, demanding mother who comes through to us, or the simple, direct, gentle, downright, fumbling, ruined father? There are two attitudes here. Lawrence (and Morel) loves his mother, but he also hates her for compelling his love; and he hates his father with the true Freudian jealousy, but he also loves him for what he is in himself, and he sympathizes more deeply with him because his wholeness has been destroyed by the mother's domination, just as his, Lawrence-Morel's, has been.

This is a psychological tension which disrupts the form of the novel and obscures its meaning, because neither the contradiction in style nor the confusion in point of view is made to right itself. Lawrence is merely repeating his emotions, and he avoids an austerer technical scrutiny of his material because it would compel him to master them. He would not let the artist be stronger than the man.

The result is that, at the same time that the book condemns the mother, it justifies her; at the same time that it shows Paul's failure, it offers rationalizations which place the failure elsewhere. The handling of the girl, Miriam, if viewed closely, is pathetic in what it signifies for Lawrence, both as man and artist. For Miriam is made the mother's scape-goat, and in a different way from the way that she was in life. The central section of the novel is shot through with alternate statements as to the source of the difficulty: Paul is unable to love Miriam wholly, and Miriam can love only his spirit. The contradictions appear sometimes within single paragraphs, and the point of view is never adequately objectified and sustained to tell us which is true. The material is never seen as material; the writer is caught in it exactly as firmly as he was caught in his experience of it. "That's how women are with me," said Paul. "They want me like mad, but they don't want to belong to me." So he might have said, and believed it; but at the end of the novel, Lawrence is still saying that, and himself believing it.

For the full history of this technical failure, one must read *Sons and Lovers* carefully and then learn the history of the manuscript from the book called *D. H. Lawrence: A Personal Record,* by one E. T., who was Miriam in life. The basic situation is clear enough. The first theme—the crippling effects of the mother's love—is developed right through to the end; and then suddenly, in the last few sentences, turns on itself, and Paul gives himself to life, not death. But all the way through, the insidious rationalizations of the second theme have crept in to destroy the artistic coherence of the work. A "split" would occur in Paul; but as the split is treated, it is superimposed upon rather than developed in support of the first theme. It is a rationalization made from it. If Miriam is made to insist on spiritual love, the meaning and the power of theme one are reduced; yet Paul's weakness is disguised.

Lawrence could not separate the investigating analyst, who must be objective, from Lawrence, the subject of the book; and the sickness was not healed, the emotion not mastered, the novel not perfected. All this, and the character of a whole career, would have been altered if Lawrence had allowed his technique to discover the fullest meaning of his subject.

*A Portrait of the Artist as a Young Man,* like *Tono-Bungay* and *Sons and Lovers,* is autobiographical, but unlike these it analyzes its material rigorously, and it defines the value and the quality of its experience not by appended comment or moral epithet, but by the texture of the style. The theme of *A Portrait,* a young artist's alienation from his environment, is explored and evaluated through three different styles and methods as Stephen Dedalus moves from childhood through boyhood into maturity. The opening pages are written in something like the stream of consciousness of *Ulysses,* as the environment impinges directly on the consciousness of the infant and the child, a strange, opening world which the mind does not yet subject to questioning, selection, or judgment. But this style changes very soon, as the boy begins to explore his surroundings, and as his sensuous experience of the world is enlarged, it takes on heavier and heavier rhythms and a fuller and fuller body of sensuous detail, until it reaches a crescendo of romantic opulence in the emotional climaxes which mark Stephen's rejection of domestic and religious values. Then gradually the style subsides into the austerer intellectuality of the final sections, as he defines to himself the outlines of the artistic task which is to usurp his maturity.

A highly self-conscious use of style and method defines the quality of experience in each of these sections, and, it is worth pointing out in connection with the third and concluding section, the style and method evaluate the experience. What has happened to Stephen is, of course, a progressive alienation from the life around him as he progressed in his initiation into it, and by the end of the novel, the alienation is complete. The final portion of the novel, fascinating as it may be for the developing aesthetic creed of Stephen-Joyce, is peculiarly bare. The life experience was not bare, as we know from *Stephen Hero;* but Joyce is forcing technique to comment. In essence, Stephen's alienation is a denial of the human environment; it is a loss; and the austere discourse of the final section, abstract and almost wholly without sensuous detail or strong rhythm, tells us of that loss. It is a loss so great that the texture of the notation-like prose here suggests that the end is really all an illusion, that when Stephen tells us and himself that he is going forth to forge in the smithy of his soul the uncreated conscience of his race, we are to infer from the very quality of the icy, abstract void he now inhabits, the implausibility of his aim. For *Ulysses* does not create the conscience of the race; it creates our consciousness.

In the very last two or three paragraphs of the novel, the style changes once more, reverts from the bare, notative kind to the romantic prose of Stephen's adolescence. "Away! Away! The spell of arms and voices; the white arms of roads, their promise of close embraces and the black arms of tall ships that stand against the moon, their tale of distant nations. They are held out to say: We are alone—come." Might one not say that the austere ambition is founded on adolescent longing? That the excessive intellectual severity of one style is the counterpart of the excessive lyric relaxation of the other? And that the final passage of *A Portrait* punctuates the illusory nature of the whole ambition?

For *Ulysses* does not create a conscience. Stephen, in *Ulysses,* is a little older, and gripped now by guilt, but he is still the cold young man divorced from the human no less than the institutional environment. The environment of urban life finds a separate embodiment in the character of Bloom, and Bloom is as lost as Stephen, though touchingly groping for moorings. Each of the two is weakened by his inability to reach out, or to do more than reach out to the other. Here, then, is the theme again, more fully stated, as it were in counterpoint.

But if Stephen is not much older, Joyce is. He is older as an artist not only because he can create and lavish his Godlike pity on a Leopold Bloom, but also because he knows now what both Stephen and Bloom mean, and *how much,* through the most brilliant technical operation ever made in fiction, they can be made to mean. Thus *Ulysses,* through the imaginative force which its techniques direct, is like a pattern of concentric circles, with the immediate human situation at its center, this passing on and out to the whole dilemma of modern life, this passing on and out beyond that to a vision of the cosmos, and this to the mythical limits of our experience. If we read *Ulysses* with more satisfaction than any other novel of this century, it is because its author held an atttiude toward technique and the technical scrutiny of subject matter which enabled him to order, within a single work and with superb coherence, the greatest amount of our experience.

4

In the United States during the last twenty-five years, we have had many big novels but few good ones. A writer like James T. Farrell apparently assumes that by endless redundancy in the description of the surface of American Life, he will somehow write a book with the scope of *Ulysses*. Thomas Wolfe apparently assumed that by the mere disgorging of the raw material of his experience he would give us at last our epic. But except in a physical sense, these men have hardly written novels at all.

The books of Thomas Wolfe were, of course, journals, and the primary role of his publisher in transforming these journals into the semblance of novels is notorious. For the crucial act of the artist, the unique act which is composition, a sympathetic editorial blue pencil and scissors were substituted. The result has excited many people, especially the young, and the ostensibly critical have observed the prodigal talent with the wish that it might have been controlled. Talent there was, if one means by talent inexhaustible verbal energy, excessive response to personal experience, and a great capacity for auditory imitativeness, yet all of this has nothing to do with the novelistic quality of the written result; until the talent is controlled, the material organized, the content achieved, there is simply the man and his life. It remains to be demonstrated that Wolfe's conversations were any less interesting as novels than his books, which is to say that his books are without interest as novels. As with Lawrence, our response to the books is determined, not by their qualities as novels but by our response to him and his qualities as a temperament.

This is another way of saying that Thomas Wolfe never really knew what he was writing *about*. Of Time and the River is merely a euphemism for Of a Man and his Ego. It is possible that had his conception of himself and of art included an adequate respect for technique and the capacity to pursue it, Wolfe would have written a great novel on his true subject—the dilemma of romantic genius; it was his true subject, but it remains his undiscovered subject, it is the subject which *we* must dig out for him, because he himself had neither the lamp nor the pick to find it in and mine it out of the labyrinths of his experience. Like Emily Brontë, Wolfe needed a point of view beyond his own which would separate his material and its effect.

With Farrell, the situation is opposite. He knows quite well what his subject is and what he wishes to tell us about it, but he hardly needs the novel to do so. It is significant that in sheer clumsiness of style, no living writer exceeds him, for his prose is asked to perform no service beyond communication of the most rudimentary kind of fact. For his ambitions, the style of the newspaper and the lens of the documentary camera would be quite adequate, yet consider the diminution which Leopold Bloom, for example, would suffer, if he were to be viewed from these, the technical perspectives of James Farrell. Under the eye of this technique, the material does not yield up enough; indeed, it shrinks.

More and more writers in this century have felt that naturalism as a method imposes on them strictures which prevent them from exploring through all the resources of technique the full amplifications of their subjects, and that thus it seriously limits the possible breadth of aesthetic meaning and response. James Farrell is almost unique in the complacency with which he submits to the blunt techniques of naturalism; and his fiction is correspondingly repetitive and flat.

That naturalism had a sociological and disciplinary value in the nineteenth century is obvious; it enabled the novel to grasp materials and make analyses which had eluded it in the past, and to grasp them boldly; but even then it did not tell us enough of what, in Virginia Woolf's phrase, is "really real," nor did it provide the means to the maximum of reality coherently contained. Even the Flaubertian ideal of objectivity seems, today, an unnecessarily limited view of objectivity, for as almost every good writer of this century shows us, it is quite as possible to be objective about subjective states as it is to be objective about the circumstantial surfaces of life. Dublin, in *Ulysses,* is a moral setting: not only a city portrayed in the naturalistic fashion of Dickens' London, but also a map of the modern psyche with its oblique and baffled purposes. The second level of reality in no way invalidates the first, and a writer like Joyce shows us that, if the artist truly respects his medium, he can be objective about both at once. What we need in fiction is a devoted fidelity to every technique which will help us to discover and to evaluate our subject matter, and more than that, to discover the amplifications of meaning of which our subject matter is capable.

Most modern novelists have felt this demand upon them. André Gide allowed one of his artist-heroes to make an observation which considerably resembles an observation we have quoted from Wells. "My novel hasn't got a subject. . . . Let's say, if you prefer it, it hasn't got *one* subject. . . . 'A slice of life,' the naturalist school said. The great defect of that school is that it always cuts its slice in the same direction; in time, lengthwise. Why not in breadth? Or in depth? As for me I should like not to cut at all. Please understand; I should like to put everything into my novel." Wells, with his equally large blob of potential material, did not know how to cut it to the novel's taste; Gide cut, of course—in every possible direction. Gide and others. And those "cuts" are all the new techniques which modern fiction has given us. None, perhaps, is more important than that inheritance from French symbolism which Huxley, in the glittering wake of Gide, called "the musicalization of fiction." Conrad anticipated both when he wrote that the novel "must strenuously aspire to the plasticity of sculpture, to the colour of painting, and to the magic suggestiveness of music—which is the art of arts," and when he said of that early but wonderful piece of symbolist fiction, *Heart of Darkness,* "It was like another art altogether. That sombre theme had to be given a sinister resonance, a tonality of its own, a continued vibration that, I hoped, would hang in the air and dwell on the ear after the last note had been struck." The analogy with music, except as a metaphor, is inexact, and except as it points to techniques which fiction can employ as fiction, not very useful to our sense of craftsmanship. It has had an approximate exactness in only one work, Joyce's final effort, and an effort unique in literary history, *Finnegans Wake,* and here, of course, those readers willing to approach the "ideal" effort Joyce demands, discovering an inexhaustible wealth and scope, are most forcibly reminded of the primary importance of technique to subject, and of their indivisibility.

The techniques of naturalism inevitably curtail subject and often leave it in its original area, that of undefined social experience. Those of our writers who, stemming from this tradition, yet, at their best, achieve a novelistic definition of social experience—writers like the occasional Sherwood Anderson, William Carlos Williams, the occasional Erskine Caldwell, Nathanael West, and Ira Wolfert in *Tucker's People,* have done so by pressing naturalism far beyond itself, into positively gothic distortions. The structural machinations of Dos Passos and the lyrical interruptions of Steinbeck are the desperate maneuvers of men committed to a method of whose limitations they despair. They are our symbolists *manqués,* who end as allegorists.

Our most accomplished novels leave no such impression of desperate and intentional struggle, yet their precise technique and their determination to make their prose work in the service of their subjects have been the measure of their accomplishment. Hemingway's *The Sun Also Rises* and Wescott's *The Pilgrim Hawk* are works of art not because they may be measured by some external, neo-classic notion of form, but because their forms are so exactly equivalent with their subjects, and because the evaluation of their subjects exists in their styles.

Hemingway has recently said that his contribution to younger writers lay in a certain necessary purification of the language· but the claim has doubtful value. The contribution of his prose was to his subject, and the terseness of style for which his early work is justly celebrated is no more valuable, as an end in itself, than the baroque involutedness of Faulkner's prose, or the cold elegance of Wescott's. Hemingway's early subject, the exhaustion of value, was perfectly investigated and invested by his bare style, and in story after story, no meaning at all is to be inferred from the fiction except as the style itself suggests that there is no meaning in life. This style, more than that, was the perfect technical substitute for the conventional commentator; it expresses and it measures that peculiar morality of the stiff lip which Hemingway borrowed from athletes. It is an instructive lesson, furthermore, to observe how the style breaks down when Hemingway moves into the less congenial subject matter of social affirmation: how the style breaks down, the effect of verbal economy as mute suffering is lost, the personality of the writer, no longer protected by the objectification of an adequate technique, begins its offensive intrusion, and the entire structural integrity slackens. Inversely, in the stories and the early novels, the technique was the perfect embodiment of the subject and it gave that subject its astonishing largeness of effect and of meaning.

One should correct Buffon and say that style is the subject. In Wescott's *Pilgrim Hawk,* a novel which bewildered its many friendly critics by the apparent absence of subject, the subject, the story, is again in the style itself. This novel, which is a triumph of the sustained point of view, is only bewildering if we try to make a story out of the narrator's observations upon others; but if we read his observations as oblique and unrecognized observations upon himself the story emerges with perfect coherence, and it reverberates with meaning, is as suited to continuing reflection as the greatest lyrics.

The rewards of such respect for the medium as the early Hemingway and the occasional Wescott have shown may be observed in every good writer we have. The involutions of Faulkner's style are the perfect equivalent of his involved structures, and the two together are the perfect representation of the moral labyrinths he explores, and of the ruined world which his novels repeatedly invoke and in which these labyrinths exist. The cultivated sensuosity of Katherine Anne Porter's style has charm in itself, of course, but no more than with these others does it have aesthetic value it inself; its values lie in the subtle means by which sensuous details become symbols, and in the way that the symbols provide a network which is the story, and which at the same time provides the writer and us with a refined moral insight by means of which to test it. When we put such writers against a writer like William Saroyan, whose respect is reserved for his own temperament, we are appalled by the stylistic irresponsibility we find in him, and by the almost total absence of theme, or defined subject matter, and the abundance of unwarranted feeling. Such a writer inevitably becomes a sentimentalist because he has no means by which to measure his emotion. Technique, at last, is measure.

These writers, from Defoe to Porter, are of unequal and very different talent, and technique and talent are, of course, after a point, two different things. What Joyce gives us in one direction, Lawrence, for all his imperfections as a technician, gives us in another, even though it is not usually the direction of art. Only in some of his stories and in a few of his poems, where the demands of technique are less sustained and the subject matter is not autobiographical, Lawrence, in a different way from Joyce, comes to the same aesthetic fulfilment. Emily Brontë, with what was perhaps her intuitive grasp of the need to establish a tension between her subject matter and her perspective upon it, achieves a similar fulfillment; and, curiously, in the same way and certainly by intuition alone, Hemingway's early work makes a moving splendor from nothingness.

And yet, whatever one must allow to talent and forgive in technique, one risks no generalization in saying that modern fiction at its best has been peculiarly conscious of itself and of its tools. The technique of modern fiction, at once greedy and fastidious, achieves as its subject matter not some singleness, some topic or thesis, but the whole of the modern consciousness. It discovers the complexity of the modern spirit, the difficulty of personal morality, and the fact of evil—all the untractable elements under the surface which a technique of the surface alone can not approach. It shows us—in Conrad's words, from *Victory*—that we all live in an "age in which we are camped like bewildered travellers in a garish, unrestful hotel," and while it puts its hard light on our environment, it penetrates, with its sharp weapons, the depths of our bewilderment. These are not two things, but only an adequate technique can show them as one. In a realist like Farrell, we have the environment only, which we know from the newspapers; in a subjectivist like Wolfe, we have the bewilderment only, which we record in our own diaries and letters. But the true novelist gives them to us together, and thereby increases the effect of each, and reveals each in its full significance.

Elizabeth Bowen, writing of Lawrence, said of modern fiction, "We want the naturalistic surface, but with a kind of internal burning. In Lawrence every bush burns." But the bush burns brighter in some places than in others, and it burns brightest when a passionate private vision finds its objectification in exacting technical search. If the vision finds no such objectification, as in Wolfe and Saroyan, there is a burning without a bush. In our committed realists, who deny the resources of art for the sake of life, whose technique forgives both innocence and slovenliness—in Defoe and Wells and Farrell, there is a bush but it does not burn. There, at first glance, the bush is only a bush; and then, when we look again, we see that, really, the thing is dead.

## Martin Turnell

### *The Language of Fiction*

The critic of fiction has a more difficult task than the critic of poetry or the drama. We all know or think we know what constitutes a poem or a play, but the critic of the novel has to begin by defining his elusive subject. A good many writers have adopted the historical approach and have tried to show that the contemporary novel is a direct development of the novel of classical times. They have selected a single concept—"character," "plot," "structure" and "form" are among the best known—and have argued that it has always been the novelist's main concern and is the clue to his art. The result is that criticism of fiction tends to be too abstract and schematic to offer the reader much assistance in the appreciation of a particular novel.

The novel is perhaps the most unwieldy of all literary forms because the novelist's experience is much less compact than the poet's or even the dramatist's. The critic is bound to rely on a comparatively small number of quotations instead of being able to quote a complete work, and this naturally increases the danger of misinterpretation. He cannot easily dispense with abstractions like character, plot, structure and form which provide him with a convenient system of reference. When properly used, they have a certain utility value and they will appear frequently in the pages that follow. It must be recognized, however, that they belong to the presentation of experience and not to the substance of the novel. The mistake lies in imagining that when we speak of a novelist's "convincing characterization," the excellence of his "plots" or his "narrative gift" we are pronouncing critical judgments, whereas in fact we are doing no more than commend the skill with which he displays his wares.

"Character" has naturally been by far the most popular of the definitions that I have mentioned, as it has been the most mischievous; and it is only during the past thirty years that critics have seriously challenged the widely accepted view that a novel or a play is no more than a biography of an imaginary person.

Now there are strong historical reasons for this belief in the supremacy of character and they are worth examining. It is sometimes said that character was an invention of the Romantic Movement, but in reality it is much older than that. It is a reflection of changing conceptions of man's nature and goes back to the emergence of the individual at the Renaissance. The Renaissance humanists diverted attention from man in society to the individual who dominates the community. The change was, perhaps, more marked in Protestant than in Catholic countries. The link between the Cornelian hero and the élite which produced him is much closer than that between the Shakespearean hero and Elizabethan society. We find an Englishman like Dryden expatiating on Shakespeare's characterization while a Frenchman like Saint-Evremond—a critic who was very much in advance of his time—was far more concerned with Corneille's impact on his audience.

The heroic age did not last long. Mr. Santayana has argued in *Winds of Doctrine* that the Copernican astronomy—Donne's "new philosophy"—struck a mortal blow at the belief that man was the centre of the universe; and more recently M. Paul Bénichou has described the part played by Pascal and La Rochefoucauld in what he calls "the demolition of the hero."[1] It always takes some time for the full effect of philosophical changes to make themselves felt on art and the life of the people. Shakespeare's "What a piece of work is man!" is echoed, mockingly, in the eighteenth century by Pope's "The glory, jest, and riddle of the world!"

[1] In *Morales du grand siècle* ("Bibliotheque des Idées"), (Paris, 1948), pp. 97–111.

"Glory" has not entirely departed, but it has become slightly ridiculous and the focus is shifting to man's enigmatic qualities. This tendency received a powerful if indirect impetus from Rousseau's *Confessions*. Man might have become less glorious, but to the eighteenth and nineteenth centuries he appeared much more interesting. The last quarter of the eighteenth century saw the publication of a number of studies of Shakespeare's characters of which the most representative was Morgann's *Essay on the Dramatic Character of Sir John Falstaff*, and this approach culminated in the next century with its speculations about Hamlet's student life and the number of Lady Macbeth's children.[2]

The disruptive tendencies of the seventeenth and eighteenth centuries were reinforced by the rise of the scientific philosophies in the nineteenth century and their influence on the novel was very marked. Balzac's monomaniacs can be traced back through Molière to Corneille and, as we shall see, they represent the final dissolution of the hero in a commercial society. Flaubert's *ratés* seem to possess a similar historical importance; they point to the demolition not merely of the hero, but of man himself. When we compare Mme de La Fayette's portrait of the Duc de Nemours with a passage from Zola's *Germinal* we can see the extent of the changes which have taken place in the short space of two hundred years:

> Mais ce prince était un chef-d'œuvre de la nature. . . . Ce qui le mettait au-dessus des autres était une valeur incomparable et un agrément dans son esprit, dans son visage et dans ses actions que l'on n'a jamais vu qu'à lui seul.

> Il y avait là des herscheurs, des moulineurs, jusqu'à des galibots de quatorze ans, toute la jeunesse des fosses, buvant plus de genièvre que de bière.

> [But this prince was nature's masterpiece. . . . What placed him above others was an incomparable valour and an attractiveness of mind, face and carriage which has never been seen except in him.

[2] See Professor L. C. Knights's *Explorations* (London, 1946), pp. 1–39.

There were putters, trammers, down to pit-lads of fourteen there, the whole of the youth of the pits, drinking more gin than beer.]

"I do not know," said Lanson of the second passage, "what he meant by *herscheurs, moulineurs, galibots,* but I have a vague picture of a cohort of miners. . . ."[3] The implication is plain. The novelist no longer sees man as an individual; he simply sees him in the mass, as part of a "cohort" of workers.

The modern novel, indeed, divides into two main schools. One concentrates on the sensitive individual who has become the prisoner of his own sensibility. The other describes the cohorts of the "party"—for naturalism led almost inevitably to the contemporary political novel—trying to destroy the last strongholds of individualism.[4]

It therefore appears that the attempt to break down the nineteenth-century idea of character was not due entirely to critical acumen; it was forced on the critic by the changes which had taken place in the conception of man's nature. The development of the inner monologue, the subtleties of Henry James and the unending meditations of Proust's narrator showed that character had lost the finality which had been claimed for it. The late C. H. Rickword drew attention to the " 'subjective' novelists' increasing tendency to rely for their effect not on set pieces of character drawing, but directly on the poetic properties of words";[5] and in a striking essay in the second volume of his *Stilstudien* Leo Spitzer remarked that Proust's syntax was "the expression of the complexity of all being."[6] It is evident that the conventional idea of character was a hindrance rather than a help in interpreting this "complexity." On the other hand, the exploits of the party member could only be measured by a non-literary criterion which made character equally irrelevant.

It is appropriate that a more suitable standard should al-

[3] *L'Art de la prose* (Paris, 1908), p. 233.

[4] See Edwin Muir's "The Natural Man and the Political Man" in *Essays on Literature and Society* (London, 1949), pp. 151–65.

[5] In *Towards Standards of Criticism* (London, 1933), p. 32.

[6] Munich, 1928, p. 396.

ready have been suggested by one of the first of the great nineteenth-century masters:

> Un roman [said Stendhal] est comme un archet, la caisse du violon *qui rend les sons,* c'est l'âme du lecteur.[7]

> [A novel is like a bow, the violin which makes the sounds is the reader's soul.]

The novelist seeks to communicate an imaginative experience to his reader. He does so by imposing the pattern of his own sensibility on him and the medium which he uses is language. The critic of the novel no less than the critic of poetry is concerned first and foremost with "arrangements of words on a page." For, said Rickword, "character is merely the term by which the reader alludes to the pseudo-objective image he composes of his responses to an author's verbal arrangements."[8] This is an extreme statement of the new attitude, but it is evident that a character is a verbal construction which has no existence outside the book. It is a vehicle for the novelist's sensibility and its significance lies in its relations with the author's other constructions. A novel is essentially a verbal pattern in which the different "characters" are strands, and the reader's experience is the impact of the complete pattern on his sensibility. The fact that we tend to consider certain characters from fiction in isolation means either that we are seeking to enlarge or add to the novelist's experience, or that he has chosen to incorporate what is most vital in his experience in one or two of his principal characters. It remains true therefore that "character" belongs to the organization and presentation of experience rather than to its substance, and when it is used as a substitute for the detailed elucidation of the text it becomes a nuisance. The study of the novels which have been written during the last two centuries can tell us a great deal about moral, social and political changes, but it is only by first submitting ourselves to the violinist's bow and listening to our own sensibility that we can say anything of value about the novelist's art.

[7] *La Vie de Henri Brulard* (Divan Edition), I, p. 227.
[8] *Op. cit.*, p. 31.

It follows from this that the study of the French novel is primarily a study of the alterations which have taken place in the French language and of the novelists' use of their resources.

## 2

When we read the *Princesse de Clèves* for the first time, it seems to have something of the elusiveness of the French classical drama. The formal, elevated prose appears as remote as the alexandrine, and we are conscious of the same lack of sensuous appeal. It is only later that we perceive the delicate emotional overtones that Mme de La Fayette conveys with her abstract words and the skilful changes of tone.

> Mais, ce qui rendait cette Cour belle et majestueuse, était le nombre infini de princes et de grands seigneurs d'un mérite extraordinaire. Ceux que je vais nommer étaient, en des manières différentes, l'ornement et l'admiration de leur siècle.
>
> Le Roi de Navarre attirait le respect de tout le monde par la grandeur de son rang et par celle qui paraissait en sa personne. Il excellait dans la guerre, et le duc de Guise lui donnait une émulation qui l'avait porté plusieurs fois à quitter sa place de général pour aller combattre auprès de lui, comme un simple soldat, dans les lieux les plus périlleux. Il est vrai aussi que ce duc avait donné des marques d'une valeur si admirable, et avait eu de si heureux succès, qu'il n'y avait point de grand capitaine qui ne dût le regarder avec envie. Sa valeur était soutenue de toutes les autres grandes qualités: il avait un esprit vaste et profond, une âme noble et élevée, et une égale capacité pour la guerre et pour les affaires.
>
> [But what made the Court fair and stately was the infinite number of princes and nobles of outstanding merit. Those whom I am about to name were, in different ways, the ornament and the admiration of their age.
>
> The King of Navarre earned the respect of all by the greatness of his state and of his bearing. He excelled in war, and the Duke of Guise so stirred his emulation that he had been

led on several occasions to leave his post as general in order to fight alongside him, as a private soldier, in the most perilous places. It is also true that the duke had given proof of such admirable valour and had enjoyed such great success that there was no great captain who could help envying him. His valour was reinforced by all the other great qualities: he had a vast and profound intelligence, a noble and lofty mind, and an equal capacity for war and for the affairs of state.]

It is evident from these passages that the *Princesse de Clèves* is a novel in the grand manner. Mme de La Fayette's prose, as surely as the alexandrine, is the product of a stable or an apparently stable society.

The first paragraph makes a general statement about the life of the Court. In the paragraphs which follow, the writer turns to individual examples of greatness and valour. The style is, intentionally, pitched in the same key; the words *grand* and *grandeur* echo and reinforce one another.

In an essay on the *Princesse de Clèves,* M. Albert Camus has defined the style of the classic artist as *une sorte de monotonie passionnée.*[9] It is an arresting phrase, but there is perhaps a danger of obscuring the variety of Mme de La Fayette's style. Its effect depends not on a blend, but on a *contrast* between "monotony" and "passion." The straightforward syntax, which is the expression of a profound belief in order and in the diverse qualities which contribute to that order, is functional. It provides a norm by which personal experience and personal feelings are tested and judged. Later in the book we read:

> "Venez, venez," me dit-il, "venez voir l'homme du monde le plus désespéré; je suis plus malheureux mille fois que je n'étais tantôt, et ce que je viens d'apprendre de Madame de Tournon est pire que sa mort."
>
> Je crus que la douleur le troublait entièrement, et je ne pouvais m'imaginer qu'il y eût quelque chose de pire que la mort d'une maîtresse que l'on aime et dont on est aimé. Je lui dis que, tant que son affliction avait eu des bornes, je l'avais

[9] *Problèmes du roman* (Brussels, 1945), p. 193.

approuvée, et que j'y étais entré; mais que je ne le plaindrais plus s'il s'abandonnait au désespoir et s'il perdait la raison.

"Je serais trop heureux de l'avoir perdue, et la vie aussi," s'écria-t-il: "Madame de Tournon m'était infidèle. . . ."

["Come here, come here," he said to me, "come and see the most despairing man in the world; I am a thousand times more unhappy than I was a few hours ago, and what I have heard about Madame de Tournon is worse than her death."

I thought that he was completely deranged by his grief, and I could not imagine that there was anything worse than the death of a woman whom one loves and by whom one is loved in return. I told him that as long as his affliction had had limits, I had approved of it; but that I should no longer sympathize with him if he gave way to despair and lost his reason.

"I should be only too happy to lose it, and life as well," he cried. "Madame de Tournon was unfaithful to me. . . ."]

This dialogue between Sancerre, who speaks first, and the Prince de Clèves illustrates the sense in which syntax is functional. For we distinguish three voices in the novel. There is the voice of the novelist which sets the tone of the book; and there are the voices of the individuals which alternately blend in with the general tone and come into conflict with it. When the Prince de Clèves asserts his belief that grief must have limits which are absolute he contributes to the preservation of order, while Sancerre's threat to abandon himself to despair is also a threat to that order. We can go on to say that the dialogue is a ceremonial which deliberately seeks to impose a check on personal emotion in the interests of the community and to preserve a balance which is already felt to be precarious. The individual speakers do not play the same parts all the time. In this passage the Prince is on the side of order, but in an exchange with his wife later in the book he says:

"Comment pouviez-vous espérer que je conservasse de la raison? Vous aviez donc oublié que je vous aimais éperdument, et que j'étais votre mari? L'un des deux peut porter aux extrémités; que ne peuvent point les deux ensemble! . . . Je n'ai que des sentiments violents et incertains dont je ne suis pas le maître: je ne me trouve plus digne de vous; vous ne me paraissez plus digne de moi; je vous adore, je vous hais; je vous offense, je vous demande pardon; je vous admire, j'ai honte de vous admirer; enfin, il n'y a plus en moi ni de calme ni de raison."

["How could you expect me to preserve my reason? Had you forgotten that I was madly in love with you, and that I was your husband? Either is enough to drive me to extremes; what can't happen with the two together! . . . I have only violent and uncertain feelings of which I am no longer master. I find that I am no longer worthy of you. You no longer appear to be worthy of me. I adore you, I hate you; I'm offensive and I ask your forgiveness; I admire you, I'm ashamed of admiring you. In short, I'm incapable of calmness or reasonableness."]

When we read this, we perceive that nearly all the characters speak with two voices—the voices of the private individual and the public personage—which maintain a perpetual dialogue. We overhear the murmur of the tormented, uneasy conscience, floating up to us from the underworld of temptation and desire, trying desperately to come to terms with itself and conform to a standard of conduct prescribed by the community.

## 3

When we come to the eighteenth century, we are at once aware of a change. The prose of Marivaux, Voltaire, Diderot and Laclos seems at first to be more subtle, more elegant and better designed to convey shades of feeling than that of their predecessors.

> Never [wrote Giraudoux] have the words "friend" or "son" or "seducer" been used more directly to designate a friend, a son, a seducer; or the word "woman" a woman. . . . Laclos has the advantage over his predecessors of a vocabulary which owes nothing to indignation or to the di-

gestion and—we shall always return to the point—which is as carefully delimited and as fundamentally pure as Racine's.[10]

It was certainly a marvellous instrument for the analysis and dissemination of ideas. Sorel reminds us that in the eighteenth century French took the place of Latin as the international language of philosophy and diplomacy, and he shows that it played an immense part in the political upheavals of the age.[11] Its characteristics, said Lanson, were "intellectualité, politesse, polissonnerie, esprit."[12] The *philosophes,* as we know, launched a full-scale attack on traditional religious and philosophical views and it was in order to prevent open scandal that they developed and perfected the qualities described by Lanson. These qualities, however, should not blind us to what was lost.

> When it is seen as it really was [said Lanson] and not according to the image which it was pleased to present of itself, the seventeenth century is overflowing with life—with energetic, fiery, brutal and even crude life. It was no doubt refined and not delicate; it submitted its fieriness and its brutality to complicated ceremonials whose very extravagance had something violent about them.[13]

That is the measure of the eighteenth century's sacrifice. Its writers possessed an instrument of extraordinary clarity. They were able, perhaps for the first time, to say exactly what they wanted; but the latent vigour, the overtones of seventeenth-century prose, the phrases which echo in the memory had disappeared. For all its elegance, Laclos' prose has a faintly tinny sound.

In a discussion of this nature there are certain reservations to be made. When we look back at the literature of an earlier century, it usually appears more uniform and more homogeneous than it really was. We are aware of a discrepancy between the reality and "the image that it was pleased to present of itself." This is due partly to the selectiveness of our reading and partly to

[10] *Littérature* (Paris, 1941), p. 71.
[11] *L'Europe et la Révolution Française,* I (Paris, 1885), pp. 147–57.
[12] *Op. cit.,* p. 143.
[13] *Ibid.,* p. 55.

a conspiracy between the leading writers. The *philosophes* were very clear-headed and very unscrupulous. They did their utmost to discredit the work of any writers whose views were opposed to their own, not out of a disinterested pursuit of truth but in order to capture the literary market. A number of its most prominent writers were profoundly rationalist and secularist, but there were other forces at work which are overlooked because they do not fit in with the official picture created by the *philosophes*. An attempt to redress the balance was made some years ago by M. Pierre Trahard. In his massive study of *Les Maîtres de la sensibilité française au dix-huitième siècle* he argues that "sensibility" and not "reason" was the keynote of the century, and he discovers "sensibility"—a term which is never satisfactorily defined—in Laclos, whom he describes as a disciple of Rousseau, as well as in the tragedies of Voltaire.[14] His book is a useful corrective to the conventional view of the eighteenth century, but it is difficult not to feel that he spoils his case by overstatement. All good writers naturally possess sensibility, but M. Trahard seems to me to make the mistake of paying insufficient attention to the quality of eighteenth-century sensibility which is often indistinguishable from mere emotionalism or mere sentimentality. It remains true, however, that the century of the Duc de Richelieu and the Comte de Tilly was also the century in which the Princesse de Condé and Mlle de Lespinasse died of love. It was the century of Voltaire, but it was also the century in which fanaticism, "illuminism" and madness were rife. Saint-Preux was probably no less representative than Valmont. The task of the literary critic is to discover the relations between these different tendencies.

> Oh! mourons, ma douce amie! mourons, la bien-aimée de mon cœur! Que faire désormais d'une jeunesse insipide dont nous avons épuisé toutes les délices? Explique-moi, si tu le peux, ce que j'ai senti dans cette nuit inconcevable; donne-moi l'idée d'une vie ainsi passée, ou laisse-m'en quitter une qui n'a plus rien de ce que je viens d'éprouver avec toi. . . . O chef-d'œuvre unique de la nature! divine Julie! possession délicieuse à laquelle tous les transports du plus ar-

[14] Four volumes (Paris, 1931–3).

dent amour suffisent à peine! . . . Rends-moi cette étroite union des âmes que tu m'avais annoncée et que tu m'as si bien fait goûter. . . . (*La Nouvelle Héloïse.*)

Comme je n'ai pas de vanité, je ne m'arrête pas aux détails de la nuit: mais vous me connaissez, et j'ai été content de moi. (*Les Liaisons dangereuses.*)

[Oh! let us die, my sweet friend, let us die, beloved of my heart! What is there left for us to do with a youth which has lost its savour and whose delights we have exhausted? Explain to me, if you can, what I felt during that inconceivable night. Make me understand what a lifetime spent like that would be like, or let me take leave of a life which no longer has anything of what I experienced with you. . . . O nature's unique masterpiece! Divine Julie! Delicious possession for which all the transports of the most ardent love are barely sufficient! . . . Give me back that close union of souls which you foretold and of which you gave me a taste. . . .

As I am not vain, I won't dwell on the details of the night: but you know me, and I was satisfied with myself.]

*La Nouvelle Héloïse* was published in 1761 and the *Liaisons dangereuses* made its appearance in 1782. It is not to be supposed that human nature had undergone a startling change in the twenty-one years which separated them. M. Trahard is no doubt right in saying that Rousseau's influence is predominant in Laclos' treatise on the education of women and in his letters to his wife, but we are not entitled to assume that the novelist and the private individual are identical. It seems to me, indeed, that these passages are the expression of two different modes of feeling which instead of combining either remained separate and distinct or undermined one another. Their existence created a dilemma for the writer which was well described by Constant at the turn of the century when he wrote in *Adolphe:*

Les sentiments de l'homme sont confus et mélangés; ils se composent d'une multitude d'impressions variées qui échappent à l'observation; et la parole, toujours trop grossière et trop générale, peut bien servir à les désigner, mais ne sert jamais à les définir.

[Men's feelings are obscure and confused; they are composed of a great number and variety of impressions which defy observation; and words, always too crude and too general, may well indicate them but can never define them.]

Constant was acutely aware of the complexity of experience and of the difficulty of finding a medium which would do justice to it. This passage is a criticism both of the French classical style and of Rousseau's experiment. The moralists and novelists of the seventeenth century shared a profound belief in the Rational Man. Their work was an attempt to control the disturbing impulses which Constant was later to describe as *impressions primitives et fougueuses,* and to help man to live a reasonable life by providing him with a series of well-tried maxims for his guidance. The writers of the Enlightenment also admired the Rational Man, but they made the mistake of trying first to eliminate the *impressions primitives et fougueuses,* then to replace *emotion* by *sensation.* Their scepticism led to an impoverishment of the novel. In the work of Laclos we feel that the novelist is operating in a gradually narrowing circle. His analysis reminds us of a mechanic taking a machine to pieces and putting it together again. For human behaviour is absolutely predictable; that his creatures should be swayed by the *transports* of Racine's or the sudden impulses described by Constant and Stendhal is practically unthinkable. When he writes of the sexual exploits of the ruling class he reveals a curious greatness; but the stiff conventional phrases of the letters of Mme de Rosemonde and the Présidente de Tourvel reflect not merely psychological but moral failure.

Rousseau undoubtedly realized that the characteristic style of both centuries was the product of a small civilized élite and was no longer an adequate vehicle for experience; but though his novels provided a release for feelings which had been excluded, his attempt to create a balance was a failure. His Man of Feeling is just as partial and incomplete as the Rational Man. The prose of the *Nouvelle Héloïse,* as we can see from the example quoted above, is a curious hybrid. In his desire to give dignity and moral seriousness to the novel he moved away from the easy conversational style of his century back to the *style oratoire* of the seventeenth century. Unfortunately, he also sacrificed that clarity for which the eighteenth century is justly famous. He did not possess the insight necessary to disentangle the complexities of experience or the classic writer's power of translating obscure feelings into exact language. In his novels language is a barrier which is interposed between the artist and his experience, and the word becomes a substitute for the feeling that it purports to describe. The psychology of the *Nouvelle Héloïse* is puerile. The characters remind us of a ventriloquist's dolls who maintain an unending stream of words and who always invoke "virtue," "chastity," "honour" and "purity" as they plunge into an adulterous couch.[15]

Paul Arbelet remarked in his admirable *Jeunesse de Stendhal* that both Constant and Stendhal were born in a barren period and he went on to argue that this accounted for what seemed to him the limitations of their work.[16] I find this view difficult to accept. It seems to me on the contrary to have been a period which was highly propitious for the great writer. It was an intermediate period—the neutral moment—which comes between the end of one age and the beginning of another. The classic virtues had not been finally lost, but there was no dominant mood, no decisive influence at work. The writer could therefore apply the whole of his talent to his books; he had no need to waste his energies trying to produce the conditions in which writing becomes possible or resisting hostile tendencies. He was free to use what seemed valuable in the classical tradition and to create new patterns of feeling. Constant and Stendhal were both influenced by Rousseau and the *philosophes*, but these influences were assimilated and transformed into something which was essentially their own.[17] Their novels exhibit those slight alterations in language which are an unmistakable sign of the great writer.

[15] Contrast "Le langage de Julie, dans la *Nouvelle Héloïse,* émeut comme celui de Bérénice . . ." (Trahard, *op. cit.,* IV, p. 277).

[16] Two volumes, Paris, 1919.

[17] Stendhal did not scruple to use the Romantic stock-in-trade of scaling ladders, lovers concealed in cupboards, log cabins and the rest, but the tone of his work is unromantic, and in the seduction of Mathilde de La Mole it becomes decidedly anti-Romantic.

Ezra Pound once remarked that Flaubert wrote much better than Stendhal, but that in Stendhal there is "a sort of solidity" which is lacking in Flaubert. He went on to define it as "a trust in the thing more than the word, which is the solid basis."[18] This "solidity" is common to Stendhal and Constant, and they owe it to the discipline which they inherited from the previous century and which was beginning to disappear.

M. Emile Henriot, quoting Anatole France, speaks of a "disaster of language which had begun under Mirabeau, extended during the Revolution and become aggravated during the Empire and the Restoration."[19] The originality of the classic style lies in "the choice and in the order of ideas." The verb is the pivot of the sentence and gives it movement, balance and stability. The fall of the old order had an immediate impact on language. It is not easy to describe it in a few words. I think we can say that it disorganized the classical syntax, that the emotional upheaval and a sudden preoccupation with material reality led to a fresh emphasis on images and vocabulary.

In a confused situation Constant and Stendhal contrived to preserve the French classical syntax, the eighteenth-century gift for analysis as well as its clarity and good sense; but by a very subtle modification of the eighteenth-century vocabulary they came to express feelings which were undreamed of in the psychology of their predecessors. Constant was occasionally guilty of a Romantic flourish—the description of the death of Mme de Charrière in *Adolphe* is an example—but these lapses throw into relief the excellence of his instrument and the skill with which he normally used it. When he writes

> Elle fixait avec une précision inquiète l'instant de mon retour.

> [She anxiously fixed the exact moment of my return.]

the *inquiète* qualifies the *précision* and extends its meaning, but it is also controlled by it. When he remarks in another place:

[18] "Letters to a Young Poet," written in 1916 and published in *The Changing World,* No. 7 (February–March–April 1949), p. 27.

[19] *Stendhaliana* (Paris, 1924), p. 209.

Nous vécûmes ainsi quatre mois dans des rapports forcés, quelquefois doux, jamais complètement libres, y rencontrant encore du plaisir, mais n'y trouvant plus de charme.

[We lived thus for four months in a forced intimacy which was sometimes sweet, but never completely free. We found pleasure in it but no more charm.]

there is a complete correspondence between the words and the perceptions which they register; but though each of the key-words—*forcés, doux, libres, plaisir* and *charme*—has a separate and unmistakable identity, they are all closely interrelated and the final impression depends on these relations. In this way Constant constructs a complex network of feelings "which is the solid basis." His central experience—the experience of falling out of love—seems to be the reverse of Mme de La Fayette's in the *Princesse de Clèves:*

Mais l'amour, ce transport des sens, cette ivresse involontaire, cet oubli de tous les intérêts, de tous les devoirs, Ellénore, je ne l'ai plus.

[But, Ellénore, I no longer feel that ecstasy of the senses, that involuntary intoxication, that forgetting of all wordly interests, of all duties—I no longer feel love.]

Yet when it comes it is thrown into relief in very much the same way and the background of "solidity" gives it its shattering reverberation.

Constant shared most of his positive qualities with Stendhal, but Stendhal's range was much wider and in spite of his apparent carelessness his style was a much more complex instrument. When he wrote of himself in *Une Position sociale,* which is "a portrait of the artist as a middle-aged man":

Du caractère en apparence le plus changeant, un mot parfois l'attendrissait jusqu'aux larmes. D'autres fois, ironique, dur par crainte d'être attendri et de se mépriser ensuite comme faible.

[He appeared to be a person of the ficklest character and sometimes a word moved him to tears. At other times, he was ironical, harsh through fear of being moved and of later despising himself for being weak.]

he hints at that blend of "tenderness" and "irony" which gives the *Chartreuse* its strange resonance. *Changeant,* too, is an important word. A great deal of Stendhal's work was directed against both the Rational Man and the Man of Feeling of the eighteenth century. They had become conventions which no longer corresponded to any living experience. For this reason he was at pains to emphasize the contradictions of human nature. He set his personal stamp on the words *singulier* and *imprévu.* They occur again and again in the novels, and they express an attitude of opposition and revolt against convention. *Rêverie* was another favourite word; but Stendhal's *rêverie* was a sign of vitality which had nothing in common with Rousseau's and Flaubert's.

Stendhal's reliance on the verb and his extremely skilful use of short sentences give his prose its lightness and mobility. It is admirably designed to express sharp contrasts and sudden changes of mood, but here his practice differs from Constant's:

> Julien atteignit un tel degré de perfection dans ce genre d'éloquence, qui a remplacé la rapidité d'action de l'empire, qu'il finit par s'ennuyer lui-même par le son de ses paroles.
>
> [Julien reached such a pitch of perfection in this sort of eloquence, which replaced the rapidity of action of the Empire, that he ended by boring himself with the sound of his own words.]

Instead of relying like Constant on the eighteenth-century antithesis, Stendhal prefers the sudden, violent juxtaposition. The process is organic and interior. When he writes:

> Dès qu'on déplaisait à Mlle de La Mole, elle savait punir par une plaisanterie si measurée, si bien choisie, si convenable en apparence, lancée si à propos, que la blessure croissait à chaque instant, plus on y réfléchissait.
>
> [Whenever anyone earned Mademoiselle de La Mole's displeasure, she knew how to punish him by a witticism so calculated, so well chosen, apparently so harmless, so aptly

> launched, that the wound it left deepened the more he thought of it.]

there is a contrast between the quietness and measure of the means used and the damage done. The wound is an internal one. We have a sense of the blood slowly seeping through the victim's clothing, and when we come to "plus on y réfléchissait" we feel him suddenly crumple up. I think that we can say that the effect of sentences like these is that of an underwater explosion.

4

With the nineteenth century proper we are on debatable ground. Admirers of Flaubert in this country are inclined to grow warm if anyone lays hands on the Master. The value of criticism naturally depends on the grounds on which it is made. I can see no excuse for the sort of attack which M. Sartre makes in *Situations II,* but there are undoubtedly grounds on which Flaubert can be legitimately criticized. A start was made nearly thirty years ago when Jacques Rivière wrote in the *Nouvelle Revue Française:*

> From Stendhal onwards, there sets in a continuous degradation of our ancient, inveterate faculty of understanding and rendering feeling. Flaubert represents the moment at which the evil becomes sensible and alarming. I do not mean that *Madame Bovary* and *L'Education sentimentale* show no knowledge of the human heart; but neither of them reveals the slightest sign of a direct view into its complexity; neither carries us a step further in our knowledge of it or gives us a frontal view of fresh aspects. There is in the writer a certain heaviness of intelligence in relation to sensibility; it follows his sensibility badly; it no longer unravels it; and it can no longer penetrate into its caprices or its nuances.[20]

This essay has, unfortunately, only recently been reprinted and it has not had the impact which it should have done. Whether

[20] "Marcel Proust et la Tradition Classique" (February 1920), p. 194. Reprinted in *Nouvelles études* (Paris, 1947), pp. 149–56.

we agree entirely with Rivière or not, it must be recognized that his criticism of Flaubert is a serious one which cannot be disregarded by admirers of that novelist. The strength of Rivière's case lies in the fact that he begins in the right place. For if we believe that after Stendhal something went wrong with the French novel, it is not sufficient to point out weaknesses in the work of individual novelists. We must try to show that, as Rivière and M. Henriot suggest, the French language itself had begun to decay. The implications of this view are very far-reaching and they are by no means confined to Flaubert. Now it does seem to me that compared with Constant and Stendhal, the language of Balzac and Flaubert reveals a fatal imprecision which can easily be illustrated:

> La longue habitude que nous avions l'un de l'autre, les circonstances variées que nous avions parcourues ensemble avaient attaché à chaque parole, presque à chaque geste, des souvenirs qui nous replaçaient tout à coup dans le passé, et nous remplissaient d'un attendrissement involontaire, comme les éclairs traversent la nuit sans la dissiper. (*Adolphe.*)
>
> . . . mais l'envie resta cachée dans le fond du cœur comme un germe de peste qui peut éclore et ravager une ville, si l'on ouvre le fatal ballot de laine où il est comprimé. (*La Cousine Bette.*)
>
> Son voyage à la Vaubyessard avait fait un trou dans sa vie, à la manière de ces grandes crevasses qu'un orage, en une seule nuit, creuse quelquefois dans les montagnes. (*Madame Bovary.*)
>
> [Accustomed to each other as we were over a long period, the various vicissitudes we had experienced together, caused every word, almost every gesture, to arouse memories which translated us into the past and filled us with an involuntary emotion, like lightning flashing through the night but not dispersing the general darkness.
>
> . . . but envy remained hidden in her secret heart, like the germ of a disease that is liable to break out and ravage a city if the fatal bale of wool in which it is hidden is ever opened.

Her journey to Vaubyessard had opened a yawning fissure in her life, a fissure that was like one of those great crevasses which a storm will sometimes make on a mountain-side in the course of one short night.]

There is nothing particularly arresting about Constant's image, but it has an obvious rightness. He is analysing the different factors in the attachment between Adolphe and Ellénore. The comparison between the "flashes of lightning" and the sudden movements of *attendrissement involontaire,* between physical night and emotional "night" has the effect of co-ordinating these different factors and fusing them into a single image. In Balzac and Flaubert the weaknesses are similar and spring from the same cause. The writers feel that the opening clause gives too faint an impression and needs reinforcing. Bette's "envy" becomes a "germ" which ravages her whole personality as though it were a town succumbing to a plague; and Emma's contact with the aristocratic world makes such a breach in her drab existence that it is compared with a huge natural cataclysm. In both cases there is a sense of strain as though the writers were using up their energies to overcome the weaknesses of their medium. In both cases the method used defeats their purpose; it disperses instead of concentrating emotion, blurs instead of clarifying the initial perception.

This is only part of a much larger problem. We are aware in Balzac of the same absence of "solidity" that Ezra Pound detected in Flaubert, but we are in a better position to appreciate the causes. Constant and Stendhal were successful because they preserved an organic connection with traditional French prose style and moulded their instrument to their needs. In poetry Baudelaire achieved something of the same sort by his adaptation of the alexandrine, but he was less successful than the novelists and far too many of the poetic clichés of the day found their way into his verse. With the later prose-writers, one feels, there was a definite breach with tradition. Although Balzac and Flaubert are alike in their weaknesses, they approached their main problems from different angles.

> We must admit once for all [writes M. Gilbert Mayer] that Balzac was content to write French as it was spoken. His style was not apart from exceptions that of an artist.[21]

This draws attention to an important distinction. Balzac is an exponent of what may broadly be described as the "natural" style and Flaubert of the "artistic" style. In an age which was remarkable for the absence of an accepted style, Balzac tried to recover "solidity" by basing his writing on the spoken word, while Flaubert's attempts to achieve the same end by artistry turned him into the greatest virtuoso of the century. I shall examine the language of both writers in greater detail in another place, but I want to comment briefly on Flaubert's virtuosity. Thibaudet has spoken of his debt to La Bruyère and to the eighteenth century. No one doubts that he learnt a great deal from both sources, but he does not seem to me to have assimilated and transformed these influences as Stendhal assimilated and transformed Rousseau and Laclos. On the contrary, what he learnt from them was a number of useful devices which he added to his repertoire. Proust once described his style as "ce grand *Trottoir Roulant* . . . au défilement continu, monotone, indéfini."[22] And he quoted a characteristic phrase from *L'Education sentimentale:*

> . . . la colline qui suivait à dorite le cours de la Seine peu à peu s'abaissa, et il en surgit une autre, plus proche, sur la rive opposée.

> [. . . the hilly ridge which followed the course of the Seine on the right grew gradually lower, and gave place to a second hill, nearer the water, on the opposite bank.]

It is scarcely possible to read a couple of pages from any of Flaubert's novels without coming across this peculiar mechanical movement which Proust well compared to a *trottoir roulant*. The

[21] *La Qualification affective dans les romans d'Honoré de Balzac* (Paris, 1940), p. 88.

[22] *Chroniques* (Paris, 1927), p. 194. "But we love those heavy materials that Flaubert's sentence lifts up and drops again with the intermittent noise of an excavator." (*Ibid.*, p. 204.)

point that I want to make here is that this artificial movement was a substitute for the natural movement of French prose and that it is the key to Flaubert's curious greatness and his strange weaknesses.[23]

It has been suggested that some of the failings of the nineteenth-century novel were due to the "decay" of the French language, but this needs some qualification. A language alternates between periods of growth and decay, but it must not be assumed that "decay" is purely negative in its effects. Balzac was thrown back on the spoken word and was driven into strange places to find words to express his particular vision of French life, but he certainly made valuable discoveries of the process. "A genuine artist like Flaubert," writes M. Charles Bruneau, "received from the hands of Balzac an instrument which was richer in possibilities than the language of *Obermann, Adolphe* or *Ourika,* or even of the *Chartreuse de Parme.*"[24] For in spite of the disabling limitations of his own sensibility, Balzac was responsible for opening up horizons which transformed the French novel. He not only provided Flaubert with an instrument which was richer in possibilities than that of any of his predecessors; he helped to forge the instrument which was used with incomparable effect by the greatest of his successors—Marcel Proust.

5

Flaubert's influence on later writers has been as potent and as pervasive as Baudelaire's. They have usually either borrowed and perfected his technical innovations or reacted strongly against his whole conception of the novel. In Proust, however, we find a combination of the two. His comment on the language of the Duchesse de Guermantes is a lucid statement of the problem which faced him as a novelist:

[23] One of the most striking examples of his virtuosity is the description of the forest of Fontainebleau in *l'Education sentimentale* where the verb changes its place in the sentence each time he mentions a different kind of tree. See Thibaudet's interesting analysis in his *Gustave Flauberi* (Paris, 1922), pp. 284–7.

[24] Ferdinand Brunot, *Histoire de la langue française des origines à nos jours,* T. XII, (*L'Epoque romantique* par Charles Bruneau) (Paris, 1948), p. 384.

> . . . it is difficult, when one is disturbed by the ideas of Kant and the nostalgia of Baudelaire, to write the exquisite French of Henri IV, so that the very purity of the Duchess's language was a sign of limitation showing that in her both intelligence and sensibility had remained closed to all the novelties.[25]

His problem was twofold. He had to rid the novel of Flaubert's mechanical syntax and restore traditional prose rhythms; and he had to devise a vocabulary—it was here that Balzac, whom he greatly admired, was of immense assistance—which was sufficiently delicate to register the new complexity which came into being during the second half of the nineteenth century.[26] Proust's own syntax was very original and highly personal, but M. Mouton is surely right in describing him as "un excellent disciple de l'ancienne rhétorique."[27] It is the "ancient rhetoric," as M. Mouton chooses to call it, which gives Proust's novel that "solidity" which was temporarily lost after Stendhal.

> One of the commonest aspects of Proust's style [writes M. Mouton] is this constant effort to find the word which will be more and more precise.[28]

When we compare Balzac's

> Cet esprit rétif, capricieux, indépendant, l'inexplicable sauvagerie de cette fille . . .

> [This stubborn, capricious, independent strain, and the inexplicable unsociableness of the girl . . .]

with Proust's picture of the sick man waiting for day

> . . . les yeux levés, l'oreille anxieuse, la narine rétive, le cœur battant . . .

[25] *Le Côté de Guermantes,* II, p. 171.

[26] Without Balzac he might possibly have found himself in a position not unlike the Duchesse de Guermantes with intelligence and sensibility "closed to all the novelties."

[27] *Le Style de Marcel Proust* (Collection "Mises au Point") (Paris, 1948), p. 151.

[28] *Ibid., loc. cit.*

[. . . my eyes staring upwards, my ears straining, my nostrils sniffing uneasily, and my heart beating . . .]

we perceive that Proust's language is capable of a far greater range of sense-perceptions than Balzac's and is at the same time far more precise. Instead of Balzac's heavy, muffled impression, Proust gives us a very sharp sensation of the *angoisse* of the patient lying in his bed at Combray. "He begins," remarks M. Mouton, "by what is most concrete, the eyes, then turns to the subtler senses, the hearing and the sense of smell. Finally, everything is summed up in a formula which symbolizes sensibility in general, *le cœur battant*, where this sensibility is entirely awakened for waiting."[29]

In other places Proust speaks of Swann's old age as

. . . cette vieillesse anormale, excessive, honteuse et méritée des célibataires . . .

[. . . that abnormal, excessive, scandalous senescence, meet only in a celibate . . .]

of rooms as having

. . . toute une vie secrète, invisible, surabondante et morale que l'atmosphère y tient en suspens . . .

[. . . a whole secret system of life, invisible, superabundant and profoundly moral, which their atmosphere holds in solution . . .]

of the difference between the sound of bells

. . . non pas le grelot profus et criard qui arrosait, qui étourdissait au passage de son bruit ferrugineux, intarissable et glacé, toute personne de la maison qui le déclanchait en entrant "sans sonner," mais le double tintement timide, ovale et doré de la clochette pour les etrangers.

[. . . not the large and noisy rattle which heralded and deafened as he approached with its ferruginous, interminable frozen sound any member of the household who had set it in

[29] *Ibid.*, pp. 148–9.

motion by coming in "without ringing," but the double peal —timid, oval, gilded—of the visitors' bell.]

There is no doubt that Proust used far too many adjectives in the early volumes of his novel, but in each of these examples we are aware of a constant effort to express highly complex impressions. His work is a reversal of the nineteenth-century novelists' use of words. Each of the epithets possesses a separate identity which relates it to what has gone before and what comes after it. In the description of Swann the first pair of adjectives conveys a psycho-physical impression and the second a moral judgment. In the second example *morale* gives us a shock of surprise. In the third he is extremely successful in distinguishing between the sound of the bells, and the influence of Symbolism is evident in the *ovale* which attempts, characteristically, to express one sense-perception in terms of another.

There has been a good deal of controversy about Proust's style. Rivière described it as a return to the French classical tradition,[30] while Mr. Edmund Wilson has called him "the first important novelist to apply the principles of Symbolism in fiction."[31] There is no conflict between the two views. Language can never stand still and there can be no such thing as a "return" to the style of an earlier age. There are certain properties which are native to all good prose. Proust did not escape the preciosity which was one of the chief failings of the Symbolists, but he did restore some of the classic virtues which had been lost in the nineteenth century and at the same time he combined them with innovations which have made him the most original prose-writer of the age. The nature of his achievment was very well expressed by Benjamin Crémieux when he called him "la fondateur du *classicisme impressionniste*."[32]

[30] *Art. cit.*

[31] *Axel's Castle* (London, 1931), p. 132. See also L. A. Bisson, "Marcel Proust in 1947," in *French Studies*, I, No. 3 (July 1947).

[32] *Du Côté de Marcel Proust* (Paris, 1929), p. 8.

# IV. What Is Character?

Virginia Woolf, "Mr. Bennett and Mrs. Brown," reprinted here by permission of Leonard Woolf and the Hogarth Press.

Nathalie Sarraute, "The Age of Suspicion," from *The Age of Suspicion*, reprinted here by permission of George Braziller, Inc. The footnotes have been numbered to run in series throughout the selection.

*The two answers to the question posed by the chapter title are polemical answers. Virginia Woolf sees herself and the younger writers of her time as "new" novelists, with new ways of capturing character which make the old "realistic" way of the Edwardians obsolete. For Nathalie Sarraute it is Virginia Woolf and her Georgians who are old and obsolete. She questions the validity of the very concept of character, as she seeks to present a theoretical justification for her own "new" kind of novel. In these essays the problem of formal realism is raised again, each time in a new context.*

## Virginia Woolf

### *Mr. Bennett and Mrs. Brown*

It seems to me possible, perhaps desirable, that I may be the only person in this room who has committed the folly of writing, trying to write, or failing to write, a novel. And when I ask myself, as your invitation to speak to you about modern fiction made me ask myself, what demon whispered in my ear and urged me to my doom, a little figure rose before me—the figure of a man, or of a woman, who said, "My name is Brown. Catch me if you can."

Most novelists have the same experience. Some Brown, Smith, or Jones comes before them and says in the most seductive and charming way in the world, "Come and catch me if you can." And so, led on by this will-o'-the-wisp, they flounder through volume after volume, spending the best years of their lives in the pursuit, and receiving for the most part very little cash in exchange. Few catch the phantom; most have to be content with a scrap of her dress or a wisp of her hair.

My belief that men and women write novels because they are lured on to create some character which has thus imposed itself upon them has the sanction of Mr. Arnold Bennett. In an article from which I will quote he says: "The foundation of good fiction is character-creating and nothing else. . . . Style counts; plot counts; originality of outlook counts. But none of these counts anything like so much as the convincingness of the characters. If the characters are real the novel will have a chance; if they are not, oblivion will be its portion. . . ." And he goes on to draw the conclusion that we have no young novelists of first-rate importance at the present moment, because they are unable to create characters that are real, true, and convincing.

These are the questions that I want with greater boldness than discretion to discuss tonight. I want to make out what we mean when we talk about "character" in fiction; to say something about the question of reality which Mr. Bennett raises; and to suggest some reasons why the younger novelists fail to create characters, if, as Mr. Bennett asserts, it is true that fail they do. This will lead me, I am well aware, to make some very sweeping and some very vague assertions. For the question is an extremely difficult one. Think how little we know about character—think how little we know about art. But, to make a clearance before I begin, I will suggest that we range Edwardians and Georgians into two camps; Mr. Wells, Mr. Bennett, and Mr. Galsworthy I will call the Edwardians; Mr. Forster, Mr. Lawrence, Mr. Strachey, Mr. Joyce, and Mr. Eliot I will call the Georgians. And if I speak in the first person, with intolerable egotism, I will ask you to excuse me. I do not want to attribute to the world at large the opinions of one solitary, ill-informed, and misguided individual.

My first assertion is one that I think you will grant—that every one in this room is a judge of character. Indeed it would be impossible to live for a year without disaster unless one practised character-reading and had some skill in the art. Our marriages, our friendships depend on it; our business largely depends on it; every day questions arise which can only be solved by its help. And now I will hazard a second assertion, which is more disputable perhaps, to the effect that on or about December 1910 human character changed.

I am not saying that one went out, as one might into a garden, and there saw that a rose had flowered, or that a hen had laid an egg. The change was not sudden and definite like that. But a change there was, nevertheless; and, since one must be arbitrary, let us date it about the year 1910. The first signs of it are recorded in the books of Samuel Butler, in *The Way of All Flesh* in particular; the plays of Bernard Shaw continue to record it. In life one can see the change, if I may use a homely illustration, in the character of one's cook. The Victorian cook lived like a leviathan in the lower depths, formidable, silent, obscure, inscrutable; the Georgian cook is a creature of sunshine and fresh air; in and out of the drawing-room, now to borrow *The Daily Herald,* now to ask advice about a hat. Do you ask for more solemn instances of the power of the human race to change? Read the *Agamemnon,* and see whether, in process of time, your sympathies are not almost entirely with Clytemnestra. Or consider the married life of the Carlyles, and bewail the waste, the futility, for him and for her, of the horrible domestic tradition which made it seemly for a woman of genius to spend her time chasing beetles, scouring saucepans, instead of writing books. All human relations have shifted—those between masters and servants, husbands and wives, parents and children. And when human relations change there is at the same time a change in religion, conduct, politics, and literature. Let us agree to place one of these changes about the year 1910.

I have said that people have to acquire a good deal of skill in character-reading if they are to live a single year of life without disaster. But it is the art of the young. In middle age and in old age the art is practised mostly for its uses, and friendships and other adventures and experiments in the art of reading character are seldom made. But novelists differ from the rest of the world because they do not cease to be interested in character when they have learnt enough about it for practical purposes. They go a step further; they feel that there is something permanently interesting in character in itself. When all the practical business of life has been discharged, there is something about people which continues to seem to them of overwhelming importance, in spite of the fact that it has no bearing whatever upon their happiness, comfort, or income. The study of character becomes to them an absorbing pursuit; to impart character an obsession. And this I find it very difficult to explain: what novelists mean when they talk about character, what the impulse is that urges them so powerfully every now and then to embody their view in writing.

So, if you will allow me, instead of analysing and abstracting, I will tell you a simple story which, however pointless, has the merit of being true, of a journey from Richmond to Waterloo, in the hope that I may show you what I mean by character in itself; that you may realise the different aspects it can wear; and the hideous perils that beset you directly you try to describe it in words.

One night some weeks ago, then, I was late for the train and jumped into the first carriage I came to. As I sat down I had the strange and uncomfortable feeling that I was interrupting a conversation between two people who were already sitting there. Not that they were young or happy. Far from it. They were both elderly, the woman over sixty, the man well over forty. They were sitting opposite each other, and the man, who had been leaning over and talking emphatically to judge by his attitude and the flush on his face, sat back and became silent. I had disturbed him, and he was annoyed. The elderly lady, however, whom I will call Mrs. Brown, seemed rather relieved. She was one of those clean, threadbare old ladies whose extreme tidiness—everything buttoned, fastened, tied together, mended and brushed up—suggests more extreme poverty than rags and dirt. There was something pinched about her—a look of suffering, of apprehension, and, in addition, she was extremely small. Her feet, in their clean little boots, scarcely touched the floor. I felt that she had nobody to support her; that she had to make up her mind for herself; that, having been deserted, or left a widow, years ago, she had led an anxious, harried life, bringing up an only son, perhaps, who, as likely as not, was by this time beginning to go to the bad. All this shot through my mind as I sat down, being uncomfortable, like most people, at travelling with fellow passengers unless I have somehow or other accounted for them. Then I looked at the man. He was no relation of Mrs. Brown's I felt sure; he was of a bigger, burlier, less refined type. He was a man of business I imagined, very likely a respectable corn-chandler from the North, dressed in good blue serge with a pocket-knife and a silk handkerchief, and a stout leather bag. Obviously, however, he had an unpleasant business to settle with Mrs. Brown; a secret, perhaps sinister business, which they did not intend to discuss in my presence.

"Yes, the Crofts have had very bad luck with their servants," Mr. Smith (as I will call him) said in a considering way, going back to some earlier topic, with a view to keeping up appearances.

"Ah, poor people," said Mrs. Brown, a trifle condescendingly. "My grandmother had a maid who came when she was fifteen and stayed till she was eighty" (this was said with a kind of hurt and aggressive pride to impress us both perhaps).

"One doesn't often come across that sort of thing nowadays," said Mr. Smith in conciliatory tones.

Then they were silent.

"It's odd they don't start a golf club there—I should have thought one of the young fellows would," said Mr. Smith, for the silence obviously made him uneasy.

Mrs. Brown hardly took the trouble to answer.

"What changes they're making in this part of the world," said Mr. Smith, looking out of the window, and looking furtively at me as he did so.

It was plain, from Mrs. Brown's silence, from the uneasy affability with which Mr. Smith spoke, that he had some power over her which he was exerting disagreeably. It might have been her son's downfall, or some painful episode in her past life, or her daughter's. Perhaps she was going to London to sign some document to make over some property. Obviously against her will she was in Mr. Smith's hands. I was beginning to feel a great deal of pity for her, when she said, suddenly and inconsequently,

"Can you tell me if an oak-tree dies when the leaves have been eaten for two years in succession by caterpillars?"

She spoke quite brightly, and rather precisely, in a cultivated inquisitive voice.

Mr. Smith was startled, but relieved to have a safe topic of conversation given him. He told her a great deal very quickly about plagues of insects. He told her that he had a brother who kept a fruit farm in Kent. He told her what fruit farmers do every year in Kent, and so on, and so on. While he talked a very odd thing happened. Mrs. Brown took out her little white handkerchief and began to dab her eyes. She was crying. But she went on listening quite composedly to what he was saying, and he went on talking, a little louder, a little angrily, as if he had seen her cry often before; as if it were a painful habit. At last it got on his nerves. He stopped abruptly, looked out of the window, then leant towards her as he had been doing when I got in, and said in a bullying menacing way, as if he would not stand any more nonsense,

"So about that matter we were discussing. It'll be all right? George will be there on Tuesday?"

"We shan't be late," said Mrs. Brown, gathering herself together with superb dignity.

Mr. Smith said nothing. He got up, buttoned his coat, reached his bag down, and jumped out of the train before it had stopped at Clapham Junction. He had got what he wanted, but he was ashamed of himself; he was glad to get out of the old lady's sight.

Mrs. Brown and I were left alone together. She sat in her corner opposite, very clean, very small, rather queer, and suffering intensely. The impression she made was overwhelming. It came pouring out like a draught, like a smell of burning. What was it composed of—that overwhelming and peculiar impression? Myriads of irrelevant and incongruous ideas crowd into one's head on such occasions; one sees the person, one sees Mrs. Brown, in the centre of all sorts of different scenes. I thought of her in a seaside house, among queer ornaments: sea-urchins, models of ships in glass cases. Her husband's medals were on the mantelpiece. She popped in and out of the room, perching on the edges of chairs, picking meals out of saucers, indulging in long, silent stares. The caterpillars and the oak-trees seemed to imply all that. And then, into this fantastic and secluded life, in broke Mr. Smith. I saw him blowing in, so to speak, on a windy day. He banged, he slammed. His dripping umbrella made a pool in the hall. They sat closeted together.

And then Mrs. Brown faced the dreadful revelation. She took her heroic decision. Early, before dawn, she packed her bag and carried it herself to the station. She would not let Smith touch it. She was wounded in her pride, unmoored from her anchorage; she came of gentlefolks who kept servants—but details could wait. The important thing was to realise her character, to steep oneself in her atmosphere. I had no time to explain why I felt it somewhat tragic, heroic, yet with a dash of the flighty, and fantastic, before the train stopped, and I watched her disappear, carrying her bag, into the vast blazing station. She looked very small, very tenacious; at once very frail and very heroic. And I have never seen her again, and I shall never know what became of her.

The story ends without any point to it. But I have not told you this anecdote to illustrate either my own ingenuity or the pleasure of travelling from Richmond to Waterloo. What I want you to see in it is this. Here is a character imposing itself upon another person. Here is Mrs. Brown making someone begin almost automatically to write a novel about her. I believe that all novels begin with an old lady in the corner opposite. I believe that all novels, that is to say, deal with character, and that it is to express character—not to preach doctrines, sing songs, or celebrate the glories of the British Empire, that the form of the novel, so clumsy, verbose, and undramatic, so rich, elastic, and alive, has been evolved. To express character, I have said; but you will at once reflect that the very widest interpretation can be put upon those words. For example, old Mrs. Brown's character will strike you very differently according to the age and country in which you happen to be born. It would be easy enough to write three different versions of the incident in the train, an English, a French, and a Russian. The English writer would make the old lady into a "character"; he would bring out her oddities and mannerisms; her buttons and wrinkles; her ribbons and warts. Her personality would dominate the book. A French writer would rub out all that; he would sacrifice the individual Mrs. Brown to give a more general view of human nature; to make a more abstract, proportioned, and harmonious whole. The Russian would pierce through the flesh; would reveal the soul—the soul alone wandering out into the Waterloo Road, asking of life some tremendous question which would sound on and on in our ears after the book was finished. And then besides age and country there is the writer's temperament to be considered. You see one thing in character, and I another. You say it means this, and I that. And when it comes to writing each makes a further selection on principles of his own. Thus Mrs. Brown can be treated in an infinite variety of ways, according to the age, country, and temperament of the writer.

But now I must recall what Mr. Arnold Bennett says. He

says that it is only if the characters are real that the novel has any chance of surviving. Otherwise, die it must. But, I ask myself, what is reality? And who are the judges of reality? A character may be real to Mr. Bennett and quite unreal to me. For instance, in this article he says that Dr. Watson in *Sherlock Holmes* is real to him: to me Dr. Watson is a sack stuffed with straw, a dummy, a figure of fun. And so it is with character after character—in book after book. There is nothing that people differ about more than the reality of characters, especially in contemporary books. But if you take a larger view I think that Mr. Bennett is perfectly right. If, that is, you think of the novels which seem to you great novels—*War and Peace, Vanity Fair, Tristram Shandy, Madame Bovary, Pride and Prejudice, The Mayor of Casterbridge, Villette*—if you think of these books, you do at once think of some character who has seemed to you so real (I do not by that mean so lifelike) that it has the power to make you think not merely of it itself, but of all sorts of things through its eyes—of religion, of love, of war, of peace, of family life, of balls in county towns, of sunsets, moonrises, the immortality of the soul. There is hardly any subject of human experience that is left out of *War and Peace* it seems to me. And in all these novels all these great novelists have brought us to see whatever they wish us to see through some character. Otherwise, they would not be novelists; but poets, historians, or pamphleteers.

But now let us examine what Mr. Bennett went on to say—he said that there was no great novelist among the Georgian writers because they cannot create characters who are real, true, and convincing. And there I cannot agree. There are reasons, excuses, possibilities which I think put a different colour upon the case. It seems so to me at least, but I am well aware that this is a matter about which I am likely to be prejudiced, sanguine, and near-sighted. I will put my view before you in the hope that you will make it impartial, judicial, and broad-minded. Why, then, is it so hard for novelists at present to create characters which seem real, not only to Mr. Bennett, but to the world at large? Why, when October comes round, do the publishers always fail to supply us with a masterpiece?

Surely one reason is that the men and women who began

writing novels in 1910 or thereabouts had this great difficulty to face—that there was no English novelist living from whom they could learn their business. Mr. Conrad is a Pole; which sets him apart, and makes him, however admirable, not very helpful. Mr. Hardy has written no novel since 1895. The most prominent and successful novelists in the year 1910 were, I suppose, Mr. Wells, Mr. Bennett, and Mr. Galsworthy. Now it seems to me that to go to these men and ask them to teach you how to write a novel—how to create characters that are real—is precisely like going to a bootmaker and asking him to teach you how to make a watch. Do not let me give you the impression that I do not admire and enjoy their books. They seem to me of great value, and indeed of great necessity. There are seasons when it is more important to have boots than to have watches. To drop metaphor, I think that after the creative activity of the Victorian age it was quite necessary not only for literature but for life, that someone should write the books that Mr. Wells, Mr. Bennett, and Mr. Galsworthy have written. Yet what odd books they are! Sometimes I wonder if we are right to call them books at all. For they leave one with so strange a feeling of incompleteness and dissatisfaction. In order to complete them it seems necessary to do something—to join a society, or more desperately, to write a cheque. That done, the restlessness is laid, the book finished: it can be put upon the shelf, and need never be read again. But with the work of other novelists it is different. *Tristram Shandy* or *Pride and Prejudice* is complete in itself; it is self-contained; it leaves one with no desire to do anything, except indeed to read the book again, and to understand it better. The difference perhaps is that both Sterne and Jane Austen were interested in things in themselves; in character in itself; in the book in itself. Therefore everything was inside the book, nothing outside. But the Edwardians were never interested in character in itself; or in the book in itself. They were interested in something outside. Their books, then, were incomplete as books, and required that the reader should finish them, actively and practically, for himself.

Perhaps we can make this clearer if we take the liberty of imagining a little party in the railway carriage—Mr. Wells, Mr. Galsworthy, Mr. Bennett are travelling to Waterloo with Mrs.

Brown. Mrs. Brown, I have said, was poorly dressed and very small. She had an anxious, harassed look. I doubt whether she was what you call an educated woman. Seizing upon all these symptoms of the unsatisfactory condition of our primary schools with a rapidity to which I can do no justice, Mr. Wells would instantly project upon the windowpane a vision of a better, breezier, jollier, happier, more adventurous and gallant world, where these musty railway carriages and fusty old women do not exist; where miraculous barges bring tropical fruit to Camberwell by eight o'clock in the morning; where there are public nurseries, fountains, and libraries, dining-rooms, drawing-rooms, and marriages; where every citizen is generous and candid, manly and magnificent, and rather like Mr. Wells himself. But nobody is in the least like Mrs. Brown. There are no Mrs. Browns in Utopia. Indeed I do not think that Mr. Wells, in his passion to make her what she ought to be, would waste a thought upon her as she is. And what would Mr. Galsworthy see? Can we doubt that the walls of Doulton's factory would take his fancy? There are women in that factory who make twenty-five dozen earthenware pots every day. There are mothers in the Mile End Road who depend upon the farthings which those women earn. But there are employers in Surrey who are even now smoking rich cigars while the nightingale sings. Burning with indignation, stuffed with information, arraigning civilisation, Mr. Galsworthy would only see in Mrs. Brown a pot broken on the wheel and thrown into the corner.

Mr. Bennett, alone of the Edwardians, would keep his eyes in the carriage. He, indeed, would observe every detail with immense care. He would notice the advertisements; the pictures of Swanage and Portsmouth; the way in which the cushion bulged between the buttons; how Mrs. Brown wore a brooch which had cost three-and-ten-three at Whitworth's bazaar; and had mended both gloves—indeed the thumb of the left-hand glove had been replaced. And he would observe, at length, how this was the non-stop train from Windsor which calls at Richmond for the convenience of middleclass residents, who can afford to go to the theatre but have not reached the social rank which can afford motor-cars, though it is true, there are occasions (he would tell us what), when they hire them from a company (he would tell us which).

And so he would gradually sidle sedately towards Mrs. Brown and would remark how she had been left a little copyhold, not freehold, property at Datchet, which, however, was mortgaged to Mr. Bungay the solicitor—but why should I presume to invent Mr. Bennett? Does not Mr. Bennett write novels himself? I will open the first book that chance puts in my way—*Hilda Lessways*. Let us see how he makes us feel that Hilda is real, true, and convincing, as a novelist should. She shut the door in a soft, controlled way, which showed the constraint of her relations with her mother. She was fond of reading *Maud;* she was endowed with the power to feel intensely. So far, so good; in his leisurely, sure-footed way Mr. Bennett is trying in these first pages, where every touch is important, to show us the kind of girl she was.

But then he begins to describe, not Hilda Lessways, but the view from her bedroom window, the excuse being that Mr. Skellorn, the man who collects rents, is coming along that way. Mr. Bennett proceeds:

"The bailiwick of Turnhill lay behind her; and all the murky district of the Five Towns, of which Turnhill is the northern outpost, lay to the south. At the foot of Chatterley Wood the canal wound in large curves on its way towards the undefiled plains of Cheshire and the sea. On the canal-side, exactly opposite to Hilda's window, was a flour-mill, that sometimes made nearly as much smoke as the kilns and the chimneys closing the prospect on either hand. From the flour-mill a bricked path, which separated a considerable row of new cottages from their appurtenant gardens, led straight into Lessways Street, in front of Mrs. Lessways' house. By this path Mr. Skellorn should have arrived, for he inhabited the farthest of the cottages."

One line of insight would have done more than all those lines of description; but let them pass as the necessary drudgery of the novelist. And now—where is Hilda? Alas. Hilda is still looking out of the window. Passionate and dissatisfied as she was, she was a girl with an eye for houses. She often compared this old Mr. Skellorn with the villas she saw from her bedroom window. Therefore the villas must be described. Mr. Bennett proceeds:

"The row was called Freehold Villas: a consciously proud name in a district where much of the land was copyhold and could only change owners subject to the payment of 'fines,' and to their feudal consent of a 'court' presided over by the agent of a lord of the manor. Most of the dwellings were owned by their occupiers, who, each an absolute monarch of the soil, niggled in his sooty garden of an evening amid the flutter of drying shirts and towels. Freehold Villas symbolised the final triumph of Victorian economics, the apotheosis of the prudent and industrious artisan. It corresponded with a Building Society Secretary's dream of paradise. And indeed it was a very real achievement. Nevertheless, Hilda's irrational contempt would not admit this."

Heaven be praised, we cry! At last we are coming to Hilda herself. But not so fast. Hilda may have been this, that, and the other; but Hilda not only looked at houses, and thought of houses; Hilda lived in a house. And what sort of a house did Hilda live in? Mr. Bennett proceeds:

"It was one of the two middle houses of a detached terrace of four houses built by her grandfather Lessways, the teapot manufacturer; it was the chief of the four, obviously the habitation of the proprietor of the terrace. One of the corner houses comprised a grocer's shop, and this house had been robbed of its just proportion of garden so that the seigneurial garden-plot might be triflingly larger than the other. The terrace was not a terrace of cottages, but of houses rated at from twenty-six to thirty-six pounds a year: beyond the means of artisans and petty insurance agents and rent-collectors. And further, it was well built, generously built; and its architecture, though debased, showed some faint traces of Georgian amenity. It was admittedly the best row of houses in the newly settled quarter of the town. In coming to it out of Freehold Villas Mr. Skellorn obviously came to something superior, wider, more liberal. Suddenly Hilda heard her mother's voice. . . ."

But we cannot hear her mother's voice, or Hilda's voice; we can only hear Mr. Bennett's voice telling us facts about rents and freeholds and copyholds and fines. What can Mr. Bennett be about? I have formed my own opinion of what Mr. Bennett is about—he is trying to make us imagine for him; he is trying to hypnotise us into the belief that, because he has made a house, there must be a person living there. With all his powers of observation, which are marvelous, with all his sympathy and humanity, which are great, Mr. Bennett has never once looked at Mrs. Brown in her corner. There she sits in the corner of the carriage—that carriage which is travelling, not from Richmond to Waterloo, but from one age of English literature to the next, for Mrs. Brown is eternal, Mrs. Brown is human nature, Mrs. Brown changes only on the surface, it is the novelists who get in and out—there she sits and not one of the Edwardian writers has so much as looked at her. They have looked very powerfully, searchingly, and sympathetically out of the window; at factories, at Utopias, even at the decoration and upholstery of the carriage; but never at her, never at life, never at human nature. And so they have developed a technique of novel writing which suits their purpose; they have made tools and established conventions which do their business. But those tools are not our tools, and that business is not our business. For us those conventions are ruin, those tools are death.

You may well complain of the vagueness of my language. What is a convention, a tool, you may ask, and what do you mean by saying that Mr. Bennett's and Mr. Wells' and Mr. Galsworthy's conventions are the wrong conventions for the Georgians? The question is difficult: I will attempt a short cut. A convention in writing is not much different from a convention in manners. Both in life and in literature it is necessary to have some means of bridging the gulf between the hostess and her unknown guest on the one hand, the writer and his unknown reader on the other. The hostess bethinks her of the weather, for generations of hostesses have established the fact that this is a subject of universal interest in which we all believe. She begins by saying that we are having a wretched May, and, having thus got into touch with her unknown guest, proceeds to matters of greater interest. So it is in literature. The writer must get into touch with his reader by putting before him something which he recognises, which therefore stimulates his imagination, and makes him willing to cooperate in the far more difficult business of intimacy. And it is of the highest importance that this common meeting-place should be reached easily, almost instinctively, in the dark, with one's eyes shut. Here is Mr. Bennett making use of this common ground in the passage which I have quoted. The problem before him was to make us believe in the reality of Hilda Lessways. So he began, being an Edwardian, by describing accurately and minutely the sort of house Hilda lived in, and the sort of house she saw from the window. House property was the common ground from which the Edwardians found it easy to proceed to intimacy. Indirect as it seems to us, the convention worked admirably, and thousands of Hilda Lessways were launched upon the world by this means. For that age and generation, the convention was a good one.

But now, if you will allow me to pull my own ancedote to pieces, you will see how keenly I felt the lack of a convention, and how serious a matter it is when the tools of one generation are useless for the next. The incident had made a great impression on me. But how was I to transmit it to you? All I could do was to report as accurately as I could what was said, to describe in detail what was worn, to say, despairingly, that all sorts of scenes rushed into my mind, to proceed to tumble them out pell-mell, and to describe this vivid, this overmastering impression by likening it to a draught or a smell of burning. To tell you the truth, I was also strongly tempted to manufacture a three-volume novel about the old lady's son, and his adventures crossing the Atlantic, and her daughter, and how she kept a milliner's shop in Westminster, the past life of Smith himself, and his house at Sheffield, though such stories seem to me the most dreary, irrelevant, and humbugging affairs in the world.

But if I had done that I should have escaped the appalling effort of saying what I meant. And to have got at what I meant I should have had to go back and back and back; to experiment with one thing and another; to try this sentence and that, referring each word to my vision, matching it as exactly as possible, and knowing that somehow I had to find a common ground between us, a convention which would not seem to you too odd, unreal, and far-fetched to believe in. I admit that I shirked that arduous undertaking. I let my Mrs. Brown slip through my fingers. I have told you nothing whatever about her. But that is partly the great Edwardians' fault. I asked them—they are my elders and betters—How shall I begin to describe this woman's character? And they said, "Begin by saying that her father kept a shop in Harrogate. Ascertain the rent. Ascertain the wages of shop assistants in the year 1878. Discover what her mother died of. Describe cancer. Describe calico. Describe—" But I cried, "Stop! Stop!" And I regret to say that I threw that ugly, that clumsy, that incongruous tool out of the window, for I knew that if I began describing the cancer and the calico, my Mrs. Brown, that vision to which I cling though I know no way of imparting it to you, would have been dulled and tarnished and vanished for ever.

That is what I mean by saying that the Edwardian tools are the wrong ones for us to use. They have laid an enormous stress upon the fabric of things. They have given us a house in the hope that we may be able to deduce the human beings who live there. To give them their due, they have made that house much better, worth living in. But if you hold that novels are in the first place about people, and only in the second about the houses they live in, that is the wrong way to set about it. Therefore, you see, the Georgian writer had to begin by throwing away the method that was in use at the moment. He was left alone there facing Mrs. Brown without any method of conveying her to the reader. But that is inaccurate. A writer is never alone. There is always the public with him—if not on the same seat, at least in the compartment next door. Now the public is a strange travelling companion. In England it is a very suggestible and docile creature, which, once you get it to attend, will believe implicitly what it is told for a certain number of years. If you say to the public with sufficient conviction, "All women have tails, and all men humps," it will actually learn to see women with tails and men with humps, and will think it very revolutionary and probably improper if you say, "Nonsense. Monkeys have tails and camels humps. But men and women have brains, and they have hearts; they think and they feel,"—that will seem to it a bad joke, and an improper one into the bargain.

But to return. Here is the British public sitting by the writer's side and saying in its vast and unanimous way, "Old women have houses. They have fathers. They have incomes. They have servants. They have hot water bottles. That is how we know that they are old women. Mr. Wells and Mr. Bennett and Mr. Galsworthy have always taught us that this is the way to recognise them. But now with your Mrs. Brown—how are we to believe in her? We do not even know whether her villa was called Albert or Balmoral; what she paid for her gloves; or whether her mother died of cancer or of consumption. How can she be alive? No; she is a mere figment of your imagination."

And old women of course ought to be made of freehold villas and copyhold estates, not of imagination.

The Georgian novelist, therefore, was in an awkward predicament. There was Mrs. Brown protesting that she was different, quite different, from what people made out, and luring the novelist to her rescue by the most fascinating if fleeting glimpse of her charms; there were the Edwardians handing out tools appropriate to house building and house breaking; and there was the British public asseverating that they must see the hot water bottle first. Meanwhile the train was rushing to that station where we must all get out.

Such, I think, was the predicament in which the young Georgians found themselves about the year 1910. Many of them—I am thinking of Mr. Forster and Mr. Lawrence in particular—spoilt their early work because, instead of throwing away those tools, they tried to use them. They tried to compromise. They tried to combine their own direct sense of the oddity and significance of some character with Mr. Galsworthy's knowledge of the Factory Acts, and Mr. Bennett's knowledge of the Five Towns. They tried it, but they had too keen, too overpowering a sense of Mrs. Brown and her peculiarities to go on trying it much longer. Something had to be done. At whatever cost of life, limb, and damage to valuable property Mrs. Brown must be rescued, expressed, and set in her high relations to the world before the train stopped and she disappeared for ever. And so the smashing and the crashing began. Thus it is that we hear all round us, in poems and novels and biographies, even in newspaper articles and essays, the sound of breaking and falling, crashing and destruction. It is the prevailing sound of the Georgian age—rather a melancholy one if you think what melodious days there have been in the past, if you think of Shakespeare and Milton and Keats or even of Jane Austen and Thackeray and Dickens; if you think of the language, and the heights to which it can soar when free, and see the same eagle captive, bald, and croaking.

In view of these facts—with these sounds in my ears and these fancies in my brain—I am not going to deny that Mr. Bennett has some reason when he complains that our Georgian writers are unable to make us believe that our characters are real. I am forced to agree that they do not pour out three immortal masterpieces with Victorian regularity every autumn. But instead of being gloomy, I am sanguine. For this state of things is, I think, inevitable whenever from hoar old age or callow youth the convention ceases to be a means of communication between writer and reader, and becomes instead an obstacle and an impediment. At the present moment we are suffering, not from decay, but from having no code of manners which writers and readers accept as a prelude to the more exciting intercourse of friendship. The literary convention of the time is so artificial—you have to talk about the weather and nothing but the weather throughout the entire visit—that, naturally, the feeble are tempted to outrage, and the strong are led to destroy the very foundations and rules of literary society. Signs of this are everywhere apparent. Grammar is violated; syntax disintegrated; as a boy staying with an aunt for the weekend rolls in the geranium bed out of sheer desperation as the solemnities of the sabbath wear on. The more adult writers do not, of course, indulge in such wanton exhibitions of spleen. Their sincerity is desperate, and their courage tremendous; it is only that they do not know which to use, a fork or their fingers. Thus, if you read Mr. Joyce and Mr. Eliot you will be struck by the indecency of the one, and the obscurity of the other. Mr. Joyce's indecency in *Ulysses* seems to me the conscious and calculated indecency of a desperate man who feels that in order to breathe he must break the windows. At moments, when the window is broken, he is magnificent. But what a waste of energy! And, after all, how dull indecency is, when it is not the overflowing of a superabundant energy or savagery, but the determined and public spirited act of a man who needs fresh air! Again, with the obscurity of Mr. Eliot. I think that Mr. Eliot has written some of the loveliest single lines in modern poetry. But how intolerant he is of the old usages and politenesses of society—respect for the weak, consideration for the dull! As I sun myself upon the intense and ravishing beauty of one of his lines, and reflect that I must make a dizzy and dangerous leap to the next, and so on from line to line, like an acrobat flying precariously from bar to bar, I cry out, I confess, for the old decorums, and envy the indolence of my ancestors who, instead of spinning madly through mid-air, dreamt quietly in the shade with a book. Again, in Mr. Strachey's books, *Eminent Victorians* and *Queen Victoria,* the effort and strain of writing against the grain and current of the times is visible too. It is much less visible, of course, for not only is he dealing with facts, which are stubborn things, but he has fabricated, chiefly from eighteenth-century material, a very discreet code of manners of his own, which allows him to sit at table with the highest in the land and to say a great many things under cover of that exquisite apparel which, had they gone naked, would have been chased by the men-servants from the room. Still, if you compare *Eminent Victorians* with some of Lord Macaulay's essays, though you will feel that Lord Macaulay is always wrong, and Mr. Strachey always right, you will also feel a body, a sweep, a richness in Lord Macaulay's essays which show that his age was behind him; all his strength went straight into his work; none was used for purposes of concealment or of conversion. But Mr. Strachey has had to open our eyes before he made us see; he has had to search out and saw together a very artful manner of speech; and the effort, beautifully though it is concealed, has robbed his work of some of the force that should have gone into it, and limited his scope.

For these reasons, then, we must reconcile ourselves to a season of failures and fragments. We must reflect that where so much strength is spent on finding a way of telling the truth the truth itself is bound to reach us in rather an exhausted and chaotic condition. Ulysses, Queen Victoria, Mr. Prufrock—to give Mrs. Brown some of the names she has made famous lately—is a little pale and dishevelled by the time her rescuers reach her. And it is the sound of their axes that we hear—a vigorous and stimulating sound in my ears—unless of course you wish to sleep, when, in the bounty of his concern, Providence has provided a host of writers anxious and able to satisfy your needs.

Thus I have tried, at tedious length, I fear, to answer some of the questions which I began by asking. I have given an account of some of the difficulties which in my view beset the Georgian writer in all his forms. I have sought to excuse him. May I end by venturing to remind you of the duties and responsibilities that are yours as partners in this business of writing books, as companions in the railway carriage, as fellow travellers with Mrs. Brown? For she is just as visible to you who remain silent as to us who tell stories about her. In the course of your daily life this past week you have had far stranger and more interesting experiences than the one I have tried to describe. You have overheard scraps of talk that filled you with amazement. You have gone to bed at night bewildered by the complexity of your feelings. In one day thousands of ideas have coursed through your brains; thousands of emotions have met, collided, and disappeared in astonishing disorder. Nevertheless, you allow the writers to palm off upon you a version of all this, an image of Mrs. Brown, which has no likeness to that surprising apparition whatsoever. In your modesty you seem to consider that writers are of different blood and bone from yourselves; that they know more of Mrs. Brown than you do. Never was there a more fatal mistake. It is this division between reader and writer, this humility on your part, these professional airs and graces on ours, that corrupt and emasculate the books which should be the healthy offspring of a close and equal alliance between us. Hence spring those sleek, smooth novels, those portentous and ridiculous biographies, that milk and watery criticism, those poems melodiously celebrating the innocence of roses and sheep which pass so plausibly for literature at the present time.

Your part is to insist that writers shall come down off their plinths and pedestals, and describe beautifully if possible, truthfully at any rate, our Mrs. Brown. You should insist that she is an old lady of unlimited capacity and infinite variety; capable of appearing in any place; wearing any dress; saying anything and doing heaven knows what. But the things she says and the things she does and her eyes and her nose and her speech and her silence have an overwhelming fascination, for she is, of course, the spirit we live by, life itself.

But do not expect just at present a complete and satisfactory presentment of her. Tolerate the spasmodic, the obscure, the fragmentary, the failure. Your help is invoked in a good cause. For I will make one final and surpassingly rash prediction—we are trembling on the verge of one of the great ages of English literature. But it can only be reached if we are determined never, never to desert Mrs. Brown.

## Nathalie Sarraute

### *The Age of Suspicion*

Although critics may prefer, like good pedagogues, to appear not to notice anything and, on the other hand, seize every opportunity to proclaim, as though announcing a fundamental truth, that the novel, unless they are very much mistaken, is and always will be, first and foremost, "a story in which characters move and have their being," that no novelist is worthy of the name unless he is able to "believe in" his characters, which is what makes it possible for him to "infuse life" into them and give them "fictional relief"; although they may continue to lavish praise on novelists who, like Balzac or Flaubert, succeed in making their hero "stand out," thus adding one more "unforgettable" figure to the unforgettable figures with which so many famous novelists have already peopled our world; although they may dangle before young writers the mirage of exquisite rewards that are supposed to await those whose faith is greatest: that moment, familiar to a few "real novelists," when the character, by virtue of the intensity of the author's belief and interest in him, actuated by some mysterious fluid, as in table-rapping, suddenly starts to move of his own momentum, and takes in tow the delighted creator who has only to let himself be guided, in his turn, by his creature; finally, however sternly critics may add threat to promise, warning novelists that if they are not vigilant, their best-armed rival, the cinema, will one day wrest the scepter from their unworthy hands—it is of no avail. Neither reproaches nor encouragements are able to revive a faith that is waning.

And, according to all appearances, not only has the novelist practically ceased to believe in his characters, but the reader, too, is unable to believe in them; with the result that the characters, having lost the twofold support that the novelist's and the reader's faith afforded them, and which permitted them to stand upright with the burden of the entire story resting on their broad shoulders, may now be seen to vacillate and fall apart.

Since the happy days of Eugénie Grandet when, at the height of his power, the character occupied the place of honor between reader and novelist, the object of their common devotion, like the Saints between the donors in primitive paintings, he has continued to lose, one after the other, his attributes and prerogatives.

At that time he was richly endowed with every asset, the recipient of every attention; he lacked for nothing, from the silver buckles on his breeches to the veined wart on the end of his nose. Since then he has lost everything: his ancestors, his carefully built house, filled from cellar to garret with a variety of objects, down to the tiniest gewgaw, his sources of income and his estates, his clothes, his body, his face. Particularly, however, has he lost that most precious of all possessions, his personality—which belonged to him alone—and frequently, even his name.

Today, a constantly rising tide has been flooding us with literary works that still claim to be novels and in which a being devoid of outline, indefinable, intangible and invisible, an anonymous, "I," who is at once all and nothing, and who as often as not is but the reflection of the author himself, has usurped the rôle of the hero, occupying the place of honor. The other characters, being deprived of their own existence, are reduced to the status of visions, dreams, nightmares, illusions, reflections, quiddities or dependents of this all-powerful "I."

Our minds might be set at rest, if we could impute this method of procedure to an egocentricity peculiar to adolescence, to the timidity or inexperience of the beginner. As it happens, however, this youthful malady has attacked some of the most important works of our time (from *Remembrance of Things Past* and *Marshlands,* to the *Miracle de la Rose,* not to mention the *Notebook of Malte Laurids Brigge, Journey to the End of the Night* and *Nausea*); in other words, works in which the authors have given immediate proof of very evident mastery and rare forcefulness.

What is revealed, in fact, by the present evolution of the character in fiction is just the opposite of regression to an infantile state.

It shows, on the part of both author and reader, an unusually sophisticated state of mind. For not only are they both wary of the character, but through him, they are wary of each other. He had been their meeting ground, the solid base from which they could take off in a common effort toward new experiments and new discoveries. He has now become the converging point of their mutual distrust, the devastated ground on which they confront each other. And if we examine his present situation, we are tempted to conclude that it furnishes a perfect illustration of Stendhal's statement that "the genius of suspicion has appeared on the scene." We have now entered upon an age of suspicion.

To begin with, today's reader is suspicious of what the author's imagination has to offer him. "There is nobody left," Jacques Tournier complains, "who is willing to admit that he invents. The only thing that matters is the document, which must be precise, dated, proven, authentic. Works of the imagination are banned, because they are invented . . . (The public), in order to believe what it is told, must be convinced that it is not being 'taken in.' All that counts now is the 'true fact' . . ."[1]

But Tournier should not be so bitter. This predilection for "true facts" which, at heart, we all share, does not indicate a timorous, sedate mind, forever ready to crush under the weight of "sound reality" all daring experiment, all impulse toward evasion. On the contrary, we must do the reader the justice of admitting that he needs a little coaxing to follow the writer along new paths. He has never really balked before the perspective of effort, and when he agreed to examine with minute attention each detail of Père Grandet's dress and each object in his house, to evaluate his poplar trees and vineyards and supervise his stock-market transactions, it was not because of a liking for sound reality, nor from a need to cuddle down snugly in the nest of a familiar world, whose contours inspired confidence. He knew well where he was being taken. Also, that it would not be plain sailing.

Something unwonted, violent, lay beneath these everyday

[1] *La Table Ronde,* Paris, January, 1948, p. 145.

appearances. Every gesture of the character was a reminder of some aspect of this fact, the most insignificant bauble reflected some facet of it. It was this that had to be brought out, explored to the very limit, investigated in its most secret recesses. Here was a compact, absolutely fresh subject-matter that required effort and fanned the passion for experimental research. Consciousness of this effort and of the validity of this research justified the cocksureness with which the author, indifferent as to whether or not he was trying the reader's patience, forced him to participate in prying housewifely inspections, to make computations that would do honor to a bank clerk or appraisals worthy of an auctioneer. It also justified the reader's tractability. They both realized that here was to be found what, at the time, was their chief concern. Here and nowhere else: as inseparable from the object as the color yellow from the lemon in a Chardin canvas—or, in a Veronese, the color blue from the sky. Just as the color yellow *was* the lemon and the color blue was the sky, and they were inconceivable one without the other, avarice *was* Père Grandet; it was his entire substance, it filled him to the very brim and, at the same time, owed its own form and vigor to him.

The stronger the framework, the better constructed and more richly ornamented the object, the richer and more delicately shaded was the subject matter.

Is it any fault of the reader if, since then, this same subject matter has taken on the mushy consistency and general insipidness of overchewed food, and the object containing it the flat appearance of painted scenery?

The sense of life to which, in the long run, all art harks back (the "intensity of life" that undoubtedly, as Gide said, "is what gives things their value"), has deserted these erstwhile promising forms and betaken itself elsewhere. By virtue of the ceaseless movement which tends to bring it ever nearer to the mobile point where, at a given moment, experiment and the peak of effort meet, it has broken through the earlier novel form and forsaken, one by one, all the old, useless accessories. Today, warts and waistcoats, characters and plots, may offer the most infinite variety without revealing anything other than a reality, the slightest particle of which we are familiar with already, from having been over and over it, in every direction. Instead of inciting the reader, as in Balzac's time, to attain to a truth whose conquest denotes hard-won struggle, all these accessories now appear to him to constitute but a dangerous concession to his inclination toward laziness—as well as to that of the author—or to his fear of change. The swiftest glance about him, the most fleeting contact, tell him more than all these external appearances, the sole aim of which is to give a semblance of likelihood to the characters. He has only to dip into the huge stock, which as a result of his own experience is constantly increasing, to compensate for what is lacking in these tiresome descriptions.

As regards the character, he realizes that it is nothing other than a crude label which he himself makes use of, without real conviction and by way of convenience, for the purpose of orienting, very approximately, his own behavior. So he is wary of the abrupt, spectacular types of action that model the character with a few resounding whacks; he is also wary of plot, which winds itself around the character like wrappings, giving it, along with an appearance of cohesiveness and life, mummy-like stiffness.

In fact, Tournier is right; the reader has grown wary of practically everything. The reason being that, for some time now, he has been learning about too many things, and he is unable to forget entirely all he has learned.

What he has learned is a matter of such common knowledge that there is no need to go into it here. He has made the acquaintance of Joyce, Proust and Freud; the trickle, imperceptible from without, of the interior monologue; the infinitely profuse growth of the psychological world and the vast, as yet almost unexplored regions of the unconscious. He has watched the watertight partitions that used to separate the characters from one another give way, and the hero become an arbitrary limitation, a conventional figure cut from the common woof that each of us contains in its entirety, and which captures and holds within its meshes the entire universe. Like the surgeon who eyes the exact spot on which his greatest effort is to be concentrated, isolating it from the rest of the sleeping body, he has been led to center all his attention and curiosity on some new psychological state, forgetting meanwhile the motionless character, who serves as its chance prop. He has seen time cease to be the swift stream that carried the plot forward, and become a stagnant pool at the bottom of which a slow, subtle decomposition is in progress; he has seen our actions lose their usual motives and accepted meanings, he has witnessed the appearance of hitherto unknown sentiments and seen those that were most familiar change both in aspect and name.

In fact, he has learned so much and learned it so well, that he has begun to doubt whether the novelist's artificially constructed object is capable of secreting the wealth of the real object. And since writers of the objective school insist that it is useless to attempt to reproduce the infinite complexity of life, and that it is up to the reader to draw on his own resources, using the instruments of investigation he already possesses to wrest its mystery from the impenetrable object they present to him, he prefers to confine his efforts to certainties, and goes in for facts.

The "true fact" has indeed an indubitable advantage over the invented tale. To begin with, that of being true. This is the source of its strength of conviction and forcefulness, of its noble indifference to ridicule and bad taste, and also of a certain quiet daring, a certain offhandedness, that allow it to break through the confining limitations in which a regard for likelihood imprisons the boldest of novelists, and to extend far afield the frontiers of reality. It allows us to attain to unknown regions into which no writer would have dared venture, and brings us, with one leap, to the edge of the "abyss."

Where is the invented story that could compete with that of Gide's *Séquestrée de Poitiers,* or with those of the concentration camps, or the Battle of Stalingrad? And how many novels, how many characters, situations and plots would be needed to furnish the reader with a subject matter equal in richness and subtlety to that offered for our curiosity and reflection by almost any well-constructed monograph?

It is, therefore, for very wholesome reasons that today's reader prefers accounts of actual experiences (or at least having the reassuring appearance of such) to the novel. Nor, as might be supposed, does the recent vogue of what, in France, is referred to as the "American" novel give the lie to this preference. On the contrary, it confirms it. This particular literature which, for the very reasons just mentioned, is looked down upon by many cultivated American readers, by transporting the French reader into a foreign universe in which he had no foothold, lulled his wariness, aroused in him the kind of credulous curiosity that travel books inspire, and gave him a delightful impression of escape into an unknown world. Now that he has more or less assimilated these exotic foods—which, despite their richness and variety, turned out to be much less tonic than had been supposed—the French reader, as well, is no longer interested.

It goes without saying that all these attitudes with regard to the novel are all the more familiar to the author who, being himself a reader, and often a very perceptive one, has also experienced them.

The result is that when he starts to tell a story and says to himself that he must make up his mind to write down for the mocking eyes of the reader, "The Marquise went out at five o'clock," he hesitates, he hasn't the heart, he simply can't bring himself to do it.

And if, after taking his courage in hand, he decides not to give the Marquise the considerate attention demanded by tradition, but to write only of what interests him today, he realizes that the impersonal tone, which is so well adapted to the needs of the old-style novel, is not suitable for conveying the complex, tenuous states that he is attempting to portray; the fact being that these states resemble certain phenomena of modern physics, which are so delicate and minute that even a ray of light falling on them disturbs and deforms them. Consequently, whenever the novelist seeks to describe them without revealing his own presence, he seems to hear the reader, like a child whose mother is reading him his first story, stop and ask: "Who said that?"

A story told in the first person satisfies the legitimate scruples of the author. In addition, it has the appearance, at least, of real experience and authenticity, which impresses the reader and dispels his mistrust.

For nobody today is entirely misled by the convenient procedure that consists, for the novelist, in parsimoniously apportioning bits of himself, which he invests with a certain likelihood by dividing them, necessarily somewhat at random (if they have been taken from a cross-section performed at a certain depth, they are identical with everyone) among his characters. By a process of decortication, the reader then removes these bits and places them, as in a game of lotto, in corresponding compartments he has discovered in himself.

Today, everybody is well aware, without being told, that *"la Bovary—c'est moi."*[2] And since the important thing now, rather than to extend indefinitely the list of literary types, is to show the co-existence of contradictory emotions and to reproduce as closely as possible the wealth and complexity of the world of the psyche, the writer, in all honesty, writes about himself.

But that's not all. However strange it may seem, this same writer, who is awed by the reader's growing perspicacity and wariness, is, himself, becoming more and more wary of the reader.

For even the most experienced reader, if left to his own devices, tends to create types; he simply can't resist it.

He does it, in fact—in the same way as the novelist, once he has begun to relax—without even noticing that he is doing it, for the convenience of everyday life and as a result of long practice. Like Pavlov's dog, in whom the tinkle of a bell stimulates the secretion of saliva, he creates characters at the slightest possible suggestion. As in the game of "statues," each one he touches turns to stone. They merely serve to swell in his memory the vast collection of inanimate figures to which, day in, day out, he is constantly adding and which, since he first learned to read, has been regularly growing as a result of the countless novels he has absorbed.

But, as has already been demonstrated, the character as conceived in the old-style novel (along with the entire old-style mechanism that was used to make him stand out) does not succeed in containing the psychological reality of today. Instead of revealing it—as used to be the case—he makes it disappear.

So that, as a result of an evolution similar to that in painting —albeit far less bold, less rapid, and interrupted by long pauses and retreats—the psychological element, like the pictorial element, is beginning to free itself imperceptibly from the object of

[2] From Flaubert's correspondence.

which it was an integral part. It is tending to become self-sufficient and, in so far as possible, to do without exterior support. The novelist's entire experimental effort is concentrated on this one point, as is also the reader's entire effort of attention.

The reader, therefore, must be kept from trying to do two things at one time. And since what the characters gain in the way of facile vitality and plausibility is balanced by a loss of fundamental truth in the psychological states for which they serve as props, he must be kept from allowing his attention to wander or to be absorbed by the characters. For this, he must be deprived as much as possible of all indications which, in spite of himself, and as a result of a natural leaning, he seizes upon in order to create illusions.

This is why the character today is reduced to a shadow of his former self. Only reluctantly does the novelist endow him with attributes that could make him too easily distinguishable: his physical aspect, gestures, actions, sensations, everyday emotions, studied and understood for so long, which contribute to giving him, at the cost of so little effort, an appearance of life, and present such a convenient hold for the reader.[3] Even a name, which is an absolutely necessary feature of his accoutrement, is a source of embarrassment to the novelist. Gide avoids use of the patronymic for his characters, for the reason that it risks situating them at once in a world too similar to that of the reader, and his preference is given to unusual forenames. Kafka's hero has for his entire name an initial only (that of Kafka himself); Joyce designates by the initials, H.C.E., of multiple interpretations, the protean hero of *Finnegans Wake*. And it would be most unfair to Faulkner's bold and very worthwhile experiments, which are so revealing of the problem of the present-day novelist, if we were to attribute to a perverse and childish desire to mystify the reader, the method used by him in *The Sound and the Fury* which consists in giving the same forename to two different characters.[4] This first name, which he shunts back and forth from one charac-

[3] "Not once," wrote Proust, "does one of my characters shut a window, wash his hands, put on his overcoat, utter a phrase of introduction. If there is anything at all new about the book, this would be it! . . ." (Letter to Robert Dreyfus).

[4] Quentin is the first name of both the uncle and the niece; Caddy, that of the mother and the daughter.

ter to the other, under the annoyed eye of the reader, like a lump of sugar under the nose of a dog, forces the reader to be constantly on the alert. Instead of letting himself be guided by the signposts with which everyday custom flatters his laziness and haste, he is obliged, in order to identify the characters, to recognize them at once, like the author himself, from the inside, and thanks to indications that are only revealed to him if, having renounced his love of comfort, he is willing to plunge into them as deeply as the author, whose vision he makes his own.

Indeed, the whole problem is here: to dispossess the reader and entice him, at all costs, into the author's territory. To achieve this, the device that consists in referring to the leading character as "I" constitutes a means that is both efficacious and simple and, doubtless for this reason, is frequently employed.

Suddenly the reader is on the inside, exactly where the author is, at a depth where nothing remains of the convenient landmarks with which he constructs the characters. He is immersed and held under the surface until the end, in a substance as anonymous as blood, a magma without name or contours. If he succeeds in finding his way, it is thanks to stakes that the author has planted for purposes of his own orientation. No reminiscences of the reader's world, no conventional concern for cohesion or likelihood, distract his attention or curb his effort. Like the author, the only barriers he encounters are those that are either inherent to all experiments of this kind or peculiar to the author's vision.

As for the secondary characters, they are deprived of all autonomous existence and reduced to mere excrescences, quiddities, experiments or dreams of the "I," with whom the author identifies himself. At the same time, this "I," not being the novelist, need not be concerned with creating a universe in which the reader will feel too much at home, nor with giving the characters the proportions and dimensions required to confer upon them their rather dangerous "resemblance." His obsessed, maniacal or visionary eye may seize upon them at will, abandon them, stretch them in a single direction, compress, enlarge, flatten or reduce them to dust, to force them to yield the new reality he is striving to find.

In the same way, the modern painter—and in this connection it might be said that, since Impressionism, all pictures have been painted in the first person—wrests the object from the universe of the spectator and deforms it in order to isolate its pictorial content.

Thus, in a movement analogous to that of painting, the novel, which only a stubborn adherence to obsolete techniques places in the position of a minor art, pursues with means that are uniquely its own a path which can only be its own; it leaves to the other arts—and, in particular, to the cinema—everything that does not actually belong to it. In the same way that photography occupies and fructifies the fields abandoned by painting, the cinema garners and perfects what is left by the novel.

The reader, instead of demanding of the novel what every good novel has more than often refused him, i.e., light entertainment, can satisfy at the cinema, without effort and without needless loss of time, his taste for "live" characters and stories.

However, the cinema too would appear to be threatened. It too is infected by the "suspicion" from which the novel suffers. Otherwise, how may we explain the uneasiness which, after that of the novelist, is now being evidenced by certain "advanced" directors who, because they feel obliged to make films in the first person, have introduced the eye of a witness and the voice of a narrator?

As for the novel, before it has even exhausted all the advantages offered by the story told in the first person, or reached the end of the blind alley into which all techniques necessarily lead, it has grown impatient and, in order to emerge from its present difficulties, is looking about for other ways out.

Suspicion, which is by way of destroying the character and the entire outmoded mechanism that guaranteed its force, is one of the morbid reactions by which an organism defends itself and seeks another equilibrium. It forces the novelist to fulfill what Arnold Toynbee, recalling Flaubert's teaching, has called "his deepest obligation: that of discovering what is new," and keeps him from committing "his most serious crime: that of repeating the discoveries of his predecessors."

[*Temps Modernes*, February, 1950.]

# V. What Is Plot?

**E. M. Forster, "The Plot," from *Aspects of the Novel*, reprinted here by permission of Harcourt, Brace and World.**

**R. S. Crane, "The Concept of Plot," from "The Concept of Plot and the Plot of *Tom Jones*" in *Critics and Criticism*, reprinted here by permission of the University of Chicago Press.**

*Both Forster and Crane are willing to assume that the abstraction "plot" exists and can be discussed in connection with that other abstraction, "character." But Forster sees an opposition between the two. He associates character with life, and plot with art, thus putting the central paradox of the novel in a special but illuminating context. Crane, on the other hand, is less concerned with the representational or mimetic aspect of the novel. He is interested in the way the novel affects its readers, and he treats plot primarily as the method by which the novelist manipulates the reader's response. He is concerned with technique, but as control rather than discovery. (The editor has taken the liberty of raising some material by R. S. Crane from the footnotes to the text.)*

## E. M. Forster

### *The Plot*

"Character," says Aristotle, "gives us qualities, but it is in actions—what we do—that we are happy, or the reverse." We have already decided that Aristotle is wrong and now we must face the consequences of disagreeing with him. "All human happiness and misery," says Aristotle, "take the form of action." We know better. We believe that happiness and misery exist in the secret life, which each of us leads privately and to which (in his characters) the novelist has access. And by the secret life we mean the life for which there is no external evidence, not, as is vulgarly supposed, that which is revealed by a chance word or a sigh. A chance word or sigh are just as much evidence as a speech or a murder: the life they reveal ceases to be secret and enters the realm of action.

There is, however, no occasion to be hard on Aristotle. He had read few novels and no modern ones—the *Odyssey* but not *Ulysses*—he was by temperament apathetic to secrecy, and indeed regarded the human mind as a sort of tub from which everything can finally be extracted; and when he wrote the words quoted above he had in view the drama, where no doubt they hold true. In the drama all human happiness and misery does and must take the form of action. Otherwise its existence remains unknown, and this is the great difference between the drama and the novel.

The speciality of the novel is that the writer can talk about his characters as well as through them or can arrange for us to listen when they talk to themselves. He has access to self-communings, and from that level he can descend even deeper and peer into the subconscious. A man does not talk to himself quite truly—not even to himself; the happiness or misery that he secretly feels proceeds from causes that he cannot quite explain, because as soon as he raises them to the level of the explicable they lose their native quality. The novelist has a real pull here. He can show the subconscious short-circuiting straight into action (the dramatist can do this too); he can also show it in its relation to soliloquy. He commands all the secret life, and he must not be robbed of this privilege. "How did the writer know that?" it is sometimes said. "What's his standpoint? He is not being consistent, he's shifting his point of view from the limited to the omniscient, and now he's edging back again." Questions like these have too much the atmosphere of the law courts about them. All that matters to the reader is whether the shifting of attitude and the secret life are convincing, whether it is πιθανόν in fact, and with his favourite word ringing in his ears Aristotle may retire.

However, he leaves us in some confusion, for what, with this enlargement of human nature, is going to become of the plot? In most literary works there are two elements: human individuals, whom we have recently discussed, and the element vaguely called art. Art we have also dallied with, but with a very low form of it: the story: the chopped-off length of the tapeworm of time. Now we arrive at a much higher aspect: the plot, and the plot, instead of finding human beings more or less cut to its requirements, as they are in the drama, finds them enormous, shadowy and intractable, and three-quarters hidden like an iceberg. In vain it points out to these unwieldy creatures the advantages of the triple process of complication, crisis, and solution so persuasively expounded by Aristotle. A few of them rise and comply, and a novel which ought to have been a play is the result. But there is no general response. They want to sit apart and brood or something, and the plot (whom I here visualize as a sort of higher government official) is concerned at their lack of public spirit: "This will not do," it seems to say. "Individualism is a most valuable quality; indeed my own position depends upon individuals; I have always admitted as much freely. Nevertheless there are certain limits, and those limits are being overstepped. Characters must not brood too long, they must not waste time running up and down ladders in their own insides, they must contribute, or higher interests will be jeopardised." How well one knows that phrase, "a contribution to the plot"! It is accorded, and of necessity, by the people in a drama: how necessary is it in a novel?

Let us define a plot. We have defined a story as a narrative of events arranged in their time-sequence. A plot is also a narrative of events, the emphasis falling on causality. "The king died and then the queen died" is a story. "The king died, and then the queen died of grief" is a plot. The time-sequence is preserved, but the sense of causality overshadows it. Or again: "The queen died, no one knew why, until it was discovered that it was through grief at the death of the king." This is a plot with a mystery in it, a form capable of high development. It suspends the time-sequence, it moves as far away from the story as its limitations will allow. Consider the death of the queen. If it is in a story we say "and then?" If it is in a plot we ask "why?" That is the fundamental difference between these two aspects of the novel. A plot cannot be told to a gaping audience of cave-men or to a tyrannical sultan or to their modern descendant the movie-public. They can only be kept awake by "and then—and then——" They can only supply curiosity. But a plot demends intelligence and memory also.

Curiosity is one of the lowest of the human faculties. You will have noticed in daily life that when people are inquisitive they nearly always have bad memories and are usually stupid at bottom. The man who begins by asking you how many brothers and sisters you have is never a sympathetic character, and if you meet him in a year's time he will probably ask you how many brothers and sisters you have, his mouth again sagging open, his eyes still bulging from his head. It is difficult to be friends with such a man, and for two inquisitive people to be friends must be impossible. Curiosity by itself takes us a very little way, nor does it take us far into the novel—only as far as the story. If we would grasp the plot we must add intelligence and memory.

Intelligence first. The intelligent novel-reader, unlike the inquisitive one who just runs his eye over a new fact, mentally picks it up. He sees it from two points of view: isolated, and related to the other facts that he has read on previous pages. Probably he does not understand it, but he does not expect to do so yet awhile. The facts in a highly organized novel (like *The Egoist*) are often of the nature of cross-correspondences and the ideal spectator cannot expect to view them properly until he is sitting up on a hill at the end. This element of surprise or mystery—the detective element as it is sometimes rather emptily called—is of great importance in a plot. It occurs through a suspension of the time-sequence; a mystery is a pocket in time, and it occurs crudely, as in "Why did the queen die?" and more subtly in half-explained gestures and words, the true meaning of which only dawns pages ahead. Mystery is essential to a plot, and cannot be appreciated without intelligence. To the curious it is just another "and then——" To appreciate a mystery, part of the mind must be left behind, brooding, while the other part goes marching on.

That brings us to our second qualification: memory.

Memory and intelligence are closely connected, for unless we remember we cannot understand. If by the time the queen dies we have forgotten the existence of the king we shall never make out what killed her. The plot-maker expects us to remember, we expect him to leave no loose ends. Every action or word ought to count; it ought to be economical and spare; even when complicated it should be organic and free from dead-matter. It may be difficult or easy, it may and should contain mysteries, but it ought not to mislead. And over it, as it unfolds, will hover the memory of the reader (that dull glow of the mind of which intelligence is the bright advancing edge) and will constantly rearrange and reconsider, seeing new clues, new chains of cause and effect, and the final sense (if the plot has been a fine one) will not be of clues or chains, but of something aesthetically compact, something which might have been shown by the novelist straight away, only if he had shown it straight away it would never have become beautiful. We come up against beauty here—for the first time in our inquiry: beauty at which a novelist should never aim, though he fails if he does not achieve it. I will conduct beauty to her proper place later on. Meanwhile please accept her as part of a completed plot. She looks a little surprised at being there, but beauty ought to look a little surprised: it is the emotion that best suits her face, as Botticelli knew when he painted her risen from the waves, between the winds and the flowers. The beauty who does not look surprised, who accepts her position as her due—she reminds us too much of a prima donna.

But let us get back to the plot, and we will do so via George Meredith.

Meredith is not the great name he was twenty or thirty years ago, when much of the universe and all Cambridge trembled. I remember how depressed I used to be by a line in one of his poems: "We live but to be sword or block." I did not want to be either and I knew that I was not a sword. It seems though that there was no real cause for depression, for Meredith is himself now rather in the trough of a wave, and though fashion will turn and raise him a bit, he will never be the spiritual power he was about the year 1900. His philosophy has not worn well. His heavy attacks on sentimentality—they bore the present generation, which pursues the same quarry but with neater instruments, and is apt to suspect anyone carrying a blunderbuss of being a sentimentalist himself. And his visions of Nature—they do not endure like Hardy's, there is too much Surrey about them, they are fluffy and lush. He could no more write the opening chapter of *The Return of the Native* than Box Hill could visit Salisbury Plain. What is really tragic and enduring in the scenery of England was hidden from him, and so is what is really tragic in life. When he gets serious and noble-minded there is a strident overtone, a bullying that becomes distressing. I feel indeed that he was like Tennyson in one respect: through not taking himself quietly enough he strained his inside. And his novels: most of the social values are faked. The tailors are not tailors, the cricket matches are not cricket, the railway trains do not even seem to be trains, the county families give the air of having been only just that moment unpacked, scarcely in position before the action starts, the straw still clinging to their beards. It is surely very odd, the social scene in which his characters are set: it is partly due to his fantasy, which is legitimate, but partly a chilly fake, and wrong. What with the faking, what with the preaching, which was never agreeable and is now said to be hollow, and what with the home counties posing as the universe, it is no wonder Meredith now lies in the trough. And yet he is in one way a great novelist. He is the finest contriver that English fiction has ever produced, and any lecture on plot must do homage to him.

Meredith's plots are not closely knit. We cannot describe the action of *Harry Richmond* in a phrase, as we can that of *Great Expectations,* though both books turn on the mistake made by a young man as to the sources of his fortune. A Meredithian plot is not a temple to the tragic or even to the comic Muse, but rather resembles a series of kiosks most artfully placed among wooded slopes, which his people reach by their own impetus, and from which they emerge with altered aspect. Incident springs out of character, and having occurred it alters that character. People and events are closely connected, and he does it by means of these contrivances. They are often delightful, sometimes touching, always unexpected. This shock, followed by the feeling, "Oh, that's all right," is a sign that all is well with the plot: characters, to be real, ought to run smoothly, but a plot ought to cause surprise. The horse-whipping of Dr. Shrapnel in *Beauchamp's Career* is a surprise. We know that Everard Romfrey must dislike Shrapnel, must hate and misunderstand his radicalism, and be jealous of his influence over Beauchamp: we watch too the growth of the misunderstanding over Rosamund, we watch the intrigues of Cecil Baskelett. As far as characters go, Meredith plays with his cards on the table, but when the incident comes what a shock it gives us and the characters too! The tragi-comic business of one old man whipping another from the highest motives—it reacts upon all their world, and transforms all the personages of the book. It is not the centre of *Beauchamp's Career,* which indeed has no centre. It is essentially a contrivance, a door through which the book is made to pass, emerging in an altered form. Towards the close, when Beauchamp is drowned and Shrapnel and Romfrey are reconciled over his body, there is an attempt to elevate the plot to Aristotelian symmetry, to turn the novel into a temple wherein dwells interpretation and peace. Meredith fails here: *Beauchamp's Career* remains a series of contrivances (the visit to France is another of them), but contrivances that spring from the characters and react upon them.

And now briefly to illustrate the mystery element in the plot: the formula of "The queen died, it was afterwards discovered through grief." I will take an example, not from Dickens (though *Great Expectations* provides a fine one), nor from Conan Doyle (whom my priggishness prevents me from enjoying), but again from Meredith: an example of a concealed emotion from the admirable plot of *The Egoist:* it occurs in the character of Laetitia Dale.

We are told, at first, all that passes in Laetitia's mind. Sir Willoughby has twice jilted her, she is sad, resigned. Then, for dramatic reasons, her mind is hidden from us, it develops naturally enough, but does not re-emerge until the great midnight scene where he asks her to marry him because he is not sure about Clara, and this time, a changed woman, Laetitia says "No." Meredith has concealed the change. It would have spoiled his high comedy if we had been kept in touch with it throughout. Sir Willoughby has to have a series of crashes, to catch at this and that, and find everything rickety. We should not enjoy the fun, in fact it would be boorish, if we saw the author preparing the booby traps beforehand, so Laetitia's apathy has been hidden from us. This is one of the countless examples in which either plot or character has to suffer, and Meredith with his unerring good sense here lets the plot triumph.

As an example of mistaken triumph, I think of a slip—it is no more than a slip—which Charlotte Brontë makes in *Villette.* She allows Lucy Snowe to conceal from the reader her discovery that Dr. John is the same as her old playmate Graham. When it comes out, we do get a good plot thrill, but too much at the expense of Lucy's character. She has seemed, up to then, the spirit of integrity, and has, as it were, laid herself under a moral obligation to narrate all that she knows. That she stoops to suppress is a little distressing, though the incident is too trivial to do her any permanent harm.

Sometimes a plot triumphs too completely. The characters have to suspend their natures at every turn, or else are so swept away by the course of Fate that our sense of their reality is weakened. We shall find instances of this in a writer who is far greater than Meredith, and yet less successful as a novelist—Thomas Hardy. Hardy seems to me essentially a poet, who conceives of his novels from an enormous height. They are to be tragedies or tragi-comedies, they are to give out the sound of hammer-strokes as they proceed; in other words Hardy arranges events with emphasis on causality, the ground plan is a plot, and the characters are ordered to acquiesce in its requirements. Except in the person of Tess (who conveys the feeling that she is greater than destiny) this aspect of his work is unsatisfactory. His characters are involved in various snares, they are finally bound hand and foot, there is ceaseless emphasis on fate, and yet, for all the sacrifices made to it, we never see the action as a living thing as we see it in *Antigone* or *Berenice* or *The Cherry Orchard*. The fate above us, not the fate working through us—that is what is eminent and memorable in the Wessex novels. Egdon Heath before Eustacia Vye has set foot upon it. The woods without the Woodlanders. The downs above Budmouth Regis with the royal princesses, still asleep, driving across them through the dawn. Hardy's success in *The Dynasts* (where he uses another medium) is complete, there the hammer-strokes are heard, cause and effect enchain the characters despite their struggles, complete contact between the actors and the plot is established. But in the novels, though the same superb and terrible machine works, it never catches humanity in its teeth; there is some vital problem that has not been answered, or even posed, in the misfortunes of Jude the Obscure. In other words the characters have been required to contribute too much to the plot; except in their rustic humours, their vitality has been impoverished, they have gone dry and thin. This, as far as I can make out, is the flaw running through Hardy's novels: he has emphasized causality more strongly than his medium permits. As a poet and prophet and visualizer George Meredith is nothing by his side—just a suburban roarer—but Meredith did know what the novel could stand, where the plot could dun the characters for a contribution, where it must let them function as they liked. And the moral—well, I see no moral, because the work of Hardy is my home and that of Meredith cannot be: still the moral from the point of these lectures is again unfavourable to Aristotle. In the novel, all human happiness and misery does not take the form of action, it seeks means of expression other than through the plot, it must not be rigidly canalized.

In the losing battle that the plot fights with the characters, it often takes a cowardly revenge. Nearly all novels are feeble at the end. This is because the plot requires to be wound up. Why is this necessary? Why is there not a convention which allows a novelist to stop as soon as he feels muddled or bored? Alas, he has to round things off, and usually the characters go dead while he is at work, and our final impression of them is through deadness. *The Vicar of Wakefield* is in this way a typical novel, so clever and fresh in the first half, up to the painting of the family group with Mrs. Primrose as Venus, and then so wooden and imbecile. Incidents and people that occurred at first for their own sake now have to contribute to the *dénouement*. In the end even the author feels he is being a little foolish. "Nor can I go on," he says, "without a reflection on those accidental meetings which, though they happen every day, seldom excite our surprise but upon some extraordinary occasion." Goldsmith is of course a light-weight, but most novels do fail here—there is this disastrous standstill while logic takes over the command from flesh and blood. If it was not for death and marriage I do not know how the average novelist would conclude. Death and marriage are almost his only connection between his characters and his plot, and the reader is more ready to meet him here, and take a bookish view of them, provided they occur later on in the book: the writer, poor fellow, must be allowed to finish up somehow, he has his living to get like anyone else, so no wonder that nothing is heard but hammering and screwing.

This—as far as one can generalize—is the inherent defect of novels: they go off at the end: and there are two explanations of it: firstly, failure of pep, which threatens the novelist like all workers: and secondly, the difficulty which we have been discussing. The characters have been getting out of hand, laying foundations and declining to build on them afterwards, and now the novelist has to labour personally, in order that the job may be done to time. He pretends that the characters are acting for him. He keeps mentioning their names and using inverted commas. But the characters are gone or dead.

The plot, then, is the novel in its logical intellectual aspect: it requires mystery, but the mysteries are solved later on: the reader may be moving about in worlds unrealized, but the novelist has no misgivings. He is competent, poised above his work, throwing a beam of light here, popping on a cap of invisibility there, and (*qua* plot-maker) continually negotiating with himself *qua* character-monger as to the best effect to be produced. He plans his book beforehand: or anyhow he stands above it, his interest in cause and effect give him an air of predetermination.

And now we must ask ourselves whether the framework thus produced is the best possible for a novel. After all, why has a novel to be planned? Cannot it grow? Why need it close, as a play closes? Cannot it open out? Instead of standing above his work and controlling it, cannot the novelist throw himself into it and be carried along to some goal that he does not foresee? The plot is exciting and may be beautiful, yet is it not a fetish, borrowed from the drama, from the spatial limitations of the stage? Cannot fiction devise a framework that is not so logical yet more suitable to its genius?

Modern writers say that it can, and we will now examine a recent example—a violent onslaught on the plot as we have defined it: a constructive attempt to put something in the place of the plot.

I have already mentioned the novel in question: *Les Faux Monnayeurs* by André Gide. It contains within its covers both the methods. Gide has also published the diary he kept while he was writing the novel, and there is no reason why he should not publish in the future the impressions he had when rereading both the diary and the novel, and in the future-perfect a still more final synthesis in which the diary, the novel, and his impressions of both will interact. He is indeed a little more solemn than an author should be about the whole caboodle, but regarded as a caboodle it is excessively interesting, and repays careful study by critics.

We have, in the first place, a plot in *Les Faux Monnayeurs* of the logical objective type that we have been considering—a plot, or rather fragments of plots. The main fragment concerns a young man called Olivier—a charming, touching and lovable character, who misses happiness, and then recovers it after an excellently contrived *dénouement*; confers it also; this fragment has a wonderful radiance and "lives," if I may use so coarse a word, it is a successful creation on familiar lines. But it is by no means the centre of the book. No more are the other logical fragments—that which concerns Georges, Olivier's schoolboy brother, who passes false coin, and is instrumental in driving a fellow-pupil to suicide. (Gide gives us his sources for all this in his diary, he got the idea of Georges from a boy whom he caught trying to steal a book off a stall, the gang of coiners were caught at Rouen, and the suicide of children took place at Clermont-Ferrand, etc.) Neither Olivier, nor Georges, nor Vincent, a third brother, nor Bernard their friend is the centre of the book. We come nearer to it in Edouard. Edouard is a novelist. He bears the same relation to Gide as Clissold does to Wells. I dare not be more precise. Like Gide, he keeps a diary, like Gide he is writing a book called *Les Faux Monnayeurs,* and like Clissold he is disavowed. Edouard's diary is printed in full. It begins before the plot-fragments, continues during them, and forms the bulk of Gide's book. Edouard is not just a chronicler. He is an actor too; indeed it is he who rescues Olivier and is rescued by him; we leave those two in happiness.

But that is still not the centre. The nearest to the centre lies in a discussion about the art of the novel. Edouard is holding forth to Bernard his secretary and some friends. He has said (what we all accept as commonplace) that truth in life and truth in a novel are not identical, and then he goes on to say that he wants to write a book which shall include both sorts of truth.

> "And what is its subject?" asked Sophroniska.
>
> "There is none," said Edouard sharply. "My novel has no subject. No doubt that sounds foolish. Let us say, if you prefer, that it will not have 'a' subject. . . . 'A slice of life,' the naturalistic school used to say. The mistake that school made was always to cut its slice in the same direction, always lengthwise, in the direction of time. Why not cut it up and down? Or across? As for me, I don't want to cut it at all. You see what I mean. I want to put everything into my novel and not snip off my material either here or there. I have been working for a year, and there is nothing I haven't put in:

all I see, all I know, all I can learn from other people's lives and my own."

"My poor man, you will bore your readers to death," cried Laura, unable to restrain her mirth.

"Not at all. To get my effect, I am inventing, as my central character, a novelist, and the subject of my book will be the struggle between what reality offers him and what he tries to make of the offer."

"Have you planned out this book?" asked Sophroniska, trying to keep grave.

"Of course not."

"Why 'of course'?"

"For a book of this type any plan would be unsuitable. The whole of it would go wrong if I decided any detail ahead. I am waiting for reality to dictate to me."

"But I thought you wanted to get away from reality."

"My novelist wants to get away, but I keep pulling him back. To tell the truth, this is my subject: the struggle between facts as proposed by reality, and the ideal reality."

"Do tell us the name of this book," said Laura, in despair.

"Very well. Tell it them, Bernard."

"*Les Faux Monnayeurs,*" said Bernard. "And now will you please tell us who these faux monnayeurs are."

"I haven't the least idea."

Bernard and Laura looked at each other and then at Sophroniska. There was the sound of a deep sigh.

The fact was that ideas about money, depreciation, inflation, forgery, etc., had gradually invaded Edouard's book—just as theories of clothing invade *Sartor Resartus* and even assume the functions of characters. "Has any of you ever had hold of a false coin?" he asked after a pause. "Imagine a ten-franc piece, gold, false. It is actually worth a couple of sous, but it will remain worth ten francs until it is found out. Suppose I begin with the idea that—"

"But why begin with an idea?" burst out Bernard, who was by now in a state of exasperation. "Why not begin with a fact? If you introduce the fact properly, the idea will follow of itself. If I was writing your *Faux Monnayeurs* I should begin with a piece of false money, with the ten-franc piece you were speaking of, and here it is!"

So saying, Bernard pulled a ten-franc piece out of his pocket and flung it on the table.

"There," he remarked. "It rings all right. I got it this morning from the grocer. It's worth more than a couple of sous, as it's coated in gold, but it's actually made of glass. It will become quite transparent in time. No—don't rub it—you're going to spoil my false coin."

Edouard had taken it and was examining it with the utmost attention.

"How did the grocer get it?"

"He doesn't know. He passed it on me for a joke, and then enlightened me, being a decent fellow. He let me have it for five francs. I thought that, since you were writing *Les Faux Monnayeurs,* you ought to see what false money is like, so I got it to show you. Now that you have looked at it, give it me back. I am sorry to see that reality has no interest for you."

"Yes," said Edouard: "it interests me, but it puts me out."

"That's a pity," remarked Bernard.[1]

This passage is the centre of the book. It contains the old thesis of truth in life versus truth in art, and illustrates it very neatly by the arrival of an actual false coin. What is new in it is the attempt to combine the two truths, the proposal that writers should mix themselves up in their material and be rolled over and over by it; they should not try to subdue any longer, they should hope to be subdued, to be carried away. As for a plot—to pot with the plot, break it up, boil it down. Let there be those "formidable erosions of contour" of which Nietzsche speaks. All that is prearranged is false.

Another distinguished critic has agreed with Gide—that old lady in the anecdote who was accused by her nieces of being illogical. For some time she could not be brought to understand what logic was, and when she grasped its true nature she was not so much angry as contemptuous. "Logic! Good gracious! What rub-

[1] Paraphrased from *Les Faux Monnayeurs,* pp. 238-246. My version, needless to say, conveys neither the subtlety nor the balance of the original.

bish!" she exclaimed. "How can I tell what I think till I see what I say?" Her nieces, educated young women, thought that she was *passée*; she was really more up to date than they were.

Those who are in touch with contemporary France say that the present generation follows the advice of Gide and the old lady and resolutely hurls itself into confusion, and indeed admires English novelists on the ground that they so seldom succeed in what they attempt. Compliments are always delightful, but this particular one is a bit of a backhander. It is like trying to lay an egg and being told you have produced a paraboloid—more curious than gratifying. And what results when you try to lay a paraboloid, I cannot conceive—perhaps the death of the hen. That seems the danger in Gide's position—he sets out to lay a paraboloid; he is not well advised, if he wants to write subconscious novels, to reason so lucidly and patiently about the subconscious; he is introducing mysticism at the wrong stage of the process. However that is his affair. As a critic he is most stimulating, and the various bundles of words he has called *Les Faux Monnayeurs* will be enjoyed by all who cannot tell what they think till they see what they say, or who weary of the tyranny by the plot and of its alternative, tyranny by characters.

## R. S. Crane

### *The Concept of Plot*

The question I wish to raise concerns not the justice of any of these estimates but rather the nature and critical adequacy of the conception of plot in general and of the plot of *Tom Jones* in particular that underlies most if not all of them. Now it is a striking fact that in all the more extended discussions of Fielding's masterpiece since 1749 the consideration of the plot has constituted merely one topic among several others, and a topic, moreover, so detached from the rest that once it is disposed of the consideration of the remaining elements of character, thought, diction, and narrative technique invariably proceeds without further reference to it. The characters are indeed agents of the story, but their values are assessed apart from this, in terms sometimes of their degrees of conformity to standards of characterization in literature generally, sometimes of the conceptions of morality they embody, sometimes of their relation to Fielding's experiences or prejudices, sometimes of their reflection, taken collectively, of the England of their time. The other elements are isolated similarly, both from the plot and from one another: what is found important in the thought, whether of the characters or of the narrator, is normally not its function as an artistic device but its doctrinal content as a sign of the "philosophy" of Fielding; the style and the ironical tone of the narrative are frequently praised, but solely as means to the general literary satisfaction of the reader; and, what is perhaps more significant, the wonderful comic force of the novel, which all have delighted to commend, is assumed to be independent of the plot and a matter exclusively of particular incidents, of the characters of some, but not all, of the persons, and of occasional passages of burlesque or witty writing.

The explanation of this procedure lies, partly, in a still unwritten chapter in the history of criticism. When works of prose fiction became objects of increasing critical attention in the eighteenth century, it was natural that the new form should be discussed in terms of its obvious analogies, both positive and negative, to drama and epic and that critics of novels should avail themselves, consequently, of the familiar categories of "fable," "characters," "sentiments," and "language" which had been long established, in the neoclassical tradition, as standard devices for the analysis of tragedies, comedies, and heroic poems. In remote origin these distinctions derived from the four qualitative "parts" which Aristotle had shown to be common to tragedy and epic (cf. *Poetics* 5. 1449$^b$15 ff.; 24. 1459$^b$8-11). In the course of their transmission to the eighteenth century, however—as a result partly of the influence of Horace and partly of a complex of more general causes operative from the beginnings of Aristotelian commentary in the Renaissance (see *Critics and Criticism* [original ed.], pp. 319-48)—the analytical significance of the scheme had undergone a radical change. For Aristotle, concerned with the construction of poetic wholes that afford "peculiar pleasures" through their imitations of different species of human actions, the four terms had designated the essential elements upon the proper handling and combination of which, relatively to the intended over-all effect, the quality of a tragedy or epic necessarily depends. They are distinct parts in the sense of being variable factors in the complex problem of composing works which, when completed, will produce their effects, synthetically, as organic wholes. Hence it is that in the *Poetics* they are treated, not discretely as co-ordinate topics, but hierarchically in a causal sequence of form-matter or end-means relationships in which plot is the most inclusive or architectonic of the four, subsuming all the others as its poetic matter; in which character, while subordinated materially to plot and effect, is similarly a formal or organizing principle with respect to thought and diction; in which thought, while functioning as matter relatively to character, incident, and effect, is the form which immediately controls the choice and arrangement of language in so far as this is employed as a means to imitative rather than ornamental ends; and in which diction, though necessarily having a form of its own by virtue of its rhythmical, syntactical, and "stylistic" figuration, is the underlying matter which, as significant speech, at once makes possible all the other "parts" and is in turn, mediately or immediately, controlled by them. The nature of the four elements is such, in short, that, although a critic in his analysis of a given tragedy or epic may take any one of them as his primary object of attention, he can make no adequate judgment of the poet's success or failure with respect to it without bringing into his discussion all the others to which it is related, directly or indirectly, either as matter or as form.

Of this causal scheme only the general outlines survived in the doctrines of subsequent critics in the "Aristotelian" line. The distinction of the four parts was retained and, along with it, the substance of the rules which Aristotle had formulated for their handling; what disappeared was precisely the rationale which in the *Poetics* had justified not only the rules but the discrimination, definition, and ordering of the parts themselves. In its place various new principles and schemes of analysis were substituted by different theorists and critics, the general tendency of which was to make of poetics a practical rather than a productive art and hence to reduce tragedy and epic to modes of ethical or rhetorical discourse designed to serve, each in its specialized way, the common purposes of all such discourse, namely, the delight and instruction of mankind. The consequence was that, although critics continued to distinguish aspects of tragedies and epics that corresponded roughly with the Aristotelian "parts" and although these served to determine the framework of the discussion at least in the most systematic treatises and essays, the discussion itself no longer turned on the nature and functional interrelations of the four parts as elements in an artistic synthesis of a particular kind but on the general qualities which the poet ought to aim at in each, in order to enhance its independent power of pleasing, moving, and edifying spectators or readers. And when this apparatus was carried over from the statement of tragic or epic theory to the practical criticism of tragedies or epics (as in Addison's papers on *Paradise Lost* or Pope's Preface to the *Iliad*), the disjunction of the four elements tended to become still more marked. They were no longer functional parts in an organic whole but so many relatively discrete *loci* of critical praise and blame; and critics could write *seriatim* of the beauties or defects in the fable, characters, sentiments, and language of a given tragedy or heroic poem without assuming any synthesizing principles more specific than the decorum of the genre or the necessity (e.g.) that the sentiments expressed should be consonant with the characters of the persons who uttered them (many illustrations of the procedure may be found in H. T. Swedenberg, Jr., *The Theory of the Epic in England, 1650-1800* [Berkeley and Los Angeles, 1944]; cf. the Index under "Fable or action," "Characters," "Sentiments in the epic," and "Language of the epic").

It was at this stage in the history of the Aristotelian "parts" that they entered into the criticism, both general and applied, of modern prose fiction. See, for example, besides many notices of novels in the *Monthly Review* and the *Critical Review*, the anonymous *Critical Remarks on Sir Charles Grandison, Clarissa, and Pamela* (1754); Arthur Murphy's "Essay on the Life and Genius of Henry Fielding," in *The Works of Henry Fielding* (1762); James Beattie's "On Fable and Romance," in his *Dissertations* (1783); and John More's "View of the Commencement and Progress of Romance," in *The Works of Tobias Smollett* (1797). In spite of the general indifference of criticism since about 1750 to questions specific to the various poetic kinds (see *C and C*, pp. 14, 459), the tradition of method thus established has persisted, especially in academic circles, to the present day; its influence still lingers in the topical divisions of treatises or textbooks dealing with the technique of fiction; and it still provides the commonplaces of a good many "studies" of novelists and novels. . . . The undoubted deficiencies of the scheme (in its neoclassical degradation) as an instrument of critical analysis and judgment have not passed unnoticed in recent years, particularly among critics of the *Scrutiny* group, who point out, justly enough, that "plot" and "character" are treated in a fashion that abstracts them unduly from the continuum of the novelist's language through which alone they affect us. These critics, however, are usually content to offer, as a positive substitute for the traditional scheme, only a still more extreme reduction of Aristotle's principles, in which everything in the discussion of a novel is made to turn on the relations between diction, in the sense of the author's "verbal arrangements," and thought, in the sense of the "experience" which he communicates by imposing "the pattern of his own sensibility" on the reader through the medium of language. See, for example, Martin Turnell, "The Language of Fiction," *Times Literary Supplement,* August 19, 1949, pp. 529-31; reprinted in his *Novel in France* (New York, 1951).

All this points to a strictly limited definition of plot as something that can be abstracted, for critical purposes, from the moral qualities of the characters and the operations of their thought. This something is merely the material continuity of the story considered in relation to the general pleasure we take in any fiction when our curiosity about the impending events is aroused, sustained, and then satisfied to a degree or in a manner we could not anticipate. A plot in this sense—the sense in which modern novelists pride themselves on having got rid of plot—can be pronounced good in terms simply of the variety of incidents it contains, the amount of suspense and surprise it evokes, and the ingenuity with which all the happenings in the beginning and middle are made to contribute to the resolution at the end. Given the definition, indeed, no other criteria are possible, and no others have been used by any of the critics of *Tom Jones* since the eighteenth century who have declared its plot to be one of the most perfect ever planned. They have uniformly judged it as interesting story merely—and this whether, as by most of the earlier writers, "the felicitous contrivance and happy extrication of the story" is taken to be the chief "beauty" of the novel or whether, as generally nowadays, preference is given to its qualities of character and thought. It is clearly of plot in no completer sense than this that Oliver Elton is thinking when he remarks that, although some "have cared little for this particular excellence, and think only of Partridge, timorous, credulous, garrulous, faithful, and an injured man; of Squire Western, and of the night at Upton, and of wit and humour everywhere," still "the common reader, for whom Fielding wrote, cares a great deal, and cares rightly, for plot; and so did Sophocles."

When plot is conceived thus narrowly, in abstraction from the peculiar characters and mental processes of the agents, it must necessarily have, for the critic, only a relatively external relation to the other aspects of the work. That is why, in most discussions of *Tom Jones,* the critical treatment of the plot (as distinguished from mere summary of the happenings) is restricted to the kind of enthusiastic general appreciation of which I have given some examples, supplemented by more particular remarks on various episodes, notably those of the Man of the Hill and of Mrs. Fitzpatrick, which appear to do little to advance the action. The plot, in these discussions, is simply one of several sources of interest and pleasure afforded by a novel peculiarly rich in pleasurable and interesting things, and the problem of its relation to the other ingredients is evaded altogether. Occasionally, it is true, the question has been faced; but even in those critics, like W. L. Cross and Oliver Elton, who have made it most explicit, the formulas suggested never give to the plot of *Tom Jones* the status of more than an external and enveloping form in relation to which the rest of the novel is content. It is not, as they see it, an end but a means, and they describe it variously, having no language but metaphor for the purpose, as a "framework" in which character (which is Fielding's "real 'bill of fare' ") is "set"; as a device, essentially "artificial," for bringing on the stage "real men and women"; as a "mere mechanism," which, except now and then in the last two books, "does not obtrude," for keeping readers alert through six volumes.

I do not believe, however, that it is necessary to remain content with this very limited and abstract definition of plot or with the miscellaneous and fragmentized criticism of works like *Tom Jones* that has always followed from it. I shall assume that any novel or drama not constructed on didactic principles is a composite of three elements, which unite to determine its quality and effect—the things that are imitated (or "rendered") in it, the linguistic medium in which they are imitated, and the manner or technique of imitation; and I shall assume further that the things imitated necessarily involve human beings interacting with one another in ways determined by, and in turn affecting, their moral characters and their states of mind (i.e., their reasonings, emotions, and attitudes). If this is granted, we may say that the plot of any novel or drama is the particular temporal synthesis effected by the writer of the elements of action, character, and thought that constitute the matter of his invention. It is impossible, therefore, to state adequately what any plot is unless we include in our formula all three of the elements or causes of which the plot is the synthesis; and it follows also that plots will differ in structure according as one or another of the three causal ingredients is employed as the synthesizing principle. There are, thus, plots of action, plots of character, and plots of thought. In the first, the synthesizing principle is a completed change, gradual or sudden, in the situation of the protagonist, determined and effected by character and thought (as in *Oedipus* and *The Brothers Karamazov*); in the second, the principle is a completed process of change in the moral character of the protagonist, precipitated or molded by action, and made manifest both in it and in thought and feeling (as in James's *The Portrait of a Lady*); in the third, the principle is a completed process of change in the thought of the protagonist and consequently in his feelings, conditioned and directed by character and action (as in Pater's *Marius the Epicurean*). All these types of construction, and not merely the first, are plots in the meaning of our definition; and it is mainly, perhaps, because most of the familiar classic plots, including that of *Tom Jones,* have been of the first kind that so many critics have tended to reduce plot to action alone. (This accounts in large part, I think, for the depreciation of "plot" in E. M. Forster's *Aspects of the Novel,* and for his notion of a rivalry between "plot" and "character," in which one or the other may "triumph." For a view much closer to that argued in this essay see Elizabeth Bowen, "Notes on Writing a Novel," *Orion,* II (1945), 18 ff.)

If this is granted, we may go farther. For a plot, in the enlarged sense here given to the term, is not merely a particular synthesis of particular materials of character, thought, and action, but such a synthesis endowed necessarily, because it imitates in words a sequence of human activities, with a power to affect our opinions and emotions in a certain way. We are bound, as we read or listen, to form expectations about what is coming and to feel more or less determinate desires relatively to our expectations. At the very least, if we are interested at all, we desire to know what is going to happen, or how the problems faced by the characters are going to be solved. This is a necessary condition of our pleasure in all plots, and there are many good ones—in the classics of pure detective fiction, for example, or in some modern psychiatric novels—the power of which depends almost exclusively on the pleasure we take in inferring progressively, from complex or ambiguous signs, the true state of affairs. For some readers and even some critics this would seem to be the chief source of delight in many plots that have obviously been constructed on more specific principles: not only *Tom Jones,* as we have seen, but *Oedipus* has been praised as a mystery story, and it is likely that much of Henry James's popularity is due to his remarkable capacity for provoking a superior kind of inferential activity. What distinguishes all the more developed forms of imitative literature, however, is that, though they presuppose this instinctive pleasure in learning, they go beyond it and give us plots of which the effects derive in a much more immediate way from the particular ethical qualities manifested in their agents' actions and thoughts vis-à-vis the human situations in which they are engaged. When this is the case, we cannot help becoming, in a greater or less degree, emotionally involved; for some of the characters we wish good, for others ill, and, depending on our inferences as to the events, we feel hope or fear, pity or satisfaction, or some modification of these or similar emotions. The peculiar power of any plot of this kind, as it unfolds, is a result of our state of knowledge at any point in complex interaction with our desires for the characters as morally differentiated beings; and we may be said to have grasped the plot in the full artistic sense only when we have analyzed this interplay of desires and expectations sequentially in relation to the incidents by which it is produced.

It is, of course, an essential condition of such an effect that the writer should so have combined his elements of action, character, and thought as to have achieved a complete and ordered whole, with all the parts needed to carry the protagonist, by probable or necessary stages, from the beginning to the end of his change: we should not have, otherwise, any connected series of expectations wherewith to guide our desires. In itself, however, this structure is only the matter or content of the plot and not its form; the form of the plot—in the sense of that which makes its matter into a definite artistic thing—is rather its distinctive "working or power," as the form of the plot in tragedy, for example, is the capacity of its unified sequence of actions to effect through pity and fear a cartharsis of such emotions.

But if this is granted, then certain consequences follow for the criticism of dramas and novels. It is evident, in the first place, that no plot of this order can be judged excellent *merely* in terms of the unity of its action, the number and variety of its incidents, or the extent to which it produces suspense and surprise. These are but properties of its matter, and their achievement, even to a high degree, in any particular plot does not inevitably mean that the emotional effect of the whole will not still be diffused or weak. They are, therefore, necessary, but not sufficient, conditions of a good plot, the positive excellence of which depends upon the power of its peculiar synthesis of character, action, and thought, as inferable from the sequence of words, to move our feelings powerfully and pleasurably in a certain definite way.

But this power, which constitutes the form of the plot, is obviously, from an artistic point of view, the most important virtue any drama or novel can have; it is that, indeed, which most sharply distinguishes works of imitation from all other kinds of literary productions. It follows, consequently, that the plot, considered formally, of any imitative work is, in relation to the work as a whole, not simply a means—a "framework" or "mere mechanism"—but rather the final end which everything in the work, if that is to be felt as a whole, must be made, directly or indirectly, to serve. For the critic, therefore, the form of the plot is a first principle, which he must grasp as clearly as possible for any work he proposes to examine before he can deal adequately with the questions raised by its parts. This does not mean that we cannot derive other relevant principles of judgment from the general causes of pleasure operative in all artistic imitations, irrespective of the particular effect, serious or comic, that is aimed at in a given work. One of these is the imitative principle itself, the principle that we are in general more convinced and moved when things are "rendered" for us through probable signs than when they are given merely in "statement," without illusion, after the fashion of a scenario. The meaning and force of this will be clear to anyone who has compared in detail the text of *The Ambassadors* with James's preliminary synopsis of the novel (*The Notebooks of Henry James* [New York, 1947], pp. 372-415. See also the excellent remarks of Allen Tate, apropos of *Madame Bovary,* in his "Techniques of Fiction" (*Forms of Modern Fiction,* ed. William Van O'Conner [Minneapolis, 1948], esp. pp. 37-45). Critical judgments, valid enough if they are not taken absolutely, may also be drawn from considerations of the general powers of language as a literary medium, of the known potentialities or requirements of a given manner of representation (e.g., dramatic or narrative), and of the various conditions of suspense and surprise. We are not likely to feel strongly the emotional effect of a work in which the worse rather than the better alternatives among these different expedients are consistently chosen or chosen in crucial scenes. The same thing, too, can be said of works in which the thought, however clearly serving an artistic use, is generally uninteresting or stale, or in which the characters of the agents, though right enough in conception for the intended effect, are less than adequately "done" or fail to impress themselves upon our memory and imagination, or in which we perceive that the most has not been made of the possibilities implicit in the incidents. And there is also a kind of judgment, distinct from any of these, the object of which is not so much the traits of a work that follow from its general character as an imitative drama or novel as the qualities of intelligence and moral sensibility in its author which are reflected in his conception and handling of its subject and which warrant us in ascribing "greatness," "seriousness," or "maturity" to some products of art and in denying these values to others no matter how excellent, in a formal sense, the latter may be.

Such criticism of parts in the light of general principles is indispensable, but it is no substitute for—and its conclusions, affirmative as well as negative, have constantly to be checked by—

the more specific kind of criticism of a work that takes the form of the plot as its starting point and then inquires how far and in what way its peculiar power is maximized by the writer's invention and development of episodes, his step-by-step rendering of the characters of his people, his use and elaboration of thought, his handling of diction and imagery, and his decisions as to the order, method, scale, and point of view of his representation.

# VI. What Is Point of View?

Percy Lubbock, "Picture, Drama, and Point of View," three chapters from *The Craft of Fiction*, reprinted here by permission of the Viking Press.

Wayne C. Booth, "Types of Narration," chapter 6 of *The Rhetoric of Fiction*, reprinted here by permission of the University of Chicago Press.

*The question of point of view must include such matters as the various ways of handling narration and the relation of this technical problem to all the other problems faced by the novelist. Lubbock's treatment of these matters is of historical importance as well as theoretical interest. Taking his cue from prefaces and essays by Henry James, he wrote the first treatise on point of view in fiction, helping to make this a major technical question for writers and critics of the past half century. The vitality of point of view as a locus for critical consideration is suggested by the difference between Lubbock's work and Booth's. Where Lubbock was content to make a few broad distinctions leading to some prescriptive advice, Booth finds the problems of description and discrimination so complex as to make dogmatizing extremely difficult. With this probing and undogmatic approach, itself a transitional chapter of a provocative book, our collection of approaches ends, in E. M. Forster's phrase, "not rounding off but opening out."*

## Percy Lubbock

### *The Craft of Fiction: Picture, Drama, and Point of View*

PICTURE

In dealing with the method that I find peculiarly characteristic of Thackeray, the "panoramic" method, I have spoken of it also as "pictorial"; and it will be noticed that I have thus arrived at another distinction which I touched upon in connection with Bovary. Picture and drama—this is an antithesis which continually appears in a novel, and I shall have much to say of it. And first of the names which I give to these contrasted manners of treatment—I do not know that they are the best names, but they express the main point of difference, and they also have this advantage, that they *have* been used technically in the criticism of fiction, with specific meaning. In writing about novels one is so rarely handling words that have ever been given close definition (with regard to the art of fiction, I mean) that it is natural to grasp at any which have chanced to be selected and strictly applied by a critic of authority. Picture and drama, therefore, I use because Henry James used them in discussing his own novels, when he reviewed them all in his later years; but I use them, I must add, in a rather more extended sense than he did. Anybody who knows the critical prefaces of his books will remember how picture and drama, to him, represented the twofold manner towards which he tended in his last novels, composed as they are in a regular alternation of dramatic dialogue and pictorial description. But *his* pictorial description was of a very special kind; and when the subject of criticism is fiction generally, not his alone, picture will take a wider meaning, as opposed to drama. It will be found to cover the panoramic manner of Thackeray.

It is a question, I said, of the reader's relation to the writer; in one case the reader faces towards the story-teller and listens to him, in the other he turns towards the story and watches it. In the drama of the stage, in the acted play, the spectator evidently has no direct concern with the author at all, while the action is proceeding. The author places their parts in the mouths of the players, leaves them to make their own impression, leaves *us,* the audience, to make what we can of it. The motion of life is before us, the recording registering mind of the author is eliminated. That is drama; and when we think of the story-teller as opposed to the dramatist, it is obvious that in the full sense of the word there is no such thing as drama in a novel. The novelist may give the very words that were spoken by his characters, the dialogue, but of course he must interpose on his own account to let us know how the people appeared, and where they were, and what they were doing. If he offers nothing but the bare dialogue, he is writing a kind of play; just as a dramatist, amplifying his play with "stage-directions" and putting it forth to be read in a book, has really written a kind of novel. But the difference between the story-teller and the playwright is not my affair; and a new contrast, within the limits of the art of fiction, is apparent when we speak of the novel by itself—a contrast of two methods, to one of which it is reasonable to give the name of drama.

I do not say that a clear line can be drawn between them; criticism does not hope to be mathematically exact. But everybody sees the diversity between the talkative, confidential manner of Thackeray and the severe, discreet, anonymous manner—of whom shall I say?—of Maupassant, for a good example, in many of his stories. It is not only the difference between the personal qualities of the two men, which indeed are also as far apart as the house of Castlewood and the Maison Tellier; it is not the difference between the kinds of story they chose to tell. They approached a story from opposite sides, and thought of it, consequently, in images that had nothing in common: not always, I dare say, but on the whole and characteristically they did so. Maupassant's idea of a story (and not peculiarly Maupassant's, of course, but his name is convenient) would suggest an object that you fashioned and abandoned to the reader, turning away and leaving him alone with it; Thackeray's would be more like the idea of a long and sociable interview with the reader, a companion with whom he must establish definite terms. Enough, the contrast is very familiar. But these are images; how is the difference shown in their written books, in Esmond and La Maison Tellier? Both, it is true, represent a picture that was in the author's mind; but the story passes into Thackeray's book as a picture still, and passes into Maupassant's as something else—I call it drama.

In Maupassant's drama we are close to the facts, against them and amongst them. He relates his story as though he had caught it in the act and were mentioning the details as they passed. There seems to be no particular process at work in his mind, so little that the figure of Maupassant, the showman, is overlooked and forgotten as we follow the direction of his eyes. The scene he evokes is contemporaneous, and there it is, we can see it as well as he can. Certainly he is "telling" us things, but they are things so immediate, so perceptible, that the machinery of his telling, by which they reach us, is unnoticed; the story appears to tell itself. Critically, of course, we know how far that is from being the case, we know with what judicious thought the showman is selecting the points of the scene upon which he touches. But the *effect* is that he is not there at all, because he is doing nothing that ostensibly requires any judgment, nothing that reminds us of his presence. He is behind us, out of sight, out of mind; the story occupies us, the moving scene, and nothing else.

But Thackeray—in *his* story we need him all the time and can never forget him. He it is who must assemble and arrange his large chronicle, piecing it together out of his experience. Becky's mode of life, in his story, is a matter of many details picked up on many occasions, and the power that collects them, the mind that contains them, is always and openly Thackeray's; it could not be otherwise. It is no question, for most of the time, of watching a scene at close quarters, where the simple, literal detail, such as anybody might see for himself, would be sufficient. A stretch of time is to be shown in perspective, at a distance; the story-teller must be at hand to work it into a single impression. And thus the general panorama, such as Thackeray displays, becomes the representation of the author's experience, and the author becomes a personal entity, about whom we may begin to ask questions. Thackeray *cannot* be the nameless abstraction that the dramatist (whether in the drama of the stage or in that of the novel) is naturally. I know that Thackeray, so far from trying to conceal himself, comes forward and attracts attention and nudges the reader a great deal more than he need; he likes the personal relation with the reader and insists on it. But do what he might to disguise it, so long as he is ranging over his story at a height, chronicling, summarizing, foreshortening, he *must* be present to the reader as a narrator and a showman. It is only when he descends and approaches a certain occasion and sets a scene with due circumspection—rarely and a trifle awkwardly, as we saw—that he can for the time being efface the thought of his active part in the affair.

So much of a novel, therefore, as is not dramatic enactment, not *scenic,* inclines always to picture, to the reflection of somebody's mind. Confronted with a scene—like Becky's great scene, once more—we forget that other mind; but as soon as the story goes off again into narrative a question at once arises. *Who* is disposing the scattered facts, whose is this new point of view? It is the omniscient author, and the point of view is his—such would be the common answer, and it is the answer we get in Vanity Fair. By convention the author is allowed his universal knowledge of the story and the people in it. But still it is a convention, and a prudent novelist does not strain it unnecessarily. Thackeray in Vanity Fair is not at all prudent; his method, so seldom strictly dramatic, is one that of its nature is apt to force this question of the narrator's authority, and he goes out of his way to emphasize the question still further. He flourishes the fact that the point of view is his own, not to be confounded with that of anybody in the book. And so his book, as one may say, is not complete in itself, not really self-contained; it does not meet and satisfy all the issues it suggests. Over the whole of one side of it there is an inconclusive look, something that draws the eye away from the book itself, into space. It is the question of the narrator's relation to the story.

However unconsciously—and I dare say the recognition is usually unconscious—the novelist is alive to this difficulty, no doubt; for we may see him, we presently shall, taking various steps to circumvent it. There is felt to be an unsatisfactory want of finish in leaving a question hanging out of the book, like a loose end, without some kind of attempt to pull it back and make it part of an integral design. After all, the book is torn away from its author and given out to the world; the author is no longer a wandering *jongleur* who enters the hall and utters his book to the company assembled, retaining his book as his own inalienable possession, himself and his actual presence and his real voice indivisibly a part of it. The book that we read has no such support; it must bring its own recognisances. And in the fictitious picture of life the effect of validity is all in all and there can be no appeal to an external authority; and so there is an inherent weakness in it if the mind that knows the story and the eye that sees it remain unaccountable. At any moment they may be questioned, and the only way to silence the question is somehow to make the mind and the eye objective, to make them facts in the story. When the point of view is definitely included in the book, when it can be recognized and verified there, then every side of the book is equally wrought and fashioned. Otherwise it may seem like a thing meant to stand against a wall, with one side left in the rough; and there is no wall for a novel to stand against.

That this is not a fanciful objection to a pictorial book like Vanity Fair, where the point of view is *not* accounted for, is proved, I think, by the different means that a novelist will adopt to authenticate his story—to dramatize the seeing eye, as I should prefer to put it. These I shall try to deal with in what seems to be their logical order; illuminating examples of any of them are not wanting. I do not suggest that if I were criticizing Vanity Fair I should think twice about this aspect of it; to do so would be very futile criticism of such a book, such a store of life. But then I am not considering it as Vanity Fair, I am considering it as a dominant case of pictorial fiction; and here is the characteristic danger of the method, and a danger which all who practise the method are not likely to encounter and override with the genius of Thackeray. And even Thackeray—he chose to encounter it once again, it is true, in Pendennis, but only once and no more, and after that he took his own precautions, and evidently found that he could move the more freely for doing so.

But to revert yet again for a moment to Bovary—which seemed on scrutiny to be more of a picture than a drama—I think it is clear how Flaubert avoided the necessity of installing himself avowedly as the narrator, in the sight of the reader. I mentioned how he constantly blends his acuter vision with that of Emma, so that the weakness of her gift of experience is helped out; and the help is mutual, for on the other hand her vision is always active as far as it goes, and Flaubert's intervention is so unobtrusive that her point of view seems to govern the story more than it does really. And therefore, though the book is largely a picture, a review of many details and occasions, the question of the narrator is never insistent. The landscape that Thackeray controls is so much wider and fuller that even with all the tact of Flaubert—and little he has of it—he could scarcely follow Flaubert's example. His book is not a portrait of character but a panorama of manners, and there is no disguising the need of some detached spectator, who looks on from without.

It is the method of picture-making that enables the novelist to cover his great spaces of life and quantities of experience, so much greater than any that can be brought within the acts of a play. As for intensity of life, that is another matter; there, as we have seen, the novelist has recourse to his other arm, the one that corresponds with the single arm of the dramatist. Inevitably, as the plot thickens and the climax approaches—inevitably, whereever an impression is to be emphasized and driven home—narration gives place to enactment, the train of events to the particular episode, the broad picture to the dramatic scene. But the limitation of drama is as obvious as its peculiar power. It is clear that if we wish to see an abundance and multitude of life we shall find it more readily and more summarily by looking for an hour into a memory, a consciousness, than by merely watching the present events of an hour, however crowded. Much may happen in that time, but in extent it will be nothing to the regions thrown open by the other method. A novelist, with a large and discursive subject before him, could not hope to show it all dramatically; much of it, perhaps the greater part, must be so marshalled that it may be swept by a travelling glance. Thackeray shows how it is done and how a vista of many facts can be made to fall into line; but he shows, too, how it needs a mind to create that vista, and how the creative mind becomes more and more perceptible, more visibly active, as the prospect widens.

Most novelists, I think, seem to betray, like Thackeray, a preference for one method or the other, for picture or for drama; one sees in a moment how Fielding, Balzac, George Eliot, incline to the first, in their diverse manners, and Tolstoy (certainly Tolstoy, in spite of his big range) or Dostoevsky to the second, the scenic way. But of course every novelist uses both, and the quality of a novelist appears very clearly in his management of the two, how he guides the story into the scene, how he picks it out of the scene, a richer and fuller story than it was before, and proceeds with his narrative. On the whole, no doubt, the possibilities of the scene are greatly abused in fiction, in the daily and familiar novel. They are doubly abused; for the treatment of the scene is neglected, and yet it recurs again and again, much too often, and its value is wasted. It has to be remembered that drama is the novelist's highest light, like the white paper or white paint of a draughtsman; to use it prodigally where it is not needed is to lessen its force where it is essential. And so the economical procedure would be to hoard it rather, reserving it for important occasions—as in Bovary, sure enough.

But before I deal with the question of the novelist's drama I would follow out the whole argument that is suggested by his reflected picture of life. This, after all, is the method which is his very own, which he commands as a story-teller pure and simple. And for a beginning I have tried to indicate its prime disadvantage, consisting of the fact that in its plain form it drags in the omniscient author and may make him exceedingly conspicuous. Why is this a disadvantage, is it asked? It is none, of course, if the author has the power to make us admire and welcome the apparition, or if his picture is so dazzling that a theoretic defect in it is forgotten. But a novel in which either of these feats is accomplished proves only the charm or genius of the author; charm and genius do what they will, there is nothing new in that. And I believe that the defect, even though at first sight it may seem a trifle, is apt to become more and more troublesome in a book as the book is re-read. It makes for a kind of thinness in the general impression, wherever the personal force of the writer is not remarkable. I should say that it may often contribute towards an air of ineffectiveness in a story, which it might otherwise be difficult to explain.

The fiction of Turgenev is on the whole a case in point, to my mind. Turgenev was never shy of appearing in his pages as the reflective story-teller, imparting the fruits of his observation to the reader. He will watch a character, let us say, cross a field and enter a wood and sit down under a tree; good, it is an opportunity for gaining a first impression of the man or woman, it is a little scene, and Turgenev's touch is quick and light. But then with perfect candour he will show his hand; he will draw the reader aside and pour into his ear a flow of information about the man or woman, information that openly comes straight from Turgenev himself, in good pictorial form, no doubt, but information which will never have its due weight with the reader, because it reposes upon nothing that he can test for himself. Who and what is this communicative participator in the business, this vocal author? He does not belong to the book, and his voice has not that compelling tone and tune of its own (as Thackeray's had) which makes a reader enjoy hearing it for its own sake. This is a small matter, I admit, but Turgenev extends it and pursues the same kind of course in more important affairs. He remains the observant narrator, to whom we are indebted for a share in his experience. The result is surely that his picture of life has less authority than its highly finished design would seem to warrant. It is evidently not a picture in which the deeps of character are sounded, and in which the heights of passion are touched, and in which a great breadth of the human world is contained; it is not a picture of such dimensions. But it has so much neat and just and even exquisite work in it that it might seem final of its kind, completely effective in what it attempts; and it falls short of this, I should say, and there is something in that constant sense of Turgenev at one's elbow, *proffering* the little picture, that may very well damage it. The thing ought to stand out by itself; it could easily be made to do so. But Turgenev was unsuspecting; he had not taken to heart the full importance of dramatizing the point of view—perhaps it was that.

The narrative, then, the chronicle, the summary, which must represent the story-teller's ordered and arranged experience, and which must accordingly be of the nature of a picture, is to be strengthened, is to be raised to a power approaching that of drama, where the intervention of the story-teller is no longer felt. The freedom which the pictorial method gives to the novelist is unknown to the playwright; but that freedom has to be paid for by some loss of intensity, and the question is how to pay as little as possible. In the end, as I think it may be shown, the loss is made good and there is nothing to pay at all, so far may the dramatizing process be followed. Method, I have said, can be imposed upon method, one kind upon another; and in analyzing the manner of certain novelists one discovers how ingeniously they will correct the weakness of one method by the force of another and retain the advantages of both. It is rather a complicated story, but the beginning is clear enough, and the direction which it is to take is also clear. Everything in the novel, not only the scenic episodes but all the rest, is to be in some sense dramatized; that is where the argument tends.

* * * * * *

## DRAMA

And now for the method by which the picture of a mind is fully dramatized, the method which is to be seen consistently applied in The Ambassadors and the other later novels of Henry James. How is the author to withdraw, to stand aside, and to let Strether's thought tell its own story? The thing must be seen from our own point of view and no other. Author and hero, Thackeray and Esmond, Meredith and Harry Richmond, have given their various accounts of emotional and intellectual adventure; but they might do more, they might bring the facts of the adventure upon the scene and leave them to make their impression. The story passes in an invisible world, the events take place in the man's mind; and we might have to conclude that they lie beyond our reach, and that we cannot attain to them save by the help of the man himself, or of the author who knows all about him. We might have to make the best of an account at second hand, and it would not occur to us, I dare say, that anything more could be forthcoming; we seem to touch the limit of the possibilities of drama in fiction. But it is not the final limit—there is fiction here to prove it; and it is this further stroke of the art that I would now examine.

The world of silent thought is thrown open, and instead of telling the reader what happened there, the novelist uses the look and behaviour of thought as the vehicle by which the story is rendered. Just as the writer of a play embodies his subject in visible action and audible speech, so the novelist, dealing with a situation like Strether's represents it by means of the movement that flickers over the surface of his mind. The impulses and reactions of his mood are the players upon the new scene. In drama of the theatre a character must bear his part unaided; if he is required to be a desperate man, harbouring thoughts of crime, he cannot look to the author to appear at the side of the stage and inform the audience of the fact; he must express it for himself through his words and deeds, his looks and tones. The playwright so arranges the matter that these will be enough, the spectator will make the right inference. But suppose that instead of a man upon the stage, concealing and betraying his thought, we watch the thought itself, the hidden thing, as it twists to and fro in his brain—watch it without any other aid to understanding but such as its own manner of bearing may supply. The novelist, more free than the playwright, could of course *tell* us, if he chose, what lurks behind this agitated spirit; he could step forward and explain the restless appearance of the man's thought. But if he prefers the dramatic way, admittedly the more effective, there is nothing to prevent him from taking it. The man's thought, in its turn, can be made to reveal its own inwardness.

Let us see how this plan is pursued in The Ambassadors. That book is entirely concerned with Strether's experience of his peculiar mission to Europe, and never passes outside the circle of his thought. Strether is despatched, it will be remembered, by a resolute New England widow, whose son is living lightly in Paris instead of attending to business at home. To win the hand of the widow, Strether must succeed in snatching the young man from the siren who is believed to have beguiled him. The mission is undertaken in all good faith, Strether descends upon Paris with a mind properly disposed and resolved. He comes as an ambassador representing principle and duty, to treat with the young man, appeal to him convincingly and bear him off. The task before him may be difficult, but his purpose is simple. Strether has reckoned, however, without his imagination; he had scarcely been aware of possessing one before, but everything grows complicated as it is touched and awakened on the new scene. By degrees and degrees he changes his opinion of the life of freedom; it is most unlike his prevision of it, and at last his purpose is actually inverted. He no longer sees a misguided young man to be saved from disaster, he sees an exquisite, bountiful world laid at a young man's feet; and now the only question is whether the young man is capable of meeting and grasping his opportunity. He is incapable, as it turns out; when the story ends he is on the verge of rejecting his freedom and going back to the world of commonplace; Strether's mission has ended successfully. But in Strether's mind the revolution is complete; there is nothing left for him, no reward and no future. The world of commonplace is no longer *his* world, and he is too late to seize the other; he is old, he has missed the opportunity of youth.

This is a story which must obviously be told from Strether's point of view, in the first place. The change in his purpose is due to a change in his vision, and the long slow process could not be followed unless his vision were shared by the reader. Strether's predicament, that is to say, could not be placed upon the stage; his outward behaviour, his conduct, his talk, do not express a tithe of it. Only the brain behind his eyes can be aware of the colour of his experience, as it passes through its innumerable gradations; and all understanding of his case depends upon seeing these. The way of the author, therefore, who takes this subject in hand, is clear enough at the outset. It is a purely pictorial subject, covering Strether's field of vision and bounded by its limits; it consists entirely of an impression received by a certain man. There can accordingly be no thought of rendering him as a figure seen from without; nothing that any one else could discern, looking at him and listening to his conversation, would give the full sense of the eventful life he is leading within. The dramatic method, as we ordinarily understand it, is ruled out at once. Neither as an action set before the reader without interpretation from within, nor yet as an action pictured for the reader by some other onlooker in the book, can this story possibly be told.

Strether's real situation, in fact, is not his open and visible situation, between the lady in New England and the young man in Paris; his grand adventure is not expressed in its incidents. These, as they are devised by the author, are secondary, they are the extension of the moral event that takes place in the breast of the ambassador, his change of mind. That is the very middle of the subject; it is a matter that lies solely between Strether himself and his vision of the free world. It is a delightful effect of irony, indeed, that he should have accomplished his errand after all, in spite of himself; but the point of the book is not there, the ironic climax only serves to bring out the point more sharply. The reversal of his own idea is underlined and enhanced by the reversal of the young man's idea in the opposite sense; but essentially the subject of the book would be unchanged if the story ended differently, if the young man held to his freedom and refused to go home. Strether would still have passed through the same cycle of unexpected experience; his errand might have failed, but still it would not have been any the more impossible for him to claim his reward, for his part, than it is impossible as things are, with the quest achieved and the young man ready to hasten back to duty of his own accord. And so the subject can only be reached through Strether's consciousness, it is plain; that way alone will command the impression that the scene makes on him. Nothing in the scene has any importance, any value in itself; what Strether sees in it—that is the whole of its meaning.

But though in The Ambassadors the point of view is primarily Strether's, and though it *appears* to be his throughout the book, there is in fact an insidious shifting of it, so artfully contrived that the reader may arrive at the end without suspecting the trick. The reader, all unawares, is placed in a better position for an understanding of Strether's history, better than the position of Strether himself. Using his eyes, we see what *he* sees, we are possessed of the material on which his patient thought sets to work; and that is so far well enough, and plainly necessary. All the other people in the book face towards him, and it is that aspect of them, and that only, which is shown to the reader; still more important, the beautiful picture of Paris and spring-time, the stir and shimmer of life in the Rue de Rivoli and the gardens of the Tuileries, is Strether's picture, *his* vision, rendered as the time and the place strike upon his senses. All this on which his thought ruminates, the stuff that occupies it, is represented from his point of view. To see it, even for a moment, from some different angle—if, for example, the author interposed with a vision of his own—would patently disturb the right impression. The author does no such thing, it need hardly be said.

When it comes to Strether's treatment of this material, however, when it is time to learn what he makes of it, turning his experience over and over in his mind, then his own point of view no longer serves. How is anybody, even Strether, to *see* the working of his own mind? A mere account of its working, after the fact, has already been barred; we have found that this of necessity is lacking in force, it is statement where we look for demonstration. And so we must see for ourselves, the author must so arrange matters that Strether's thought will all be made intelligible by a direct view of its surface. The immediate flaw or ripple of the moment, and the next and the next, will then take up the tale, like the speakers in a dialogue which gradually unfolds the subject of the play. Below the surface, behind the outer aspect of his mind, we do not penetrate; this is drama, and in drama the spectator must judge by appearances. When Strether's mind is dramatized, nothing is shown but the passing images that anybody might detect, looking down upon a mind grown visible. There is no drawing upon extraneous sources of information; Henry

James knows all there is to know of Strether, but he most carefully refrains from using his knowledge. He wishes us to accept nothing from him, on authority—only to watch and learn.

For suppose him to begin sharing the knowledge that he alone possesses, as the author and inventor of Strether; suppose that instead of representing only the momentary appearance of Strether's thought he begins to expound its substance: he must at once give us the whole of it, must let us into every secret without delay, or his exposition is plainly misleading. It is assumed that he tells all, if he once begins. And so, too, if the book were cast autobiographically and Strether spoke in person; he could not hold back, he could not heighten the story of his thought with that touch of suspense, waiting to be resolved, which stamps the impression so firmly into the memory of the onlooker. In a tale of murder and mystery there is one man who cannot possibly be the narrator, and that is the murderer himself; for if he admits us into his mind at all he must do so without reserve, thereby betraying the secret that we ought to be guessing at for ourselves. But by this method of The Ambassadors the mind of which the reader is made free, Strether's mind, is not given away; there is no need for it to yield up all its secrets at once. The story in it is played out by due degrees, and there may be just as much deliberation, refrainment, suspension, as in a story told scenically upon the stage. All the effect of true drama is thus at the disposal of the author, even when he seems to be describing and picturing the consciousness of one of his characters. He arrives at the point where apparently nothing but a summary and a report should be possible, and even there he is precluded from none of the privileges of a dramatist.

It is necessary to show that in his attitude towards his European errand Strether is slowly turning upon himself and looking in another direction. To announce the fact, with a tabulation of his reasons, would be the historic, retrospective, undramatic way of dealing with the matter. To bring his mind into view at the different moments, one after another, when it is brushed by new experience—to make a little scene of it, without breaking into hidden depths where the change of purpose is proceeding—to multiply these glimpses until the silent change is apparent, though no word has actually been said of it: this is Henry James's way, and though the *method* could scarcely be more devious and roundabout, always refusing the short cut, yet by these very qualities and precautions it finally produces the most direct impression, for the reader has *seen.* That is why the method is adopted. The author has so fashioned his book that his own part in the narration is now unobtrusive to the last degree; he, the author, could not imaginably figure there more discreetly. His part in the effect is no more than that of the playwright, who vanishes and leaves his people to act the story; only instead of men and women talking together, in Strether's case there are innumerable images of thought crowding across the stage, expressing the story in their behaviour.

But there is more in the book, as I suggested just now, than Strether's vision and the play of his mind. In the *scenic* episodes, the colloquies that Strether holds, for example, with his sympathetic friend Maria Gostrey, another turn appears in the author's procedure. Throughout these clear-cut dialogues Strether's point of view still reigns; the only eyes in the matter are still his, there is no sight of the man himself as his companion sees him. Miss Gostrey is clearly visible, and Madame de Vionnet and little Bilham, or whoever it may be; the face of Strether himself is never turned to the reader. On the evening of the first encounter between the elderly ambassador and the young man, they sat together in a café of the boulevards and walked away at midnight through quiet streets; and all through their interview the fact of the young man's appearance is strongly dominant, for it is this that first reveals to Strether how the young man has been transformed by his commerce with the free world; and so his figure is sharply before the reader as they talk. How Strether seemed to Chad—this, too, is represented, but only by implication, through Chad's speech and manner. It is essential, of course, that it should be so, the one-sided vision is strictly enjoined by the method of the whole book. But though the seeing eye is still with Strether, there is a noticeable change in the author's way with him.

In these scenic dialogues, on the whole, we seem to have edged away from Strether's consciousness. He sees, and we with him; but when he *talks* it is almost as though we were outside him and away from him altogether. Not always, indeed; for in many of the scenes he is busily brooding and thinking throughout, and we share his mind while he joins in the talk. But still, on the whole, the author is inclined to leave Strether alone when the scene is set. He talks the matter out with Maria, he sits and talks with Madame de Vionnet, he strolls along the boulevards with Chad, he lounges on a chair in the Champs Elysées with some one else—we know the kind of scene that is set for Strether, know how very few accessories he requires, and know that the scene marks a certain definite climax, wherever it occurs, for all its everyday look. The occasion is important, there is no doubt about that; its importance is in the air. And Strether takes his part in it as though he had almost become what he cannot be, an objective figure for the reader. Evidently he cannot be that, since the centre of vision is still within him; but by an easy sleight of hand the author gives him almost the value of an independent person, a man to whose words we may listen expectantly, a man whose mind is screened from us. Again and again the stroke is accomplished, and indeed there is nothing mysterious about it. Simply it consists in treating the scene as dramatically as possible—keeping it framed in Strether's vision, certainly, but keeping his consciousness out of sight, his thought unexplored. He talks to Maria; and to us, to the reader, his voice seems as much as hers to belong to somebody whom we are *watching*—which is impossible, because our point of view is his.

A small matter, perhaps, but it is interesting as a sign, still another, of the perpetual tendency of the novel to capture the advantages which it appears to forego. The Ambassadors is without doubt a book that deals with an entirely non-dramatic subject; it is the picture of an *état d'âme*. But just as the chapters that are concerned with Strether's soul are in the key of drama, after the fashion I have described, so too the episode, the occasion, the scene that crowns the impression, is always more dramatic in its method than it apparently has the means to be. Here, for instance, is the central scene of the whole story, the scene in the old Parisian garden, where Strether, finally filled to the brim with the sensation of all the life for which his own opportunity has passed, overflows with his passionate exhortation to little Bilham

—warning him, adjuring him not to make *his* mistake, not to let life slide away ungrasped. It is the hour in which Strether touches his crisis, and the first necessity of the chapter is to show the sudden lift and heave of his mood within; the voices and admonitions of the hour, that is to say, must be heard and felt as he hears and feels them himself. The scene, then, will be given as Strether's impression, clearly, and so it is; the old garden and the evening light and the shifting company of people appear as their reflection in his thought. But the scene is *also* a piece of drama, it strikes out of the book with the strong relief of dramatic action; which is evidently an advantage gained, seeing the importance of the hour in the story, but which is an advantage that it could not enjoy, one might have said.

The quality of the scene becomes clear if we imagine the story to be told by Strether himself, narrating in the first person. Of the damage that this would entail for the picture of his brooding mind I have spoken already; but suppose the book to have taken the form of autobiography, and suppose that Strether has brought the story up to this point, where he sits beside little Bilham in Gloriani's garden. He describes the deep and agitating effect of the scene upon him, calling to him of the world he has missed; he tells what he thought and felt; and then, he says, I broke out with the following tirade to little Bilham—and we have the energetic outburst which Henry James has put into his mouth. But is it not clear how the incident would be weakened, so rendered? That speech, word for word as we have it, would lose its unexpected and dramatic quality, because Strether, arriving at it by narration, could not suddenly spring away from himself and give the impression of the worn, intelligent, clear-sighted man sitting there in the evening sun, strangely moved to unwonted eloquence. His narration must have discounted the effect of his outburst, leading us up to the very edge of it, describing how it arose, explaining where it came from. He would be *subjective,* and committed to remain so all the time.

Henry James, by his method, can secure this effect of drama, even though his Strether is apparently in the position of a narrator throughout. Strether's are the eyes, I said, and they are more so than ever during this hour in the garden; he is the sentient creature in the scene. But the author, who all through the story has been treating Strether's consciousness as a play, as an action proceeding, can at any moment use his talk almost as though the source from which it springs were unknown to us from within. I remember that he himself, in his critical preface to the book, calls attention to the way in which a conversation between Strether and Maria Gostrey, near the beginning, puts the reader in possession of all the past facts of the situation which it is necessary for him to know; a *scene* thus takes the place of that "harking back to make up," as he calls it, which is apt to appear as a lump of narrative shortly after the opening of a story. If Strether were really the narrator, whether in the first person or the third, he could not use his own talk in this manner; he would have to tell us himself about his past. But he has never *told* us his thought, we have looked at it and drawn our inferences; and so there is still some air of dramatic detachment about him, and his talk may seem on occasion to be that of a man whom we know from outside. The advantage is peculiarly felt on that crucial occasion at Gloriani's, where Strether's sudden flare of vehemence, so natural and yet so unlike him, breaks out with force unimpaired. It strikes freshly on the ear, the speech of a man whose inmost perturbations we have indeed inferred from many glimpses of his mind, but still without ever learning the full tale of them from himself.

The Ambassadors, then, is a story which is seen from one man's point of view, and yet a story in which that point of view is itself a matter for the reader to confront and to watch constructively. Everything in the novel is now dramatically rendered, whether it is a page of dialogue or a page of description, because even in the page of description nobody is addressing us, nobody is reporting his impression to the reader. The impression is enacting itself in the endless series of images that play over the outspread expanse of the man's mind and memory. When the story passes from these to the scenes of dialogue—from the silent drama of Strether's meditation to the spoken drama of the men and women—there is thus no break in the method. The same law rules everywhere—that Strether's changing sense of his situation shall appeal directly to the onlooker, and not by way of any summarizing picture-maker. And yet *as a whole* the book is all pictorial, an indirect impression received through Strether's intervening consciousness, beyond which the story never strays. I conclude that on this paradox the art of dramatizing the picture of somebody's experience—the art I have been considering in these last chapters —touches its limit. There is indeed no further for it to go.

## POINT OF VIEW

The whole intricate question of method, in the craft of fiction, I take to be governed by the question of the point of view—the question of the relation in which the narrator stands to the story. He tells it as *he* sees it, in the first place; the reader faces the story-teller and listens, and the story may be told so vivaciously that the presence of the minstrel is forgotten, and the scene becomes visible, peopled with the characters of the tale. It may be so, it very often is so for a time. But it is not so always, and the story-teller himself grows conscious of a misgiving. If the spell is weakened at any moment, the listener is recalled from the scene to the mere author before him, and the story rests only upon the author's direct assertion. Is it not possible, then, to introduce another point of view, to set up a fresh narrator to bear the brunt of the reader's scrutiny? If the story-teller is *in* the story himself, the author is dramatized; his assertions gain in weight, for they are backed by the presence of the narrator in the pictured scene. It is advantage scored; the author has shifted his responsibility, and it now falls where the reader can see and measure it; the arbitrary quality which may at any time be detected in the author's voice is disguised in the voice of his spokesman. Nothing is now imported into the story from without; it is self-contained, it has no associations with anyone beyond its circle.

Such is the first step towards dramatization, and in very many a story it may be enough. The spokesman is there, in recognizable relation with his matter; no question of his authority can arise. But now a difficulty may be started by the nature of the tale that he tells. If he has nothing to do but to relate what he has seen, what anyone might have seen in his position, his account will serve very well; there is no need for more. Let him unfold his chronicle as it appears in his memory. But if he is himself the subject of his story, if the story involves a searching exploration of his own consciousness, an account in his own words, after the fact, is not by any means the best imaginable. Far better it would be to see him while his mind is actually at work in the agitation, whatever it may be, which is to make the book. The matter would then be objective and visible to the reader, instead of reaching him in the form of a report at second hand. But how to manage this without falling back upon the author and *his* report, which has already been tried and for good reasons, as it seemed, abandoned? It is managed by a kind of repetition of the same stroke, a further shift of the point of view. The spectator, the listener, the reader, is now himself to be placed at the angle of vision; not an account or a report, more or less convincing, is to be offered him, but a direct sight of the matter itself, while it is passing. Nobody expounds or explains; the story is enacted by its look and behaviour at particular moments. By the first stroke the narrator was brought into the book and set before the reader; but the action appeared only in his narrative. Now the action is there, proceeding while the pages are turned; the narrator is forestalled, he is watched while the story is in the making. Such is the progress of the writer of fiction towards drama; such is his method of evading the drawbacks of a mere reporter and assuming the advantages, as far as possible, of a dramatist. How far he may choose to push the process in his book—that is a matter to be decided by the subject; it entirely depends upon the kind of effect that the theme demands. It may respond to all the dramatization it can get, it may give all that it has to give for less. The subject dictates the method.

And now let the process be reversed, let us start with the purely dramatic subject, the story that will tell itself in perfect rightness, unaided, to the eye of the reader. This story never deviates from a strictly scenic form; one occasion or episode follows another, with no interruption for any reflective summary of events. Necessarily it must be so, for it is only while the episode is proceeding that no question of a narrator can arise; when the scene closes the play ceases till the opening of the next. To glance upon the story from a height and to give a general impression of its course—this is at once to remove the point of view from the reader and to set up a new one somewhere else; the method is no longer consistent, no longer purely dramatic. And the dramatic story is not only scenic, it is also limited to so much as the ear can hear and the eye see. In rigid drama of this kind there is naturally no admission of the reader into the private mind of any of the characters; their thoughts and motives are transmuted into action. A subject wrought to this pitch of objectivity is no doubt given weight and compactness and authority in the highest degree; it is like a piece of modelling, standing in clear space, casting its shadow. It is the most finished form that fiction can take.

But evidently it is not a form to which fiction can aspire in general. It implies many sacrifices, and these will easily seem to be more than the subject can usefully make. It is out of the question, of course, wherever the main burden of the story lies within some particular consciousness, in the study of a soul, the growth of a character, the changing history of a temperament; there the subject would be needlessly crossed and strangled by dramatization pushed to its limit. It is out of the question, again, wherever the story is too big, too comprehensive, too widely ranging, to be treated scenically, with no opportunity for general and panoramic survey; it has been discovered, indeed, that even a story of this kind *may* fall into a long succession of definite scenes, under some hands, but it has also appeared that in doing so it incurs unnecessary disabilities, and will likely suffer. These stories, therefore, which will not naturally accommodate themselves to the reader's point of view, and the reader's alone, we regard as rather pictorial than dramatic—meaning that they call for some narrator, somebody who *knows,* to contemplate the facts and create an impression of them. Whether it is the omniscient author or a man in the book, he must gather up his experience, compose a vision of it as it exists in his mind, and lay *that* before the reader. It is the reflection of an experience; and though there may be all imaginable diversity of treatment within the limits of the reflection, such is its essential character. In a pictorial book the principle of the structure involves a point of view which is not the reader's.

It is open to the pictorial book, however, to use a method in its picture-making that is really no other than the method of drama. It is somebody's experience, we say, that is to be reported, the general effect that many things have left upon a certain mind; it is a fusion of innumerable elements, the deposit of a lapse of time. The straightforward way to render it would be for the narrator—the author or his selected creature—to view the past retrospectively and discourse upon it, to recall and meditate and summarize. That is picture-making in its natural form, using its own method. But exactly as in drama the subject is distributed among the characters and enacted by them, so in picture the effect may be entrusted to the elements, the reactions of the moment, and *performed* by these. The mind of the narrator becomes the stage, his voice is no longer heard. His voice *is* heard so long as there is narrative of any sort, whether he is speaking in person or is reported obliquely; his voice is heard, because in either case the language and the intonation are his, the direct expression of his experience. In the drama of his mind there is no personal voice, for there is no narrator; the point of view becomes the reader's once more. The shapes of thought in the man's mind tell their own story. And that is the art of picture-making when it uses the dramatic method.

But it cannot always do so. Constantly it must be necessary to offer the reader a summary of facts, an impression of a train of events, that can only be given as somebody's narration. Suppose it were required to render the general effect of a certain year in a man's life, a year that has filled his mind with a swarm of many memories. Looking into his consciousness after the year has gone, we might find much there that would indicate the nature of the year's events without any word on his part; the flickers and flashes of thought from moment to moment might indeed tell us much. But we shall need an account from him too, no doubt; too much has happened in a year to be wholly acted, as I call it, in the movement of the man's thought. He must narrate—he must make; that is to say, a picture of the events as he sees them, glancing back. Now if he speaks in the first person there can, of course, be no uncertainty in the point of view; he has his fixed position, he cannot leave it. His description will represent the face that the facts in their sequence turned towards *him;* the field of vision is defined with perfect distinctness, and his story cannot stray outside it. The reader, then, may be said to watch a reflection of the facts in a mirror of which the edge is nowhere in doubt; it is rounded by the bounds of the narrator's own personal experience.

This limitation may have a convenience and a value in the story, it may contribute to the effect. But it need not be forfeited, it is clear, if the first person is changed to the third. The author may use the man's field of vision and keep as faithfully within it as though the man were speaking for himself. In that case he retains this advantage and adds to it another, one that is likely to be very much greater. For now, while the point of view is still fixed in space, still assigned to the man in the book, it is free in *time;* there no longer stretches, between the narrator and the events of which he speaks, a certain tract of time, across which the past must appear in a more or less distant perspective. All the variety obtainable by a shifting relation to the story in time is thus in the author's hand; the safe serenity of a far retrospect, the promising or threatening urgency of the present, every gradation between the two, can be drawn into the whole effect of the book, and all of it without any change of the seeing eye. It is a liberty that may help the story indefinitely, raising this matter into strong relief, throwing that other back into vaguer shade.

And next, still keeping mainly and ostensibly to the same point of view, the author has the chance of using a much greater latitude than he need appear to use. The seeing eye is with somebody in the book, but its vision is reinforced; the picture contains more, becomes richer and fuller, because it is the author's as well as his creature's, both at once. Nobody notices, but in fact there are now two brains behind the eye; and one of them is the author's, who adopts and shares the *position* of his creature, and at the same time supplements his wit. If you analyse the picture that is now presented, you find that it is not all the work of the personage whose vision the author has adopted. There are touches in it that go beyond any sensation of his, and indicate that some one else is looking over his shoulder—seeing things from the same angle, but seeing more, bringing another mind to bear upon the scene. It is an easy and natural extension of the personage's power of observation. The impression of the scene may be deepened as much as need be; it is not confined to the scope of one mind, and yet there is no blurring of the focus by a double point of view.

And thus what I have called the sound of the narrator's voice (it is impossible to avoid this mixture of metaphors) is less insistent in oblique narration, even while it seems to be following the very same argument that it would in direct, because another voice is speedily mixed and blended with it.

So this is another resource upon which the author may draw according to his need; sometimes it will be indispensable, and generally, I suppose, it will be useful. It means that he keeps a certain hold upon the narrator *as an object;* the sentient character in the story, round whom it is grouped, is not utterly subjective, completely given over to the business of seeing and feeling on behalf of the reader. It is a considerable point; for it helps to meet one of the great difficulties in the story which is carefully aligned towards a single consciousness and consistently so viewed. In that story the man or woman who acts as the vessel of sensation is always in danger of seeming a light, uncertain weight compared with the other people in the book—simply because the other people are objective images, plainly outlined, while the seer in the midst is precluded from that advantage, and must see without being directly seen. He, who doubtless ought to bulk in the story more massively than any one, tends to remain the least recognizable of the company, and even to dissolve in a kind of impalpable blur. By his method (which I am supposing to have been adopted in full strictness) the author is of course forbidden to look this central figure in the face, to describe and discuss him; the light cannot be turned upon him immediately. And very often we see the method becoming an embarrassment to the author in consequence, and the devices by which he tries to mitigate it, and to secure some reflected sight of the seer, may even be tiresomely obvious. But the resource of which I speak is of a finer sort.

It gives to the author the power of imperceptibly edging away from the seer, leaving his consciousness, ceasing to use his eyes—though still without substituting the eyes of another. To revert for a moment to the story told in the first person, it is plain that in that case the narrator has no such liberty; his own consciousness must always lie open; the part that he plays in the story can never appear in the same terms, on the same plane, as that of the other people. Though he is not visible in the story to the reader, as the others are, he is at every moment *nearer* than they, in his capacity of the seeing eye, the channel of vision; nor can he put off his function, he must continue steadily to see and to report. But when the author is reporting *him* there is a margin of freedom. The author has not so completely identified himself, as narrator, with his hero that he can give him no objective weight whatever. If necessary he can allow him something of the value of a detached and phenomenal personage, like the rest of the company in the story, and that without violating the principle of his method. He cannot make his hero actually visible—there the method is uncompromising; he cannot step forward, leaving the man's point of view, and picture him from without. But he can place the man at the same distance from the reader as the other people, he can almost lend him the same effect, he can make of him a dramatic actor upon the scene.

And how? Merely by closing (when it suits him) the open consciousness of the seer—which he can do without any look of awkwardness or violence, since it conflicts in no way with the rule of the method. That rule only required that the author, having decided to share the point of view of his character, would not proceed to set up another of his own; it did not debar him from allowing his hero's act of vision to lapse, his function as the sentient creature in the story to be intermitted. The hero (I call him so for convenience—he may, of course, be quite a subordinate onlooker in the story) can at any moment become impenetrable, a human being whose thought is sealed from us; and it may seem a small matter, but in fact it has the result that he drops into the plane of the people whom he has hitherto been seeing and judging. Hitherto subjective, communicative in solitude, he has been in a category apart from them; but now he may mingle with the rest, engage in talk with them, and his presence and his talk are no more to the fore than theirs. As soon as some description or discussion of them is required, then, of course, the seer must resume his part and unseal his mind; but meanwhile, though the reader gets no direct view of him, still he is there in the dialogue with the rest, his speech (like theirs) issues from a hidden mind and has the same dramatic value. It is enough, very likely, to harden our image of him, to give precision to his form, to save him from dissipation into that luminous blur of which I spoke just now. For the author it is a resource to be welcomed on that account, and not on that account alone.

For besides the greater definition that the seer acquires, thus detached from us at times and relegated to the plane of his companions, there is much benefit for the subject of the story. In the tale that is quite openly and nakedly somebody's narrative there is this inherent weakness, that a scene of true drama is impossible. In true drama nobody *reports* the scene; it *appears,* it is constituted by the aspect of the occasion and the talk and the conduct of the people. When one of the people who took part in it sets out to report the scene, there is at once a mixture and a confusion of effects; for his own contribution to the scene has a different quality from the rest, cannot have the same crispness and freshness, cannot strike in with a new or unexpected note. This weakness may be well disguised, and like everything else in the whole craft it may become a positive and right effect in a particular story, for a particular purpose; it is always there, however, and it means that the full and unmixed effect of drama is denied to the story that is rigidly told from the point of view of one of the actors. But when that point of view is held in the manner I have described, when it is open to the author to withdraw from it silently and to leave the actor to play his part, true drama—or something so like it that it passes for true drama—is always possible; all the figures of the scene are together in it, one no nearer than another. Nothing is wanting save only that direct, unequivocal sight of the hero which the method does indeed absolutely forbid.

Finally there is the old, immemorial, unguarded, unsuspicious way of telling a story, where the author entertains the reader, the minstrel draws his audience round him, the listeners rely upon his word. The voice is then confessedly and alone the author's; he imposes no limitation upon his freedom to tell what he pleases and to regard his matter from a point of view that is solely his own. And if there is anyone who can proceed in this fashion without appearing to lose the least of the advantages of a more cautious style, for him the minstrel's license is proper and appropriate; there is no more to be said. But we have yet to discover him; and it is not very presumptuous in a critic, as things are, to declare that a story will never yield its best to a writer who takes the easiest way with it. He curtails his privileges and chooses a narrower method, and immediately the story responds; its better condition is too notable to be forgotten, when once it has caught the attention of a reader. The advantages that it gains are not nameless, indefinable graces, pleasing to a critic but impossible to fix in words; they are solid, we can describe and recount them. And I can only conclude that if the novel is still as full of energy as it seems to be, and is not a form of imaginative art that, having seen the best of its day, is preparing to give place to some other, the novelist will not be willing to miss the inexhaustible opportunity that lies in its treatment. The easy way is no way at all; the only way is that by which the most is made of the story to be told, and the most was never made of any story except by a choice and disciplined method.

## Wayne C. Booth

### *Types of Narration*

We have seen that the author cannot choose to avoid rhetoric; he can choose only the kind of rhetoric he will employ. He cannot choose whether or not to affect his readers' evaluations by his choice of narrative manner; he can only choose whether to do it well or poorly. As dramatists have always known, even the purest of dramas is not purely dramatic in the sense of being entirely presented, entirely shown as taking place in the moment. There are always what Dryden called "relations" to be taken care of, and try as the author may to ignore the troublesome fact, "some parts of the action are more fit to be represented, some to be related."[1] But related by whom? The dramatist must decide, and the novelist's case is different only in that the choices open to him are more numerous.

If we think through the many narrative devices in the fiction we know, we soon come to a sense of the embarrassing inadequacy of our traditional classification of "point of view" into three or four kinds, variables only of the "person" and the degree of omniscience. If we name over three or four of the great narrators—say Cervantes' Cid Hamete Benengeli, Tristram Shandy, the "I" of *Middlemarch,* and Strether, through whose vision most of *The Ambassadors* comes to us, we realize that to describe any of them with terms like "first-person" and "omniscient" tells us nothing about how they differ from each other, or why they

[1] *An Essay of Dramatic Poesy* (1668). Though this quotation comes from Lisideius, in his defense of French drama, and not from Neander, who seems to speak more nearly for Dryden, the position is taken for granted in Neander's reply; the only dispute is over which parts are more fit to be represented.

succeed while others described in the same terms fail.[2] It should be worth our while, then, to attempt a richer tabulation of the forms the author's voice can take. . . .

## PERSON

Perhaps the most overworked distinction is that of person. To say that a story is told in the first or the third person[3] will tell us nothing of importance unless we become more precise and describe how the particular qualities of the narrators relate to specific effects. It is true that choice of the first person is sometimes unduly limiting; if the "I" has inadequate access to necessary information, the author may be led into improbabilities. And there are other effects that may dictate a choice in some cases. But we can hardly expect to find useful criteria in a distinction that throws all fiction into two, or at most three, heaps. In this pile we see *Henry Esmond*, "A Cask of Amontillado," *Gulliver's Travels*, and *Tristram Shandy*. In that, we have *Vanity Fair*, *Tom Jones*, *The Ambassadors*, and *Brave New World*. But in *Vanity Fair* and *Tom Jones* the commentary is in the first person, often resembling more the intimate effect of *Tristram Shandy* than that of many third-person works. And again, the effect of *The Ambassadors* is much closer to that of the great first-person novels, since Strether in large part "narrates" his own story, even though he is always referred to in the third person.

Further evidence that this distinction is less important than

[2] There is no point in listing any of the conventional classifications here in order to reject them. They range from the simplest and least useful, in a clever popular essay by C. E. Montague ("'Sez 'e' or 'Thinks 'e,' " *A Writer's Notes on His Trade* [London, 1930; Pelican ed., 1952], pp. 34–35) to the valuable study by Norman Friedman ("Point of View," *PMLA*, LXX [December, 1955], 1160–84).

[3] Efforts to use the second person have never been very successful, but it is astonishing how little real difference even this choice makes. When I am told, at the beginning of a book, "You have put your left foot. . . . You slide through the narrow opening. . . . Your eyes are only half open . . . ," the radical unnaturalness is, it is true, distracting for a time. But in reading Michel Butor's *La Modification* (Paris, 1957), from which this opening comes, it is surprising how quickly one is absorbed into the illusory "present" of the story, identifying one's vision with the "vous" almost as fully as with the "I" and "he" in other stories.

has often been claimed is seen in the fact that all of the following functional distinctions apply to both first- and third-person narration alike.

## DRAMATIZED AND UNDRAMATIZED NARRATORS

Perhaps the most important differences in narrative effect depend on whether the narrator is dramatized in his own right and on whether his beliefs and characteristics are shared by the author.

*The implied author* (*the author's "second self"*).—Even the novel in which no narrator is dramatized creates an implicit picture of an author who stands behind the scenes, whether as stage manager, as puppeteer, or as an indifferent God, silently paring his fingernails. This implied author is always distinct from the "real man"—whatever we may take him to be—who creates a superior version of himself, a "second self," as he creates his work.[4]

In so far as a novel does not refer directly to this author, there will be no distinction between him and the implied, undramatized narrator; in Hemingway's "The Killers," for example, there is no narrator other than the implicit second self that Hemingway creates as he writes.

*Undramatized narrators.*—Stories are usually not so rigorously impersonal as "The Killers"; most tales are presented as passing through the consciousness of a teller, whether an "I" or a "he." Even in drama much of what we are given is narrated by someone, and we are often as much interested in the effect on the narrator's own mind and heart as we are in learning what *else* the author has to tell us. When Horatio tells of his first encounter with the ghost in *Hamlet,* his own character, though never mentioned, is important to us as we listen. In fiction, as soon as we encounter an "I," we are conscious of an experiencing mind

[4] A fine account of the subtleties that underlie the seemingly simple relations between real authors and the selves they create as they write can be found in "Makers and Persons," by Patrick Cruttwell, *Hudson Review,* XII (Winter, 1959–60), 487–507.

whose views of the experience will come between us and the event. When there is no such "I," as in "The Killers," the inexperienced reader may make the mistake of thinking that the story comes to him unmediated. But no such mistake can be made from the moment that the author explicitly places a narrator into the tale, even if he is given no personal characteristics whatever.

*Dramatized narrators.*—In a sense even the most reticent narrator has been dramatized as soon as he refers to himself as "I," or, like Flaubert, tells us that "we" were in the classroom when Charles Bovary entered. But many novels dramatize their narrators with great fulness, making them into characters who are as vivid as those they tell us about (*Tristram Shandy, Remembrance of Things Past, Heart of Darkness, Dr. Faustus*). In such works the narrator is often radically different from the implied author who creates him. The range of human types that have been dramatized as narrators is almost as great as the range of other fictional characters—one must say "almost" because there are some characters who are not fully qualified to narrate or "reflect" a story (Faulkner can use the idiot for *part* of his novel only because the other three parts exist to set off and clarify the idiot's jumble).

We should remind ourselves that many dramatized narrators are never explicitly labeled as narrators at all. In a sense, every speech, every gesture, narrates; most works contain disguised narrators who are used to tell the audience what it needs to know, while seeming merely to act out their roles.

Though disguised narrators of this kind are seldom labeled so explicitly as God in Job, they often speak with an authority as sure as God's. Messengers returning to tell what the oracle said, wives trying to convince their husbands that the business deal is unethical, old family retainers expostulating with wayward scions —these often have more effect on us than on their official auditors; the king goes ahead with his obstinate search, the husband carries out his deal, the hell-bound youth goes on toward hell as if nothing had been said, but we know what we know—and as surely as if the author himself or his official narrator had told us. "She's laughing at you to your face, brother," Cleante says to Orgon in *Tartuffe*, "and frankly, without meaning to anger you, I must say she's quite right. Has there ever been the like of such a whim? . . . You must be mad, brother, I swear."[5] And in tragedy there is usually a chorus, a friend, or even a forthright villain, to speak truth in contrast to the tragic mistakes of the hero.

The most important unacknowledged narrators in modern fiction are the third-person "center of consciousness" through whom authors have filtered their narratives. Whether such "reflectors," as James sometimes called them, are highly polished mirrors reflecting complex mental experience, or the rather turbid, sense-bound "camera eyes" of much fiction since James, they fill precisely the function of avowed narrators—though they *can* add intensities of their own.

> Gabriel had not gone to the door with the others. He was in a dark part of the hall gazing up the staircase. A woman was standing near the top of the first flight, in the shadow also. He could not see her face but he could see the terracotta and salmon-pink panels of her skirt which the shadow made appear black and white. It was his wife. She was leaning on the banisters, listening to something. . . . He asked himself what is a woman standing on the stairs in the shadow, listening to distant music, a symbol of [Joyce's "The Dead"].

The very real advantages of this method, for some purposes, have provided a dominant theme in modern criticism. Indeed, so long as our attention is on such qualities as naturalness and vividness, the advantages seem overwhelming. Only as we break out of the fashionable assumption that all good fiction tries for the same kind of vivid illusion in the same way are we forced to recognize disadvantages. The third-person reflector is only one mode among many, suitable for some effects but cumbersome and even harmful when other effects are desired.

### OBSERVERS AND NARRATOR-AGENTS

Among dramatized narrators there are mere observers (the "I" of *Tom Jones, The Egoist, Troilus and Criseyde*), and there

[5] From an unpublished translation by Marcel Gutwirth.

are narrator-agents, who produce some measurable effect on the course of events (ranging from the minor involvement of Nick in *The Great Gatsby,* through the extensive give-and-take of Marlow in *Heart of Darkness,*[6] to the central role of Tristram Shandy, Moll Flanders, Huckleberry Finn, and—in the third person—Paul Morel in *Sons and Lovers*). Clearly, any rules we might discover about observers may not apply to narrator-agents, yet the distinction is seldom made in talk about point of view.

## SCENE AND SUMMARY

All narrators and observers, whether first or third person, can relay their tales to us primarily as scene ("The Killers," *The Awkward Age,* the works of Ivy Compton-Burnett and Henry Green), primarily as summary or what Lubbock called "picture" (Addison's almost completely non-scenic tales in *The Spectator*), or, most commonly, as a combination of the two.

Like Aristotle's distinction between dramatic and narrative manners, the somewhat different modern distinction between showing and telling does cover the ground. But the trouble is that it pays for broad coverage with gross imprecision. Narrators of all shapes and shades must either report dialogue alone or support it with "stage directions" and description of setting. But when we think of the radically different effect of a scene reported by Huck Finn and a scene reported by Poe's Montresor, we see that the quality of being "scenic" suggests very little about literary effect. And compare the delightful summary of twelve years given in two pages of *Tom Jones* (Book III, chap. i) with the tedious showing of even ten minutes of uncurtailed conversation in the hands of a Sartre when he allows his passion for "durational realism" to dictate a scene when summary is called for. As was shown in

[6] For a careful interpretation of the development and functions of Marlow in Conrad's works, see W. Y. Tindall, "Apology for Marlow," in *From Jane Austen to Joseph Conrad,* ed. Robert C. Rathburn and Martin Steinmann, Jr. (Minneapolis, Minn., 1958), pp. 274–85. Though Marlow is often himself a victim of Conrad's ironies, he is generally a reliable reflector of the clarities and ambiguities of the implied author. A much fuller treatment, and a remarkable work for an undergraduate, is James L. Guetti, Jr., *The Rhetoric of Joseph Conrad* ("Amherst College Honors Thesis," No. 2 [Amherst, Mass., 1960]).

chapters i and ii [not included here], the contrast between scene and summary, between showing and telling, is likely to be of little use until we specify the kind of narrator who is providing the scene or the summary.

### COMMENTARY

Narrators who allow themselves to tell as well as show vary greatly depending on the amount and kind of commentary allowed in addition to a direct relating of events in scene and summary. Such commentary can, of course, range over any aspect of human experience, and it can be related to the main business in innumerable ways and degrees. To treat it as a single device is to ignore important differences between commentary that is merely ornamental, commentary that serves a rhetorical purpose but is not part of the dramatic structure, and commentary that is integral to the dramatic structure, as in *Tristram Shandy*.

### SELF-CONSCIOUS NARRATORS

Cutting across the distinction between observers and narrator-agents of all these kinds is the distinction between *self-conscious narrators*, aware of themselves as writers (*Tom Jones*, *Tristram Shandy*, *Barchester Towers*, *The Catcher in the Rye*, *Remembrance of Things Past*, *Dr. Faustus*), and narrators or observers who rarely if ever discuss their writing chores (*Huckleberry Finn*) or who seem unaware that they are writing, thinking, speaking, or "reflecting" a literary work (Camus's *The Stranger*, Lardner's "Haircut," Bellow's *The Victim*).

### VARIATIONS OF DISTANCE

Whether or not they are involved in the action as agents or as sufferers, narrators and third-person reflectors differ markedly according to the degree and kind of distance that separates them from the author, the reader, and the other characters of the story. In any reading experience there is an implied dialogue among author, narrator, the other characters, and the reader. Each of the four can range, in relation to each of the others, from identification to complete opposition, on any axis of value, moral, intellectual, aesthetic, and even physical. (Does the reader who stammers react to the stammering of H. C. Earwicker as I do? Surely not.) The elements usually discussed under "aesthetic distance" enter in of course; distance in time and space, differences of social class or conventions of speech or dress—these and many others serve to control our sense that we are dealing with an aesthetic object, just as the paper moons and other unrealistic stage effects of some modern drama have had an "alienation" effect. But we must not confuse these with the equally important effects of personal beliefs and qualities, in author, reader, narrator, and all others in the cast of characters.

1. The *narrator* may be more or less distant from the *implied author*. The distance may be moral (Jason vs. Faulkner, the barber vs. Lardner, the narrator vs. Fielding in *Jonathan Wild*). It may be intellectual (Twain and Huck Finn, Sterne and Tristram Shandy on the influence of noses, Richardson and Clarissa). It may be physical or temporal: most authors are distant from even the most knowing narrator in that they presumably know how "everything turns out in the end." And so on.

2. The *narrator* also may be more or less distant from the *characters* in the story he tells. He may differ morally, intellectually, and temporally (the mature narrator and his younger self in *Great Expectations* or *Redburn*); morally and intellectually (Fowler the narrator and Pyle the American in Greene's *The Quiet American,* both departing radically from the author's norms but in different directions); morally and emotionally (Maupassant's "The Necklace," and Huxley's "Nuns at Luncheon," in which the narrators affect less emotional involvement than Maupassant and Huxley clearly expect from the reader); and thus on through every possible trait.

3. The *narrator* may be more or less distant from the *reader's* own norms; for example, physically and emotionally (Kafka's *The Metamorphosis*); morally and emotionally (Pinkie

in *Brighton Rock,* the miser in Mauriac's *Knot of Vipers,* and the many other moral degenerates that modern fiction has managed to make into convincing human beings).

With the repudiation of omniscient narration, and in the face of inherent limitations in dramatized reliable narrators, it is hardly surprising that modern authors have experimented with unreliable narrators whose characteristics change in the course of the works they narrate. Ever since Shakespeare taught the modern world what the Greeks had overlooked in neglecting character change (compare *Macbeth* and *Lear* with *Oedipus*), stories of character development or degeneration have become more and more popular. But it was not until authors had discovered the full uses of the third-person reflector that they could effectively show a narrator changing *as he narrates.* The mature Pip, in *Great Expectations,* is presented as a generous man whose heart is where the reader's is supposed to be; he watches his young self move away from the reader, as it were, and then back again. But the third-person reflector can be shown, technically in the past tense but in effect present before our eyes, moving toward or away from values that the reader holds dear. Authors in the twentieth century have proceeded almost as if determined to work out all of the possible plot forms based on such shifts: start far and end near; start near, move far, and end near; start far and move farther; and so on. Perhaps the most characteristic, however, have been the astonishing achievements in the first of these, taking extremely unsympathetic characters like Faulkner's Mink Snopes and transforming them, both through character change and technical manipulation, into characters of dignity and power. We badly need thoroughgoing studies of the various plot forms that have resulted from this kind of shifting distance.

4. The *implied author* may be more or less distant from the *reader.* The distance may be intellectual (the implied author of *Tristram Shandy,* not of course to be identified with Tristram, more interested in and knowing more about recondite classical lore than any of his readers), moral (the works of Sade), or aesthetic. From the author's viewpoint, a successful reading of his book must eliminate all distance between the essential norms of his implied author and the norms of the postulated reader. Often

enough, there is very little fundamental distance to begin with; Jane Austen does not have to convince us that pride and prejudice are undesirable. A bad book, on the other hand, is often most clearly recognizable because the implied author asks that we judge according to norms that we cannot accept.

5. The *implied author* (carrying the reader with him) may be more or less distant from *other characters*. Again, the distance can be on any axis of value. Some successful authors keep most of their characters very far "away" in every respect (Ivy Compton-Burnett), and they may work very deliberately, as William Empson says of T. F. Powys, to maintain an artificiality that will keep their characters "at a great distance from the author."[7] Others present a wider range from far to near, on a variety of axes. Jane Austen, for example, presents a broad range of moral judgment (from the almost complete approval of Jane Fairfax in *Emma* to the contempt for Wickham in *Pride and Prejudice*), of wisdom (from Knightley to Miss Bates or Mrs. Bennet), of taste, of tact, of sensibility.

It is obvious that on each of these scales my examples do not begin to cover the possibilities. What we call "involvement" or "sympathy" or "identification," is usually made up of many reactions to author, narrators, observers, and other characters. And narrators may differ from their authors or readers in various kinds of involvement or detachment, ranging from deep personal concern (Nick in *The Great Gatsby,* MacKellar in *The Master of Ballantrae,* Zeitblom in *Dr. Faustus*) to a bland or mildly amused or merely curious detachment (Waugh's *Decline and Fall*).

For practical criticism probably the most important of these kinds of distance is that between the fallible or unreliable narrator and the implied author who carries the reader with him in judging the narrator. If the reason for discussing point of view is to find how it relates to literary effects, then surely the moral and intellectual qualities of the narrator are more important to our judgment than whether he is referred to as "I" or "he," or whether he is privileged or limited. If he is discovered to be untrust-

[7] *Some Versions of Pastoral* (London, 1935), p. 7. For an excellent discussion of Powys' deliberate artificiality, see Martin Steinmann's "The Symbolism of T. F. Powys," *Critique,* I (Summer, 1957), 49–63.

worthy, then the total effect of the work he relays to us is transformed.

Our terminology for this kind of distance in narrators is almost hopelessly inadequate. For lack of better terms, I have called a narrator *reliable* when he speaks for or acts in accordance with the norms of the work (which is to say, the implied author's norms), *unreliable* when he does not. It is true that most of the great reliable narrators indulge in large amounts of incidental irony, and they are thus "unreliable" in the sense of being potentially deceptive. But difficult irony is not sufficient to make a narrator unreliable. Nor is unreliability ordinarily a matter of lying, although deliberately deceptive narrators have been a major resource of some modern novelists (Camus' *The Fall,* Calder Willingham's *Natural Child,* etc.).[8] It is most often a matter of what James calls *inconscience;* the narrator is mistaken, or he believes himself to have qualities which the author denies him. Or, as in *Huckleberry Finn,* the narrator claims to be naturally wicked while the author silently praises his virtues behind his back.

Unreliable narrators thus differ markedly depending on how far and in what direction they depart from their author's norms; the older term "tone," like the currently fashionable terms "irony" and "distance," covers many effects that we should distinguish. Some narrators, like Barry Lyndon, are placed as far "away" from author and reader as possible, in respect to every virtue except a kind of interesting vitality. Some, like Fleda Vetch, the reflector in James's *The Spoils of Poynton,* come close to representing the author's ideal of taste, judgment, and moral

[8] Alexander E. Jones in a recent essay argued convincingly for a "straight" reading of *The Turn of the Screw,* offering as one reason that "the basic convention of first-person fiction is necessarily a confidence in the narrator. . . . Unless James has violated the basic rules of his craft, the governess cannot be a pathological liar" (*PMLA,* LXXIV [March, 1959], 122). Whatever may have been true in James's time, it is clear that in modern fiction there is no longer any such convention. The only convention that can be relied on . . . is that if a narrator presents himself as speaking or writing to the reader, he really is doing so. The content of what he says may turn out to be dream (Schwartz's "In Dreams Begin Responsibilities"), or falsehood (Jean Cayrol's *Les corps étrangers*), or it may not "turn out" at all—that is, it may be left indeterminately between dream, falsehood, fantasy, and reality (Unamuno's *Mist,* Beckett's *Comment c'est*).

sense. All of them make stronger demands on the reader's powers of inference than do reliable narrators.

### VARIATIONS IN SUPPORT OR CORRECTION

Both reliable and unreliable narrators can be unsupported or uncorrected by other narrators (Gully Jimson in *The Horse's Mouth,* Henderson in Bellow's *Henderson the Rain King*) or supported or corrected (*The Master of Ballantrae, The Sound and the Fury*). Sometimes it is almost impossible to infer whether or to what degree a narrator is fallible; sometimes explicit corroborating or conflicting testimony makes the inference easy. Support or correction differs radically, it should be noted, depending on whether it is provided from within the action, so that the narrator-agent might benefit from it in sticking to the right line or in changing his own views (Faulkner's *Intruder in the Dust*), or is simply provided externally, to help the reader correct or reinforce his own views as against the narrator's (Graham Greene's *The Power and the Glory*). Obviously, the effects of isolation will be extremely different in the two cases.

### PRIVILEGE

Observers and narrator-agents, whether self-conscious or not, reliable or not, commenting or silent, isolated or supported, can be either privileged to know what could not be learned by strictly natural means or limited to realistic vision and inference. Complete privilege is what we usually call omniscience. But there are many kinds of privilege, and very few "omniscient" narrators are allowed to know or show as much as their authors know.

We need a good study of the varieties of privilege and limitation and their function. Some limitations are only temporary, or even playful, like the ignorance Fielding sometimes imposes on his "I" (as when he doubts his own powers of narration and invokes the Muses for aid [*Tom Jones,* Book XIII, chap. i]). Some are more nearly permanent but subject to momentary relaxation, like the generally limited, humanly realistic Ishmael in *Moby Dick,* who can yet break through his human limitations when the story requires ("'He waxes brave, but nevertheless obeys; most careful bravery that!' murmured Ahab"—with no one present to report to the narrator). And some are confined to what their literal condition would allow them to know (first person, Huck Finn; third person, Miranda and Laura in Katherine Anne Porter's stories).

The most important single privilege is that of obtaining an inside view of another character, because of the rhetorical power that such a privilege conveys upon a narrator. There is a curious ambiguity in the term "omniscience." Many modern works that we usually classify as narrated dramatically, with everything relayed to us through the limited views of the characters, postulate fully as much omniscience in the silent author as Fielding claims for himself. Our roving visitation into the minds of sixteen characters in Faulkner's *As I Lay Dying,* seeing nothing but what those minds contain, may seem in one sense not to depend on an omniscient author. But this method is omniscience with teeth in it: the implied author demands our absolute faith in his powers of divination. We must never for a moment doubt that he knows everything about each of these sixteen minds or that he has chosen correctly how much to show of each. In short, impersonal narration is really no escape from omniscience—the true author is as "unnaturally" all-knowing as he ever was. If evident artificiality were a fault—which it is not—modern narration would be as faulty as Trollope's.

Another way of suggesting the same ambiguity is to look closely at the concept of "dramatic" storytelling. The author can present his characters in a dramatic situation without in the least presenting them in what we normally think of as a dramatic manner. When Joseph Andrews, who has been stripped and beaten by thieves, is overtaken by a stagecoach, Fielding presents the scene in what by some modern standards must seem an inconsistent and undramatic mode. "The poor wretch, who lay motionless a long time, just began to recover his senses as a stagecoach came by. The postilion, hearing a man's groans, stopped his horses, and told the coachman, he was certain there was a dead man lying in the ditch. . . . A lady, who heard what the postilion said, and likewise heard the groan, called eagerly to the coachman to stop and see what was the matter. Upon which he bid the postilion alight, and look into the ditch. He did so, and returned, 'That there was a man sitting upright, as naked as ever he was born.' " There follows a splendid description, hardly meriting the name of scene, in which are recorded the selfish reactions of each passenger. A young lawyer points out that they might be legally liable if they refuse to take Joseph up. "These words had a sensible effect on the coachman, who was well acquainted with the person who spoke them; and the old gentleman above mentioned, thinking the naked man would afford him frequent opportunities of showing his wit to the lady, offered to join with the company in giving a mug of beer for his fare; till, partly alarmed by the threats of the one, and partly by the promises of the other, and being perhaps a little moved with compassion at the poor creature's condition, who stood bleeding and shivering with the cold, he at length agreed." Once Joseph is in the coach, the same kind of indirect reporting of the "scene" continues, with frequent excursions, however superficial, into the minds and hearts of the assembly of fools and knaves, and occasional guesses when complete knowledge seems inadvisable. If to be dramatic is to show characters dramatically engaged with each other, motive clashing with motive, the outcome depending upon the resolution of motives, then this scene is dramatic. But if it is to give the impression that the story is taking place by itself, with the characters existing in a dramatic relationship vis-à-vis the spectator, unmediated by a narrator and decipherable only through inferential matching of word to word and word to deed, then this is a relatively undramatic scene.

On the other hand, an author can present a character in this latter kind of dramatic relationship with the reader without involving that character in any internal drama at all. Many lyric poems are dramatic in this sense and undramatic in any other. "That is no country for old men—" Who says? Yeats, or his "mask," says. To whom? To us. How do we know that it is Yeats and not some character as remote from him as Caliban is remote from Browning in "Caliban upon Setebos"? We infer it as the dramatized statement unfolds; the need for the inference is what makes the lyric dramatic in this sense. Caliban, in short, is dramatic in two senses; he is in a dramatic situation with other characters, and he is in a dramatic situation over against us. Yeats's poem is dramatic in only one sense.

The ambiguities of the word dramatic are even more complicated in fiction that attempts to dramatize states of consciousness directly. Is *A Portrait of the Artist as a Young Man* dramatic? In some respects, yes. We are not told about Stephen. He is placed on the stage before us, acting out his destiny with only disguised helps or comments from his author. But it is not his actions that are dramatized directly, not his speech that we hear unmediated. What is dramatized is his mental record of everything that happens. We see his consciousness at work on the world. Sometimes what it records is itself dramatic, as when Stephen observes himself in a scene with other characters. But the report itself, the internal record, is dramatic in the second sense only. The report we are given of what goes on in Stephen's mind is a monologue uninvolved in any modifying dramatic context. And it is an infallible report, even less subject to critical doubts than the typical Elizabethan soliloquy. We accept, by convention, the claim that what is reported as going on in Stephen's mind really goes on there, or in other words, that Joyce knows how Stephen's mind works. "The equation of the page of his scribbler began to spread out a widening tail, eyed and starred like a peacock's; and, when the eyes and stars of its indices had been eliminated, began slowly to fold itself together again. The indices appearing and disappearing were eyes opening and closing; the eyes opening and closing were stars. . . ." Who says so? Not Stephen, but the omniscient, infallible author. The report is direct, and it is clearly unmodified by any "dramatic" context—that is, unlike a speech in a dramatic scene, it does not lead us to suspect that the thoughts have been in any way aimed at an effect. We are thus in a dramatic relation with Stephen only in a limited sense—the sense in which a lyric poem is dramatic.[9]

[9] I am aware that my terminology here contrasts with Joyce's own use of the triad, *lyric, epic,* and *dramatic*. *Portrait* is dramatic in Joyce's sense, but in that sense only.

## Inside Views

Finally, narrators who provide inside views differ in the depth and the axis of their plunge. Boccaccio can give inside views, but they are extremely shallow. Jane Austen goes relatively deep morally, but scarcely skims the surface psychologically. All authors of stream-of-consciousness narration presumably attempt to go deep psychologically, but some of them deliberately remain shallow in the moral dimension.[10] We should remind ourselves that any sustained inside view, of whatever depth, temporarily turns the character whose mind is shown into a narrator; inside views are thus subject to variations in all of the qualities we have described above, and most importantly in the degree of unreliability. Generally speaking, the deeper our plunge, the more unreliability we will accept without loss of sympathy.

Narration is an art, not a science, but this does not mean that we are necessarily doomed to fail when we attempt to formulate principles about it. There are systematic elements in every art, and criticism of fiction can never avoid the responsibility of trying to explain technical successes and failures by reference to general principles. But we must always ask where the general principles are to be found.

It is not surprising to hear practicing novelists report that

[10] Discussion of the many devices covered by the loose term "stream-of-consciousness" has generally concentrated on their service to psychological realism, avoiding the moral effect of different degrees of depth. Even unfriendly critics—Mauriac in *Le romancier et ses personnages* (Paris, 1933), for example—have generally pointed to their amorphousness, their lack of clear control and their obvious artifice, not to their moral implications. Too often, both attack and defense have assumed that there is a single device which can be assessed as good or bad, once and for all, for such-and-such general reasons. Melvin Friedman (*Stream of Consciousness* [New Haven, Conn., 1955]) concludes that it is "almost axiomatic that no further work of the first order can be done within this tradition," since the method depended on a "certain literary mentality which died out with Joyce, Virginia Woolf, and the early Faulkner" (p. 261). But the works he treats make use of dozens of varieties of stream-of-consciousness, some of which are now an established part of the novelist's repertory. Most of them are likely to find new uses in the future.

they have never had any help from critics about point of view. In dealing with point of view the novelist must always deal with the individual work: which particular character shall tell this particular story, or part of a story, with what precise degree of reliability, privilege, freedom to comment, and so on. Shall he be given dramatic vividness? Even if the novelist has decided on a narrator who will fit one of the critic's classifications—"omniscient," "first person," "limited omniscient," "objective," "roving," "effaced," or whatever—his troubles have just begun. He simply cannot find answers to his immediate, precise, practical problems by referring to statements such as that the "omniscient is the most flexible method," or that "the objective is the most rapid or vivid." Even the soundest of generalizations at this level will be of little use to him in his page-by-page progress through his novel.

As Henry James's detailed records show, the novelist discovers his narrative technique as he tries to achieve for his readers the potentialities of his developing idea. The majority of his choices are consequently choices of degree, not kind. To decide that your narrator shall not be omniscient decides practically nothing. The hard question is: Just how *inconscient* shall he be? Again, to decide on first-person narration settles only a part of one's problem, perhaps the easiest part. What kind of first person? How fully characterized? How much aware of himself as narrator? How reliable? How much confined to realistic inference; how far privileged to go beyond realism? At what points shall he speak truth and at what points utter no judgment or even utter falsehood? These questions can be answered only by reference to the potentialities and necessities of particular works, not by reference to fiction in general, or the novel, or rules about point of view.

There are no doubt *kinds* of effect to which the author can refer; for example, if he wants to make a scene more amusing, poignant, vivid, or ambiguous, or if he wants to make a character more sympathetic or more convincing, such-and-such practices may be indicated. But we can understand why in his search for help in his decisions, the novelist should find the practice of his peers more helpful than the abstract rules of the textbooks: the sensitive author who reads the great novels finds in them a storehouse of precise examples, of how *this* effect, as distinct from all other possible effects, was heightened by the proper narrative choice. In dealing with the types of narration, the critic must always limp behind, referring constantly to the varied practice which alone can correct his temptations to overgeneralize. In place of our modern "fourth unity," in place of abstract rules about consistency and objectivity in the use of point of view, we need more painstaking, specific accounts of how great tales are told.

# A SUGGESTION ABOUT FURTHER READING

A suggestion, not suggestions; an idea, not a list, is offered here. It amounts quite simply to building on what is in this book. Read, if you have not read them, the works discussed by these critics. Read novels, that is, and keep criticism in its proper perspective as a means to the end of understanding fiction, just as fiction itself is a means to the end of living a richer, more humane life. For further critical reading, you would do best to turn first to the works where the materials collected here are to be found in the full context of their authors' developed thought: *Mimesis, Anatomy of Criticism, The Rise of the Novel, The Gates of Horn, The Rhetoric of Fiction,* and the others. Beyond these, the editor of this collection can recommend, as an earnest effort to present a total theory of narrative, Scholes and Kellogg, *The Nature of Narrative* (Oxford University Press, 1966).